Forks in the Digital Road

Forks in the Digital Road

Key Decisions in the History of the Internet

SCOTT J. SHACKELFORD

AND

SCOTT O. BRADNER

FOREWORD BY VINT CERF

OXFORD
UNIVERSITY PRESS

Oxford University Press is a department of the University of Oxford. It furthers
the University's objective of excellence in research, scholarship, and education
by publishing worldwide. Oxford is a registered trade mark of Oxford University
Press in the UK and certain other countries.

Published in the United States of America by Oxford University Press
198 Madison Avenue, New York, NY 10016, United States of America.

© Oxford University Press 2024

All rights reserved. No part of this publication may be reproduced, stored in
a retrieval system, or transmitted, in any form or by any means, without the
prior permission in writing of Oxford University Press, or as expressly permitted
by law, by license, or under terms agreed with the appropriate reproduction
rights organization. Inquiries concerning reproduction outside the scope of the
above should be sent to the Rights Department, Oxford University Press, at the
address above.

You must not circulate this work in any other form
and you must impose this same condition on any acquirer.

CIP data is on file at the Library of Congress

ISBN 978–0–19–761777–9 (pbk.)
ISBN 978–0–19–761776–2 (hbk.)

DOI: 10.1093/oso/9780197617762.001.0001

To our loving spouses, Emily and Cheryl.

CONTENTS

List of Figures ix

Foreword by Vint Cerf xi

Preface xv

Acknowledgments xix

Abbreviations xxi

PART I Setting the Stage

1. Core Technical Decisions That Created the Internet 3

2. "Layer 9"—Core Policy Decisions That Gave Us the Internet We Have 34

PART II A Play in Five Acts

3. A Flaw in the Design? 67

4. The Web for Free 86

5. Regulating Online Speech 99

6. Why We're Still Living in 1995: ISP Wars and Net Neutrality 115

7. What Passed for Internet Governance 126

PART III Curtains

8. Taking Stock: The Internet We Deserve 143

Conclusion—Our Meta Future? 158

Notes 161
Index 199

FIGURES

1.1 Paul Baran's Figure of a Distributed Network 11

1.2 ARPANET Geographic Map, October 1980 14

1.3 The "Bread Truck" 29

1.4 How TCP/IP Works 31

3.1 Robert Tappan Morris in 2008, Courtesy of Wikimedia 71

3.2 Nevil Maskelyne in 1903, Courtesy of Wikimedia 73

3.3 Creeper, the World's First Internet Worm 76

4.1 First World Wide Website 87

5.1 Tim Berners-Lee (2014) 114

6.1 Turning Points in an Increasingly Commercialized Web 120

7.1 Jon Postel with Map of Internet Top-Level Domains (1994) 132

FOREWORD

Looking at the arc of history, one can't help but wonder where key turning points were and how things might have come out differently had alternatives prevailed. That's the intriguing thesis of this book and, as one who has lived through the past 50+ years of Internet history and its prehistory, it has been fascinating to see this evolution through the eyes of contemporaries. No one's sense of history is ever the same as another's. That's a bit like the famous notion that you cannot step twice into the same stream since the water you touched has long since moved on. While I might have chosen a few different forks in the road, I think the ones these authors have chosen are reasonable milestones at which different outcomes could have been anticipated.

There are aspects of the datagram and layering concepts that I consider to be fundamental to the success of the Internet. The first is that the packets don't know how they are carried and don't care. It seemed to me very important that knowledge of the underlying network characteristics was unknown to the IP layer of protocol. When new transmission technologies came along, notably optical fiber networks in the 1980s, the protocol did not need to change. Moreover, because the IP layer is ignorant of the meaning of the bits in the payload of the Internet's packets, adding a new application that reinterprets the meaning of the bits does not require any change to the IP layer of protocol. It is fair to say, of course, that the speed and latency of transport do have effects and that some applications will not work well if latency is too high or if the data rates are inadequate for the task. Think of all the streaming audio and video that have been exercised during the Covid pandemic period that only worked because wired and wireless speeds have increased dramatically since the Internet was formally made operational in 1983.

Cryptography has been a much-debated topic and so it is in this book. Even in the earliest days of Internet design, Bob Kahn and I knew that we would need new forms of packet cryptography to secure a military instance of the system. A system for packet encryption on the Advanced Projects Research Agency Network (ARPANET) called "Private Line Interface" that used military-grade cryptography was in development in 1975 and had limited but approved capacity to handle key distribution and protection of classified, encrypted packets across the ARPANET. We knew we needed something more flexible, and to that end, work also began in 1975 with NSA under the Advanced Projects Research Agency (ARPA) support to craft a new breed of encryptor that could manage to deal with out-of-order and lossy delivery and still successfully decrypt the contents of arriving packets. We also recognized the need for carrying end/end plaintext packets and their content as encrypted content in the payloads of otherwise unencrypted packets. The plain text ("red") content and packet headers would be fully encrypted using symmetric keys shared by each end of the logical connection and carried, hop-by-hop, through a lower-level Internet ("black"). We used the DES and Triple-DES open cryptography algorithms for testing these architectural concepts to simplify the operational testing of the design. Until the arrival of public-key cryptography, key distribution had to be done in a more centralized fashion, which was not considered as scalable as one would need if the system expanded to the size we see today.

When the 1976 paper by Diffie and Hellman was published, effectively announcing new directions in cryptography, I was excited to learn more. It would be a couple more years before the famous Rivest-Shamir-Adleman (RSA) algorithms emerged. At that point, I was already at ARPA managing the Internetting program and eager to test the TCP/IP system in a live setting. Given that I was already convinced we understood how to do packet cryptography at the IP layer, it seemed more important at the time to focus on successfully implementing and demonstrating basic TCP/IP functionality on multiple platforms and networks. So it was that the famous November 22, 1977, three-network demonstration took place without the benefit of cryptography.

Since that time, a variety of ways to introduce cryptographic methods have been developed including IPSEC at the IP layer, and Secure Sockets Layer (SSL) and subsequently Transport Layer Security (TLS), and more recently Quick User Datagram Protocol Internet Connections (QUIC) at the transport layer of the protocol stack. In addition, new methods of validating domain name binding to associated IP address(s) (DNSSEC—Domain Name System Security Extensions) and Route Public Key Cryptography (RPKI) have been introduced.

It is evident that the work is not yet done, given a continuing need for improved validation of identity and provenance of traffic on the Internet. The World Wide Web introduced new opportunities for mischief and risk as downloaded HTML files are ingested into browsers and then interpreted (executed) in the middle of popular operating systems of the day.

Another milestone, if not a fork, was the arrival of the smartphone in the form of the iPhone in 2007. The dramatic increase in accessibility to the Internet was made manifest by millions of "apps" that were developed and placed in "application stores" run by Apple, Google, and others. Subsequently, millions of devices of the "Internet of Things" (IoT) type are showing up and increasingly at risk for lack of commonly agreed security and authentication methods.

Finally, it must be said that content is another quagmire because its correctness is not always verifiable. Indeed, there are many ways in which misinformation and disinformation can arrive via browsers and other Internet-enabled applications. This is a huge topic in and of itself. Governments around the world, private sector players, and academia are all wrestling with the potential of social media to distribute deliberately or inadvertently misleading content.

This look at the arc of the Internet's history and some of its milestones is an important contribution to our understanding of how the system is likely to evolve over the next few years and decades that lie ahead. We are headed off the planet with an Interplanetary variant of the terrestrial Internet, which uses yet another suite of protocols (Bundle Protocols) that is organized to deal with the highly variable delay and disruption of deep space communication. In another decade or two, it may be timely to look back once again to see where we have come, how we got there, and what the implications are of operations across the solar system.

—Vint Cerf, March 2023

PREFACE

Science fiction has long featured various visions of cyberspace. From the original "shared hallucination" in William Gibson's *Neuromancer*, which first coined the term "cyberspace," to the dystopian metaverse of the *Matrix*, authors and fans alike have been fascinated by how interconnected technologies that are being developed today will shape our collective future, for better and worse. Less common is an urge to look back and understand how decisions made by a relatively small number of entrepreneurs, graduate students, researchers, and government officials have given us the Internet we have. But if we don't know where we've been, it's tough to understand where we are, to say nothing of where we're headed.

Consider that only some 50 years ago, a UCLA computer science professor and his student sent the first message over the predecessor to the Internet, a network called ARPANET. On October 29, 1969, Leonard Kleinrock and Charley Kline sent Stanford University researcher Bill Duval a two-letter message: "lo."[1] It was not meant to be a biblical reference. The intended message, the full word "login," was truncated by a computer crash.

Much more traffic than that travels through the Internet these days, with billions of emails sent and searches conducted daily. Indeed, from these humble beginnings to this writing in 2022, there are more than 5.5 billion Internet users visiting some 2 billion available websites. Each day, these users conduct more than 6 billion Google searches, post nearly 1 million posts on X, and watch more than 1 billion hours of YouTube videos—including, yes, loads of cat videos, which have collectively been seen more than 25 billion times alone.[2] Beyond usage statistics, the Internet is massively complex, much more so than many of us appreciate. Every time you send an email, it might travel through myriad networks owned by Internet service providers (ISPs), potentially being carried as pulses of light on fiberoptic cables at the bottom of the ocean, or even being bounced off orbiting satellites; in many ways, all Internet users are part of a living, dynamic, and global digital ecosystem. The more than 40,000 networks comprising this Internet ecosystem talk to each other through a common language, TCP/IP, which was developed by two DARPA researchers in the 1970s, Vint Cerf and Bob Kahn. Their decisions on the structure of the protocol itself—along with, of course, many others—have done more to shape our daily lives both on and offline than many of us can appreciate.

The goal of this book is to, for the first time in a single volume, revisit some of these key decision points in the history of cybersecurity and Internet governance, revealing the potential alternative options that existed at the time, and engage with that perennial question—what if? What if encryption had been built into the Internet's architecture from the beginning? What if Section 230, which shields Internet platforms from civil liability, had taken a different form? What if Cerf and Kahn had structured TCP/IP differently? What if Tim Berners-Lee had taken the advice of counsel and patented the World Wide Web? And what if the U.S. government had not helped to establish the Internet Corporation for Assigned Names and Numbers (ICANN) in 1998 or elected not to help launch a new era of cyber conflict in 2006?

This book answers these questions, and many more. We also offer practical ideas for how you can join the effort to help address the issues stemming from these decisions and, in the process, help build a new vision of cyberspace that is as secure, private, efficient, and, yes, even as fun as possible. At a time when the future of cyberspace has never been more in doubt—with the potential for a new Digital Cold War, or even a "splinternet" having the potential to fracture cyberspace into a series of national-level intranets in the wake of the war in Ukraine, the time is ripe to take both a look back, and ahead.

PREFACE   xvii

The decision points we discuss in this book—the forks—can be roughly divided into two categories: choices between somewhat equivalent technologies, and economic or policy decisions about the use of a given technology. This book is structured to better understand these key decisions and their impacts in three parts. In Part I, "Setting the Stage," we lay a foundation by surveying some of the core technical and policy decisions that created the Internet. Chapter 1, "Core Technical Decisions That Created the Internet," does this by describing the series of inventions and technical decisions that led to the protocols and architecture that comprise today's Internet, along with analyzing the key decisions about the use of a given technology. Chapter 2, "'Layer 9'—Core Policy Decisions That Gave Us the Internet We Have," then describes the series of nontechnical decisions that led to the prominence of the Internet and explores how it operates today.

In Part II, "A Play in Five Acts," we take a deeper dive into some of the key decisions beginning in Chapter 3, "A Flaw in the Design?," which discusses the often-repeated point that the Internet was not developed with security in mind. This chapter investigates how the choices made in the 1970s and '80s led to this decision by running through a brief history of cybersecurity, focusing on the key fork of "What if the Internet Protocol had been encrypted?" and its wider implications for cyber conflict, the Internet of things, and encryption back doors. Chapter 4, "The Web for Free," focuses on the story of Tim Berners-Lee, creator of the World Wide Web, and his decision not to patent his invention and its wider implications for net neutrality, social networks, and cyber sovereignty. Chapter 5, "Regulating Online Speech," offers a brief history of speech regulation in the United States and how that shaped the road to Section 230 of the Communications Decency Act, which is the now (in) famous "twenty-six words that created the Internet," according to Jeff Kosseff.[3] Wider implications including widespread misinformation and disinformation online—and how an array of countries around the world are dealing with the fallout—are analyzed in turn. Chapter 6, "Why We're Still Living in 1995: ISP Wars and Net Neutrality," describes the gradual commercialization of the Internet and how things could have turned out very differently. In Chapter 7, "What Passed for Internet Governance," we summarize a brief history of attempts to govern the Internet, focusing on the period from APRANET in the 1970s through the establishment of ICANN in the late 1990s. We then discuss the wider implications such as China's Digital Silk Road, digital isolation in the aftermath of the war in Ukraine, and even the rollout of an Interplanetary Protocol.

The book concludes with Part III, "Curtains," and Chapter 8, "Taking Stock: The Internet We Deserve," which distills lessons learned from the common threads of these forks in the digital road. It then moves in a normative direction to discuss not the Internet we have, but the one we deserve, including the prospects for cyber peace, equitable Internet governance, and how we can deploy these insights to ensure that the right digital forks are taken as we grapple with new technologies such as blockchain, the Internet of things, and the metaverse. After all, inaction is itself a choice, and as Franklin Delano Roosevelt said, "Democracy cannot succeed unless those who express their choice are prepared to choose wisely."[4] As with elections and public policy, so too with Internet governance. Let us choose wisely, informed by history and a clear-eyed view of the diverse cultures and perspectives that comprise the Internet as we look back and ahead at the vision of cyberspace that we leave to our children and posterity.

ACKNOWLEDGMENTS

This book would not have been possible without the help and support of numerous scholars, practitioners, policymakers, and research assistants. First and foremost, we would like to thank the Belfer Center for Science and International Affairs for first introducing us, and the Center for International Law and Governance at the Fletcher School, Tufts University, for pairing us up to work on our first collaborative project entitled, "Have You Updated Your Toaster? Transatlantic Approaches for Governing the Internet of Things," which was published by the *Hastings Law Journal* in 2022.

An extremely talented team of graduate students worked hard to help bring this book to fruition, including: Aderinsola Oluwafeyisayo Adesida, Jay Bhatia, Maria del mar Diez, Sergei Dmitriachev, Kari McMullen, Kalea Miao, Alexandra Reibel, Samuel Troyer, and Kara Williams. We are indebted to them for their invaluable research and cite-checking support. My thanks also go to the Kelley School of Business administration, staff, and colleagues in the Department of Business Law and Ethics for their much-appreciated support and enthusiasm for this project, along with the faculty affiliates and staff at the Ostrom Workshop, and the Center for Applied Cybersecurity Research.

In addition, we would like to thank Angela Chnapko and the staff at Oxford University Press for taking a chance on this book, and for their incredible professionalism, patience, and dedication throughout every stage of the production process.

Above all, we are indebted in countless ways to our wonderful families, who have made all of this possible.

ABBREVIATIONS

ACM	Association for Computing Machinery
AIDS	Acquired Immunodeficiency Syndrome
AOL	America Online
ARPA	Advanced Projects Research Agency
ARPANET	Advanced Research Projects Agency Network
AT&T	American Telephone and Telegraph Company
ATM	Asynchronous Transfer Mode
AUP	acceptable use policy
BBN	Bolt Beranek and Newman Inc.
BSD	Berkeley Software Distribution
CBS	Columbia Broadcasting System
CCITT	Consultative Committee for International Telephony and Telegraphy
CDA	Communications Decency Act
CDN	content delivery networks
CERN	Conseil Européen pour la Recherche Nucléaire
CHM	common heritage of mankind
CIS	CompuServe Information Service
CNNIC	China Internet Network Information Center
CSAIL	Computer Science and Artificial Intelligence Laboratory
CSNET	Computer Science Network
DAO	decentralized autonomous organization
DARPA	Defense Advanced Research Projects Agency

DDoS	distributed denial of service
DEC	Digital Equipment Corporation
DEC VAX	Digital Equipment Company Virtual Address eXtension
DECnet	Digital Equipment Corporation network
DNS	domain name system
DoD	Department of Defense
DSR	Digital Silk Road
e2e	end to end
EFF	Electronic Frontier Foundation
ENQUIRE	Enquire-Within-upon-Everything
ESPRIT	European Strategic Programme on Research in Information Technology
EU	European Union
FCC	Federal Communications Commission
FIPS	Federal Information Processing Standard
FNC	Federal Networking Council
FSB	Federalnaya Sluzhba Bezopasnosti
GDP	gross domestic product
GDPR	General Data Protection Regulation
GOSIP	Government Open Systems Interconnection Profile
HTML	Hypertext Markup Language
HTTP	Hypertext Transfer Protocol
httpd	Hypertext Transfer Protocol daemon
IAB	Internet Architecture Board
IANA	Internet Assigned Numbers Authority
IBM	International Business Machines
ICANN	Internet Corporation for Assigned Names and Numbers
IEEE	Institute of Electrical and Electronics Engineers
IETF	Internet Engineering Task Force
IGF	Internet Governance Forum
IMPs	Interface Message Processors
INWG	International Packet Network Working Group
IP	Internet Protocol
IPv6	Internet Protocol version 6

IPX	Internetwork Packet Exchange
IRTF	Internet Research Task Force
ISI	Information Sciences Institute
ISO	International Organization for Standardization
ISP	Internet service provider
ITU	International Telecommunication Union
JvNC	John von Neuman Center
KGB	Komitet Gosudarstvennoy Bezopasnosti
MCI	MCI Mail; MCI Corporation
MIT	Massachusetts Institute of Technology
MOI	Mine of Information
NASA	National Aeronautics and Space Administration
NATO	North Atlantic Treaty Organization
NCSA	National Center for Supercomputing Applications
NERC	North American Electric Reliability Corporation
NFT	non-fungible token
NGN	next-generation network
NGO	nongovernmental organization
NIST	National Institute of Standards and Technology
NSA	National Security Agency
NSC	Network Secure Communication
NSF	National Science Foundation
NSFNET	National Science Foundation Network
NSI	Network Solutions, Inc.
NTIA	National Telecommunications and Information Administration
OSI	Open System Interconnection
PaCSON	Pacific Cyber Security Operational Network
PII	personally identifiable information
PSINET	Performance Systems International
PTTs	postal, telegraph, and telephone services
QoS	quality of service
QUIC	Quick User Datagram Protocol Internet Connections
RAND	research and development

RARE	Réseaux Associés pour la Recherche Européenne
RFCs	Requests for Comments
RFQ	request for quotation
ROSE	Research Open System for Europe
RSA	Rivest-Shamir-Adleman
RT	Russia Today
SAGE	Semi-Automatic Ground Environment
SC6	Subcommittee 6
SNA	Systems Network Architecture
SSL	Secure Sockets Layer
TCP	Transmission Control Protocol
TIM	The Information Mine
TLD	top-level domain
UCLA	The University of California, Los Angeles
UDI	universal document identifier
UDP	User Datagram Protocol
URI	uniform resource identifier
URL	universal resource locator
USSR	Union of Soviet Socialist Republics
UUNET	Unix to Unix NETwork
VAX	Virtual Address eXtension
VINES	Virtual Integrated NEtwork Service
VoIP	Voice over Internet Protocol
VPNs	virtual private networks
W3C	World Wide Web Consortium
WWW	World Wide Web
XNS	Xerox Network Systems
ZDNet	Ziff-Davis Network

PART I

Setting the Stage

1

Core Technical Decisions That Created the Internet

It seems reasonable to envision, for a time 10 or 15 years hence, a "thinking center" that will incorporate the functions of present-day libraries together with anticipated advances in information storage and retrieval. The picture readily enlarges itself into a network of such centers, connected to one another by wide-band communication lines and to individual users by leased-wire services. In such a system, the speed of the computers would be balanced, and the cost of the gigantic memories and the sophisticated programs would be divided by the number of users.

—J. C. R. LICKLIDER, *computer scientist and founding father of the ARPANET*[1]

Perhaps surprisingly to some, there have only been a handful of purely technical choices that got us to the Internet we have today, and the choices were made by a relatively small number of people. Subsequent chapters explore the nontechnical and policy choices. This chapter digs into these key technical digital forks, gives credit to the people who made them in the rooms where they happened, explains why a particular choice was made, tracks some of the wider implications of the choices made, and for each choice asks the key question—what if another path had been chosen?

Forks in the Digital Road. Scott J. Shackelford and Scott O. Bradner, Oxford University Press. © Oxford University Press 2024.
DOI: 10.1093/oso/9780197617762.003.0001

INTRODUCTION

The story of the Internet starts after the end of World War II. The design of digital computers had progressed significantly during the war years, and by the mid-1950s IBM was selling computers to businesses. By the end of that decade, it already sold over 10,000.[2] During the same period, IBM developed and put into service the nationwide Semi-Automatic Ground Environment (SAGE) air defense system in which multiple computers were interconnected over telephone lines.[3] SAGE was a self-contained, purpose-built system completely unlike the expandable, multipurpose, multiuser networks such as the Advanced Research Projects Agency Network (ARPANET) and the Internet, which were to come later and are discussed further in Chapter 8, though SAGE was a wide-area intercomputer network and, thus, a harbinger of things to come.

During this same period, visionaries like the public intellectual Vannevar Bush were thinking about just how computers might be used in the future, imagining beyond simple business applications such as managing payroll and keeping track of sales to the general storage, relating, and retrieving of vast amounts of information.[4] Multiple researchers expanded on Bush's thinking and adapted it to changing computer technology; for example, J. C. R. Licklider at MIT explored the ways in which people would be able to interact with computers and computers interact with other computers. Licklider ("Lick" to his friends, and perhaps even some of his enemies) envisioned data centers "connected to one another by wide-band communication lines and to individual users by leased-wire services."[5]

By the early 1960s, it had become clear that people were going to need to communicate with computers and computers were going to need to communicate with other computers over some sort of data network. This data network evolved into the Internet that we know and tolerate, if not always enjoy, today.

The four technical forks we will discuss in this chapter that led to this point are:

Packets: Should the data network of the future continue to use the circuit-switched technology that was the foundation of the worldwide telephone system, or were there more flexible alternatives?

Routers: How should the computers in the data network of the future be interconnected, and what should they know about the network?

Datagram: Should the data network of the future provide intelligent support for applications, or be ignorant of what applications are using the network?

Split TCP: Should the data network of the future only offer reliable data delivery like telephone networks, or were there reasons to not insist on reliability in some cases?

Each of these topics is addressed in turn.

1.1. Should the Network of the Future Use Circuits, Messages, or Packets?

Requiem of the ARPANET
It was the first, and being first, was best,
but now we lay it down to ever rest.
Now pause with me a moment, shed some tears.
For auld lang syne, for love, for years and years
of faithful service, duty done, I weep.
Lay down thy packet, now, O friend, and sleep.
— VINT CERF, *Father of the Internet*[6]

FORK 1: CAN YOU BUILD THE FUTURE ON TELEPHONE NETWORK TECHNOLOGY?

At the beginning of the 1960s, the only option for computer-to-computer data connections was the same facility used for people-to-people voice connections—circuit-switched telephone networks. Some researchers were also talking about the use of message switching. And, by the beginning of the 1970s, a new contender was just starting to show itself—a contender that would, in time, come to replace essentially all circuit- and message-switched facilities. This new contender was packet switching.[7]

The key difference between circuit- and packet-switching technologies lies in how the information to be communicated is communicated. In circuit-switched communications the information is transferred over a continuous connection from the start of the communication, such as a phone call, to the end, when one of the parties hangs up the phone. Thus, the resources, including the wires to the computers at the ends of the call, are busy from the start to the end of the call. In message-switched networks, on the other hand, the connection is only tied up for as long as it takes to transmit a single message.

Another feature of circuit-switched networks is that all the network devices, all of which are telephone switches in the case of the telephone network, have to know about the phone call and reserve network capacity for it for the duration of the call. A byproduct of this requirement for a stored call state in the telephone switches means that if one switch fails, or the link to the switch fails, then the call state is lost and the call has to be terminated.

Packet-switched communications can be seen as message-switched communications with a limit on the maximum size of a message. Specifically, the information, for example the digitized voices of the people on a phone call, are broken up into short chunks called packets for transmission to a destination.

We review the circuit, message, and packet-switching technologies, and why choosing to build the network of the future with packet switching made all the difference. All of these techniques are centered on the question of how best to communicate information of all kinds—from instant messages to images of the Mona Lisa.

CIRCUIT SWITCHING

Up until the early 1960s, the only way that people knew how to interconnect computers was with wires. Engineers either used their own wires to connect computers together that were near to each other or rented wires from a telephone company if the computers were further apart. The latter system became that much more important with the rise of long-distance calling, eventually laying the groundwork for the global networks that we take for granted today.

From the earliest days, the telephone system operated by establishing a pair of electrical connections between a telephone that originated a call to a telephone that was to receive the call, one for each direction. These connections were made by using telephone switches to link together a series of point-to-point circuits, starting with the origin telephone's connection to its local telephone switch, continuing through one or more intermediate telephone switches to the telephone switch the destination phone was connected to, and then on to the called telephone itself. The second series of point-to-point connections was required for the reverse direction.[8] Each of the switches in such a network needs to keep track of all of the phone calls passing through it so the switch could maintain the circuit. The circuits were maintained for as long as needed to complete the call, then "torn down" when the call was finished such that the wires were then freed up to support other calls. If this all sounds complicated, it was. Initially, the setup and tear down were done manually by telephone operators working in telephone offices, but by the early 1900s these functions were controlled by the user dialing a destination phone number, which caused electromechanical switches to automatically make and terminate these connections.

The setup and tear-down process became known as circuit switching—specifically, a connection ("circuit") needed to be switched on between two endpoints, be they telephones or computers, before information (voice or data) could be exchanged.[9] This circuit setup process could take a long time (up to multiple seconds), which is fine if the caller is a human setting up a phone call but not so good if the caller is a computer with only a short message to exchange, such as an email invitation to dinner that only takes a few milliseconds to transmit. In such a case, the circuit setup and teardown can be many times the length of the actual data transmission.

Over the years the internal technology of the telephone system was updated by a move from electromechanical switching to all electronic switching, though the circuit-switching concept remained the operating principle of the telephone world. Using telephone company–switched circuits to interconnect computers was accomplished by connecting each computer that was going to intercommunicate to a local telephone switch. Computer-to-computer communications, though, still needed to be bidirectional like voice calls because the receiving computer must let the sending computer know that a communication had been successfully received. The circuits would be maintained for as long as the computers needed to communicate and then were torn down.

Store-and-forward message switching had been developed for the telegraph network and was seen by some researchers as a possible alternative to circuit switching.

MESSAGE SWITCHING

Message switching involves sending a whole message, whatever its length, from a source computer to an adjacent switching node. The switching node then stores the message and, when it gets a chance, forwards the message to another switch that is closer to the ultimate destination. Messages can range in length from a few characters in the case of a short email to millions of characters in the case of a large picture. Message switching makes far more efficient use of communication links than does circuit switching because such links are only tied up for as long as it takes to send a single message to transmit rather than for the duration of a phone call. In addition, message-switching systems are more resilient to the failure of a single link or switch since the stored message can be resent when the failure is corrected, or, if an alternate path existed, the message could be sent to the destination via that path.

An early example of message switching was the telegraph. In the 1870s, advances in telegraph transmission technology meant that the actual transmission of telegraphs over wires had become far faster than the capacity of the individual human operators using the then-standard techniques. So, instead of using a telegraph key directly connected to the transmission line, operators started using a keyboard that was connected to a paper tape punch.[10] Each telegraph would be punched onto a length of paper tape, and the tape would be torn off and placed in a basket associated with a transmission line going to a particular telegraph office. Multiple operators were kept busy creating these short tapes of telegraph messages, not exactly the most exciting occupation. An additional operator would be in charge of taking tapes out of a basket and feeding them into an electronic telegraph transmitter that operated at a far higher speed than humans ever could. Equipment at each of the receiving telegraph offices would punch the telegraphs onto a paper tape, which would then be torn into individual pieces, each representing an individual telegraph. The received tapes would be put into baskets for outgoing connections to another telegraph office closer to the intended destination telegraph office. If a particular line was down or too busy, the messages could be sent on a different line as long as the line went to a switch closer to the destination telegraph office. Thus, telegraph messages were stored and then forwarded.[11]

Message switching is the same as circuit switching when used for interactive continuous communications such as voice calls since the communications line in each direction is tied up for the full duration of the voice call—even if no one is talking. Message switching of arbitrarily long messages provides for efficient usage of communication lines. But since long messages take quite a long time to transmit, the communications lines will be tied up for unknown periods, which interferes with interactive uses such as remote computer access.

For interactive types of communications and for other types of communications that involve lots of short messages, a different kind of technology was needed: specifically, something that efficiently used transmission lines like message switching, while supporting continuous voice communications as well as real-time interactive remote login applications. That something else would become known as packet switching.

PACKET SWITCHING

In the early 1960s, Paul Baran, a researcher working under a U.S. Air Force contract at RAND, a U.S. defense contractor, was researching ways to build a command-and-control network for the U.S. military that would survive a nuclear first strike. Born in Grodno, Poland (now Belarus), Baran's family moved to Philadelphia in 1928. He studied electrical engineering at Drexel University and UCLA before becoming a researcher at RAND.[12]

While there, Baran had an idea that was initially published in 1962 to break up communications, both voice and data, into "standardized message blocks" like what was done for message switching but with a limit on the maximum length of each message block.[13] If a specific message was longer than the maximum message block size, it would be split into multiple message blocks. If the maximum message block length was short enough, then a network using them would be able to support both continuous data streams and interactive use. In Baran's concept, each of the message blocks contained enough information (specifically the address of another computer connected to the network) for the message block to be routed through a distributed network of many redundantly interconnected switching nodes. Baran's 1962 diagram of such a network is shown in Figure 1.1.

Even if a number of the switching nodes were to be destroyed or to fail, which would be the case in the event of a nuclear attack, the message blocks would be rerouted and get through, as long as at least one path survived.[14] In addition, one computer could communicate with multiple other computers over the same wire since the network would direct each message block to the correct computer; thus, a single wire could handle multiple simultaneous communications that were operating at different rates of speed to different other computers. Baran and his fellow researchers expanded on his concepts in a multivolume series published in 1964.[15] An aspect of Baran's work illustrates his personal philosophy— almost all of his work was unclassified—he wanted the Soviet Union to have the same technology so no one in the U.S. government would think

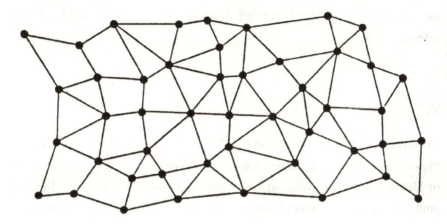

Figure 1.1. Paul Baran's Figure of a Distributed Network
Paul Baran, *On Distributed Communications Networks*, RAND, 1, 4 (1962), https://www.rand.org/pubs/papers/P2626.html.

that a nuclear first strike on the Soviet Union would keep the Soviets from retaliating.[16]

A few years later, working independently, Welsh researcher Donald Davies from the United Kingdom's National Physical Laboratory (NPL) developed the same basic concepts as Baran. Davies called his message blocks "packets" and the overall concept "packet switching."[17] Prior to coining the term "packets," Davies had studied physics and mathematics at Imperial College, London.[18]

Although on opposite sides of the pond, both Baran and Davies faced strong resistance to their ideas from the established telephone operators, including AT&T.[19] In the end, the U.S. Air Force, which had funded Baran's research, did not build the network Baran had described.[20] But Davies did build a working packet-switched network that went live in 1969.[21]

While the Air Force did not build a packet-based network in the mid-1960s, the Advanced Projects Research Agency (ARPA), part of the U.S. Defense Department, did so a few years later. That packet-based network was called the ARPANET, and it provided proof that, despite conventional wisdom, worldwide packet-based networks could be built, operated, and efficiently used for many different purposes, eventually morphing into the Internet. ARPA is further discussed in Chapters 2, and 3, but is introduced below.

ARPA

In response to the Soviet Union's 1957 launch of the Sputnik satellite, U.S. President Dwight Eisenhower established ARPA in the U.S. Department of Defense with a mission to "to prevent technological surprise like the launch of Sputnik."[22] Specifically, DoD directive 5105.15, which established ARPA, was very open-ended and authorized ARPA to "acquire or construct such research, development, and test facilities and equipment as may be approved by the Secretary of Defense."[23] It took time for this body to reach national, and eventually global, prominence, resulting in calls for "ARPA-everything,"[24] but that journey was hastened by its pioneering support of ARPANET, which led to the Internet we know today.

ARPANET

By the mid-1960s, ARPA was funding myriad researchers at nearly as many universities, each of which, it seemed, wanted their own computer to support their research—something that even ARPA could not afford despite its $283 million budget (which works out to $2.6 billion in 2023 dollars).[25] MIT researcher Larry Roberts moved to ARPA in 1966 and started to work on finding a way to share computing resources so that each researcher would not have a justification for their own computers. Born in 1937 and raised in Westport, Connecticut, to parents who both held doctorates in chemistry from Yale, Roberts was frequently hospitalized as a child as a result of chemistry experiments gone awry.[26]

Eventually earning a doctorate in electrical engineering, Roberts began working on a network to interconnect remote researchers to the existing ARPA-sponsored, time-shared computers. He called the network the ARPANET. Roberts knew about electronic message-switching systems but felt they were "too slow and laborious."[27] He presented the general concept at several conferences, including one in Gatlinburg, Tennessee, in 1967.[28] His presentation included why such a network would be useful and what services it would offer. Roger Scantlebury from Donald Davies's lab presented a paper at the same conference describing packet switching. Scantlebury's paper included references to Baran's work.[29] During the conference, Scantlebury and Roberts talked about the potential use of packet switching for the ARPANET. Later, it turned out that Roberts had copies of Baran's papers in his office but had not read them, which he did when he got back home.[30] Based on the discussions and papers Roberts decided to use the concept of packet switching for the ARPANET instead of circuit or message switching. This fortuitous meeting over coffee at a conference in Tennessee continues to have ripple effects to this day.

NOT THE BOMB

Note that Roberts, who managed the building of the ARPANET, was creating the network to share computing resources so ARPA could avoid buying each researcher his own computer. Roberts was not building a network to survive a nuclear attack, so, even though Roberts was using a packet-switched network of the general design that Baran had conceived of to survive a nuclear attack, the ARPANET itself was not developed in response to the Cold War nuclear threat.[31] But since the money came from the Defense Department there may have been people in the Pentagon who had other objectives.[32]

The devices connected to the ARPANET were timeshare computers and terminal servers. A researcher could be connected to their own local computer, which could communicate with other computers by exchanging packets through the ARPANET, and they would appear as a terminal user on the timeshare computer. Or a researcher could connect his or her own computer terminal to an ARPANET terminal server and then, via packets through the ARPANET, to a timeshare computer. Multiple researchers could be connected to a timeshare computer simultaneously either from

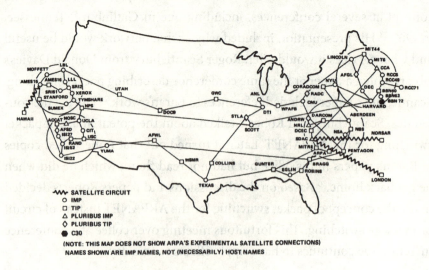

Figure 1.2. ARPANET Geographic Map, October 1980
APRANET (October 1980), https://mappa.mundi.net/maps/maps_001/.

terminals connected via the ARPANET or from directly connected local terminals. The packet-switched network scaled well in that adding an additional computer only required that the new computer have a unique address and a single wire into the network.

The ARPANET started small, and by today's standards, stayed small—after a decade there were less than 200 computers connected to it,[33] and there were not many more than that connected before the ARPANET was shut down in 1990. But the small number of nodes belies the geographic scale of the ARPANET—it covered half the globe, from Hawaii to Norway—as is illustrated in Figure 1.2.

WHAT IF ROBERTS HAD CHOSEN MESSAGE OR CIRCUIT SWITCHING?

Larry Roberts had three possible networking technologies he could have chosen to implement a resource-sharing network in the late 1960s: circuit switching, message switching, and packet switching. Of these, packet switching was the newest and, at least in the traditional networking community, the least trusted. Roberts nonetheless chose to use packet switching. Would we have the Internet of today if he had opted for one of the other two more proven technologies?

As Paul Baran and Bruce Davies had found out, the traditional telecommunications experts in the mid-1960s did not think that packet switching was good for much of anything. Almost universally, these experts favored using switched circuit services from a telephone company. Even after the ARPANET had been running successfully for a number of years, AT&T did not respond to an offer to take over its operations because packet-switched networks were not in AT&T's plan.[34]

If Roberts had chosen to use circuit switching, he would have found a lot of support in the telecommunications community of the day, but he would have built a network with little flexibility, one that could not have supported the vast variety of applications and users that the Internet supports today. The use of a circuit-switched network would have meant that every communication between computers would have been implemented as a phone call. Each of the computers in the system would have had to have multiple connections into the circuit-switched network, one connection for every possible simultaneous outgoing or incoming connection. Such a network could not have feasibly scaled to billions of computers. And, of course, the telephone companies would have wanted to charge for each call, which would have made the system expensive to use and far out of reach for many of the people that rely on the Internet for an increasing share of their personal and professional lives, thus exacerbating digital divides.

If Roberts had decided to use a message-forwarding network, it would have scaled better than a circuit-switched one because only a single connection is needed per computer, but message-switched networks cannot support continuous applications such as voice or streaming video. Today's Internet would be much less than it is if that were the case, since essentially all telephone calls are carried over Internet technology, along with audio and video streaming. Message-switched networks cannot support real-time interactive gaming, for example.

Roberts's decision to use packet switching in his network directly led to a technology that has scaled in connections from 4 computers in 1969 to over 20 billion by the end of 2018.[35] It led to a network that scaled in link speed, too, from the ARPANET's 56,000 bits per second in 1969 to 100 billion bits per second by 2020.[36] Additionally, it led to a network that went from supporting simple file transfer and interactive connections on timeshare computers to replacing essentially the entire telecommunication infrastructure of a large part of the world; supporting an almost infinite range of applications in the process, as is explored further in Part II.

1.2. What Should the Topology of the Network of the Future Look Like?

> Why have central control? Why not have small machines?
>
> —Attributed to Wesley Clark[37]

Fork 2: Will an Additional Box Help the Design?

After Larry Roberts had decided to use packets for his new network, there were some basic design issues to be addressed, including what the network topology should be, and what role the computers being interconnected should play in directing the traffic through the network.

In deciding to build a network so that computers could talk with each other, Roberts was venturing into uncharted territory. At that time there was very little experience with computers talking with other computers, much less doing so at a distance. Roberts had personal experience with one of the few attempts at transcontinental computer communication. In 1966, he had arraigned for a connection between a TX-2 computer that he used at MIT's Lincoln Labs in Lincoln, Massachusetts and a computer at Systems Development Corporation in Santa Monica, California.[38]But since Roberts was planning to build a network over which about two dozen computers would communicate,[39] this single link did not provide much help in defining an overall network design.

Robert's original idea was to implement a star topology with a large controlling computer located somewhere in the center of the country. A star topology simplifies directing messages between computers. Each of the participating computers would be connected to it with leased telephone lines.[40] Then, the participating computers would just need to send a message to the central computer, which would then forward the message to the correct destination. But a star topology is expensive when it comes to telephone circuits and does not scale all that well.

Luckily, Roberts was convinced that there was a better way for both the topology and directing the message traffic.

MOVING AWAY FROM A STAR

Roberts presented his star topology at an ARPA contractors meeting.[41] Several issues with the idea were discussed at the meeting, including the amount of computing resources in the end computers that would have to be dedicated to network operations and the requirement to update the computer software as the network evolved. Star topologies are also fragile since a computer could easily be cut off if one of the long-haul telephone circuits failed.

Wesley Clark, a researcher who was at the meeting, had a different idea, which he explained to Roberts during a cab ride after the meeting.[42] A physicist by training who saw the future "15 years before everyone else,"[43] Clark's suggestion was to get rid of the central controlling computer and make use of small special-purpose computers that would handle the network operations. These special-purpose computers would be connected to the researcher's computers and to each other. This would free up the researcher's computers to do more research. The use of separate, small computers to manage the network itself would also mean that the research computers could use standard network interface hardware and software and would not have to be updated every time the network changed. The fact that the special-purpose computers could be made cheaply meant that there could be more of them so that the network topology could be more flexible and redundant.

As it happens, Paul Baran's original 1962 paper described using just this type of special-purpose computer as the backbone of a data network, though there is no indication that Clark knew of Bran's work.[44]

Roberts adopted the idea and issued a request for quotation (RFQ) for routers, which he called Interface Message Processors (IMPs), for the ARPANET in 1969.[45] The contract was awarded to Bolt Beranek and Newman Inc. (BBN) in Cambridge, Massachusetts. After the award, Massachusetts Senator Ted Kennedy sent BBN a telegram saying that they were "to be congratulated on winning the contract for the interfaith message processor."[46]

Each IMP could be used to connect one or more computers to the network and to two or more other IMPs. The connections between the IMP and the researcher's computers used a defined standard that was implemented by different computer manufactures and did not have to change as the ARPANET itself evolved. The IMPs handled all the network operations, including maintaining an internal map of the network topology so that the IMP would know how to forward a packet to the correct destination. Offloading these functions to the IMPs greatly simplified the software needed in the computer, and the IMPs isolated the researcher's computers from the network so network issues would not impact the computers. Connecting each IMP to two or more other IMPs provided redundant paths that could be used if a particular telephone link were to fail.

The concept of using special-purpose computers to implement the network itself became even more important a few years later when the ARPANET evolved into the Internet, as is discussed in Chapters 2 and 3.

The Internet Protocol that the pioneers Vint Cerf and Robert Kahn developed assumed that the network was a network of networks. The network of networks extended to the multiple networks in an enterprise or even in a home to the worldwide network of networks that is the Internet. These networks would be joined together by IMP-like special computers, which they referred to as gateways.[47] When a gateway receives a packet going through the network, its primary function was to decide where to send the packet next, not unlike the ring gates in *Stargate*, a function that Cerf and Kahn called "routing."[48] Thus, it was natural that when companies began to manufacture these gateways for sale, they called them "routers."

Internet routers provide for logical and managerial separation between networks. Each router has two or more interfaces, each of which is connected to a network. The networks need not be managed by the same people, but they can be. An organization such as Harvard has dozens of routers to support the many dozens of individual networks, one or more in each building. Harvard also has a few routers that are used to connect Harvard's network, the collection of all of those individual networks, to Internet service providers (ISPs), which, in turn, provide connectivity to the worldwide Internet. ISPs themselves have many routers that interconnect the network links that make up the ISP's network and that connect to routers in other ISPs.

WHAT IF WESS CLARK HAD NOT SUGGESTED EXTERNAL DEVICES TO RUN THE NETWORK?

Without routers, the Internet as we know it could not exist. Routers enable the interconnection of millions of separately operated networks so that the Internet looks like a single network. Routers also enable the interconnection of the telephone cellular networks to the rest of the Internet so you can read email on your smartphone. Routers also mean that your smartphone can participate on the Internet because the routers in the network take care of directing the data packets toward the destination, rather than requiring the smartphone to know enough about the topology of the overall Internet to know how to direct the packets.

With routers, adding another network to the Internet is as simple as connecting a router on the new network to a router on an ISP.

1.3. The Users or the Carriers: Who Should Control the Network of the Future?

> You could see it in the eyes of the idolaters—FEAR! I say FEAR of the DATAGRAM was upon them! They realized that they wuz in the midst of an epiphany—AN EPIPHANY, and SOMETHING DIED! The CIRCUIT as the atomic abstraction had been STRUCK DOWN by a MIGHTY BLAST of INSIGHT and the smokin' ruin just lay there on the floor, the unmistakable odor of lost hegemony stinkin' up the place.
>
> SOULS WERE SAVED THAT DAY from a life of unceasing DIAL TONE!
>
> The MIGHTY POUZIN finally bid the crowd disperse, but the fire lit that day in fact, changed lives.
>
> For which I'm eternally grateful.
>
> —INTERNET SAGE MIKE O'DELL[49]

FORK 3: DO WE HAVE TO CEDE CONTROL TO THE CARRIERS?
The following is the background.

The ARPANET that Roberts had built was based on packets. The packet-based ARPANET provided for great multiplexing of applications, including applications that ran at very different speeds. Initially, Robert's original ARPANET itself provided a reliable data delivery service by the IMPs correcting any transmission errors before passing the communications on to the host computers. (More on that aspect in the next section.) The original ARPANET was also a single network, not a network of networks.

By the mid-1970s, ARPA was supporting more than just the ARPANET; it was also supporting a Packet radio network, as well as a packet satellite system.[50] The packet radio network and the ARPANET were very different networks—they operated at very different speeds, they used different packet sizes, and they had different operating assumptions about the reliability of packet delivery. Bob Kahn, then a manager at ARPA, thought it would be good to link these networks together with the ARPANET so researchers could access resources on the various networks, so he went looking for help to develop a communications protocol that could support communications between computers connected to networks with different characteristics.[51] He found Vint Cerf.

Born in New Haven, Connecticut, the son of Muriel and Vinton Cerf, Vint attended high school with the other legendary figure in the history of Internet governance, Jon Postel. He worked at the contractor Rocketdyne on the Apollo program and earned a degree in mathematics from Stanford University. Tellingly, both he and his wife Sigrid have hearing aids, making them proponents for accessibility, which may have informed his later work on Internet governance. Cerf received his MS and Ph.D. from UCLA, where he worked under Professors Gerald Estrin and Leonard Kleinrock, who were, you recall, responsible for connecting the first two nodes of the ARPANET in 1969. He later worked as an assistant professor at Stanford and at DARPA through 1982 on various projects, including TCP/IP, before going on to found the first commercial email system (MCI Mail) to be connected to the Internet.

Cerf met Bob Kahn at UCLA. Before Kahn became a "Father of the Internet" who was instrumental in ARPANET's success, Kahn had been an electrical engineer from Brooklyn. He had earned both his master's and doctoral degrees from Princeton before joining DARPA.[52] While there, he spearheaded the billion-dollar Strategic Computing Program, which at that point was "the largest computer research and development program ever undertaken by the federal government."[53] Kahn became convinced that the ARPANET design of a single network would not scale, so he reached out to Cerf, who was still a graduate student, to put together the concept of what became the Internet, as described below.

Instead, the path that Cerf and Kahn could have taken was to continue the ARPANET design of having the network itself ensure the reliable delivery of information, but they decided to take a different path. The path that Cerf and Kahn chose enabled innovation and disenfranchised telephone carriers, with many positive results for users. In short, they chose to build a stupid network rather than assume a smart network.

WHY STUPID IS SOMETIMES SMART

The original IMP-based ARPANET was a "smart network." Smart in the sense that it was able to detect and correct transmission errors. The IMPs were able to detect corrupted packets and discard them, detect duplicated packets and discard one of the duplicates, detect packets that were reordered in the network and rearrange them into the proper order, and retransmit any lost packets.[54]

Around the time that Cerf and Kahn were starting to figure out how to interconnect the ARPA-funded packet networks telephone standards organizations were working on a standard for smart packet-switched network technology called X.25.[55] X.25 supported reliable communications through the use of virtual circuits and by correcting any packet transmission errors. Virtual circuit protocols attempt to make a packet-switched network indistinguishable from a switched circuit network.[56] A major advantage of X.25 and its virtual circuit service, as well as the general smart network concept, from the point of view of the telephone carrier, was that it put the carrier in control of what the network could be used for since the network operator was in the loop of the management of the virtual circuits. The telephone companies even made a point of advertising their network design as "The Intelligent Network."[57]

IBM introduced System Network Architecture (SNA) at about the same time, which was a smart network technology targeted at enterprise networks. In general, the smart network concept was quite popular among traditional network professionals at the time. It seemed to make a great deal of sense—why wouldn't everybody want a network that understands its customers' needs and provides for reliable information exchange?

But this "smart network" model is very limiting. Users must get the network operator's permission to run new types of applications, and the network operator has to reconfigure the network equipment to support the new application—and, of course, the user could have to pay extra for the privilege of having their desired application supported.

STUPID NETWORK?

French network researcher Louis Pouzin was faced with the constraints of the smart network model and came up with a different concept—the datagram. Born in 1931, the son of a sawmill operator, Pouzin studied engineering at France's famous engineering university, the École Polytechnique.[58] After graduating in 1952, he designed machine tools for the French national telecommunications monopoly but was soon drawn to a new technology—computing.[59]

While at the French national computing lab, Pouzin and his team developed the datagram concept, which is not about the unit of data transfer even though if you do an Internet search for "what is the difference between a datagram and a packet," you will get a lot of responses that say they are the same thing; that is not the case. Those responses are missing the point, which is that the difference is more structural than definitional. The key point of Pouzin's datagram concept is that the network just delivers the datagrams (i.e., the packets)—the network does not provide any kind of service other than to attempt to deliver packets as best as it can—what became known as "best-effort" delivery. The network does not know what application is being run and does not need to, since the best-effort service is the same in all cases.

In the Pouzin datagram model, the computers on the two ends of a communication are completely responsible for all aspects of the communication, including deciding at what rate they need to send the packets to support the application they are running, and implementing any reliability mechanisms to make up for the fact that packets can be lost, reordered, or duplicated in transit.[60] The end systems only do so if the application they are running needs such reliability. As we will see in the next section, interactive voice is made worse if it is done over a connection that ensures reliable packet delivery. On the other hand, bulk data transfer needs both reliability and good rate control to ensure the data does not get corrupted in transit and that the rate of data flow does not overwhelm the receiving computer.

Leaving it to the end nodes to decide what type of information transfer they need for the particular application they are running is also called the end-to-end (e2e) model. The principles behind the e2e model are well described in the 1981 paper *End-to-End Arguments in System Design* by Saltzer, Reed, and Clark.[61]

The Pouzin datagram model has the effect of totally disintermediating the network operator—that is, the telephone company—so network operators did not like it very much,[62] as was colorfully described in the quote at the start of this section from network guru Mike O'Dell. Cerf and Kahn adopted the Pouzin datagram model for the new network and network protocol to interconnect the ARPA-supported networks. The network model they adopted is what we use today for the Internet, and the network protocol they developed—TCP/IP—is the protocol that created the Internet's network of networks, as is discussed further in Part II.

The importance of choosing a stupid datagram-based network design rather than a smart network design is also discussed in David Isenberg's seminal paper "The Rise of the Stupid Network"[63] and in the wonderful *Wired* magazine article, "Netheads vs Bellheads."[64]

WHAT IF CERF AND KAHN HAD DECIDED THAT X.25 WAS A GOOD ENOUGH INTERNET PROTOCOL?

A common way to describe today's Internet environment is that it supports "permissionless innovation."[65] In the case of the Internet, this means that someone with a new idea for an Internet service or application does not need to get prior permission before developing and trying out the idea. For example, if you come up with a shopping website that you think is better than Amazon, you do not have to get permission from your Internet service provider before you launch and market the site.

Today's permissionless innovation Internet is primarily a result of Cerf and Kahn deciding to support datagrams and the end-to-end architectural model rather than depending on a smart network to manage communications. That is because the alternative to the Pouzin datagram model is a network service model in which the network operator determines what applications the user can run and how much each application would cost to run. Although there may be a benefit for security, as is discussed in Chapter 3, this is a model that the telephone companies have repeatedly tried to deploy but to date have failed. The telephone standards bodies and telephone companies have tried X.25, ATM,[66] NGN,[67] and most recently, 5G.[68] The network service model would mean innovation would only have taken place at the pace that phone companies innovate, glacial at best.

1.4. Is Unreliability Useful?

> Realtime is like milk: keep the newest
> Non-realtime is like wine: keep the oldest
> —Danny Cohen, Internet speech researcher[69]

Fork 4: Should the Protocol Assume Reliability Is Required?

As discussed in the last section, in the mid-1970s the standard network information delivery service offering from the telephone companies and IBM, as well as from the ARPANET, ensured that the information was reliably delivered. Thus, it was natural that the new Internet end-to-end protocol that Cerf and Kahn developed was one that only provided reliable information delivery even though they had adopted the datagram model for the network itself. The software in the end systems running the Cerf/Kahn "Internet Transmission Control Program" watched for datagrams that had been lost, duplicated, or reordered and then corrected any errors it found.

It certainly seemed to make sense; after all, who would want to use an unreliable data network? It turns out, we all do, whether we realize it or not. There are several applications that work far better over communication links that do not try to provide reliable data transport—interactive voice being an important example. After quite a bit of discussion, Cerf & Kahn revised their Internet TCP to include an ability to pass datagrams to the user applications without any error correction. This change enabled many services that are seen as basic Internet services today such as Voice over IP and video streaming, enabling firms like Netflix and offerings like YouTube to exist. The way that people actually interact in a conversation dictates that you cannot have large gaps in interactive voice such as phone calls or have people talk over each other.

HOW PEOPLE TALK

Research done in the 1930s at AT&T Bell Labs determined that normal human conversation, at least among North American English speakers, occurred in bursts separated by short pauses.[70] One person, Person A, would talk for a while (a "talkspurt") and then pause to see if the other person wanted to talk. If Person A did not hear the other person, Person B, start talking within a short period of time (the "resumption time"), then Person A would resume talking. The research showed that the median resumption time in the conversations they recorded was 0.6 seconds (600 milliseconds [ms]). In other words, if Person A did not hear Person B start talking within 600 ms of pausing, then Person A would start talking again—in the process talking right over Person B, thus defeating the purpose of the call and the technology.[71]

This observation was important in the telephone world because it defined the maximum end-to-end round-trip delay that could be tolerated in a telephone connection before people would start talking over each other. This magic value of 600 ms maximum round-trip delay has been enshrined in numerous telephone-related documents.[72] But the mechanisms that are required to support reliable data transfer often cause large pauses in the data transfer.

RELIABLE INFORMATION TRANSFER

Protocols that provide a reliable data transfer service need to recover from lost, corrupted, reordered, or duplicated packets. The protocols have various mechanisms to provide reliability, but most of them include sequence numbers in the individual packets to detect that a packet has been lost, packets have been reordered, or packets have been duplicated. Dealing with duplicated or reordered packets is easy and quick—the software just discards a packet if it has already seen a packet in the communication with the same sequence number, and the software makes sure it forwards packets in the correct sequence order.

Dealing with lost packets can be much more time-consuming—if the software detects a gap in the sequence numbers in the packets it receives, the software usually must wait a period of time—known as a timeout time—to see if the packet was actually lost or maybe just reordered or otherwise delayed. If the packet was lost, then it must be retransmitted to patch the gap in the data stream. The timeout time can be multiple seconds, during which time no data is forwarded to the receiving computer.[73]

Large gaps in the data stream are fine for file transfer; the overall transfer takes a bit longer, but the data is reliability transferred. Such gaps are not so good for interactive voice since it can cause garbled conversations if the gaps exceed 600 ms. People would talk over each other or just hang up.

The gap issue is not quite as stark as it might seem since it turns out that the Vocoders, the devices that turn packet data into audio, can deal with some missed packets; the resulting sound may have minor glitches but can be perfectly understandable. Yet that is only the case if there are infrequent gaps. This Vocoder feature means that, for voice, it is better to ignore lost packets rather than to add the gaps that would result from the timeouts and retransmissions required to ensure reliable data transfer.[74] In addition, in the case of badly delayed packets, for voice, unlike for file transfer, it is better to throw them away than to worry about recovering them as noted by Danny Cohen at the beginning of this section.

ARPA NETWORK SECURE COMMUNICATION (NSC) PROGRAM:

ARPA started a Network Secure Communication (NSC) program in 1973 to develop interactive packet voice technology over the ARPANET.[75] Harvard student and eventual faculty member, Danny Cohen was one of the researchers working on the ARPA NSC program. Born in Israel, Cohen "developed the first real-time visual flight simulator on a general purpose computer" but ran into issues when he tried to make his creation available over ARPANET.[76] The problems stemmed from trying to support speech over a reliable transport protocol since the NSC project was trying to run speech over the old ARPANET that implemented, by default, reliable information delivery.[77] In order to avoid the gaps introduced by the reliable information delivery process, Cohen got rare permission to make use of a special mode in the IMP software that bypassed the reliability functions.[78] This bypass mode just delivered the packets and did not try to correct errors in any way. Using the bypass mode, Cohen and the team from the Information Sciences Institute (ISI), which is part of the University of Southern California, and, at that time, a primary contractor for the ARPA NSC program, were able to demonstrate intelligible voice over the ARPANET.[79] As such, Cohen became the first to implement "packet video" and "packet voice," and all in the name of playing a cool new videogame online.

INTERNET TRANSMISSION CONTROL PROGRAM

Cerf and Kahn's first proposal to link the multiple ARPA-sponsored networks together into a "network of networks" (an "Internet") was called "Internet Transmission Control Program" (TCP) and was published in late 1974.[80] The specification described programs that would reside in network end systems that would send and receive datagrams, perform error control, and offer a reliable information transfer service to applications running on the end systems.

After this effort the two began to work even more together closely, culminating in another red-letter date in the history of Internet governance and cybersecurity on November 22, 1977. On that day, a message was sent from a repurposed delivery van known as the "bread truck," (see Figure 1.3) parked in San Francisco and equipped with a wireless transmitter, to Norway via a satellite and back to California.[81] This first communion of the Internet demonstrated not just a single transmission, proving a new communications technology as with ARPANET; rather, according to Kahn, "It was a whole system of network protocols being demonstrated over three different networks."[82] The Internet, after all, is an ecosystem of disparate networks, of which ARPANET had become but one.

The road to that parking lot in 1977, though, was full of twists and turns. An important mile marker was when Kahn traveled to Stanford, where Cert was an assistant professor at the time, saying simply, "I have a problem."[83] The issue was that Kahn wanted to control a network of computers "from the computers that connected to it" but not permit any one machine to dominate.[84] "The problem is that if you are serious about using computers, you better be able to put them in mobile vehicles,

Figure 1.3. The "Bread Truck"

ships at sea, and aircraft, as well as at fixed installations," Cerf said.[85] This presaging of what has become the Internet of Things underscored for a single protocol not to rule them all exactly, but to act as a sort of universal translator vis-à-vis *Star Trek*.

Based on his work on packet speech in the NSC project, Cohen was convinced that having a way to bypass the reliability features of a transport protocol was critical for a whole range of applications but in particular for interactive speech.[86] Many sources describe a meeting that Cohen had with Cerf, David Reed, John Shoch, and Jon Postel in a corridor or maybe a conference room at ISI. This conversation was the culmination of a multiyear effort by Cohen and others to persuade Cerf and Kahn to add a reliability bypass to TCP.[87]

David Reed, born in 1952 and educated at MIT, who would later become famous for postulating "Reed's Law," which is the idea that "the utility of large networks, can scale exponentially with the size of the network,"[88] worked closely with Postel. Born in 1943 in Altadena, California, Jon Postel would go on to attend UCLA, where he earned a doctorate in computing in 1974.[89]

The result of the meeting between Reed, Postel, Cerf, and Kahn was that Cerf agreed that a way to bypass the reliability function in TCP could be useful. That way turned out to be to restructure TCP to split the IP (the send-and-receive datagram part) from the TCP (the error correcting part) and add, in parallel to TCP, a User Datagram Protocol (UDP) to support real-time applications. UDP itself was designed, if designed is the right term, by David Reed.[90] UDP bypassed the reliability features of TCP and, like the bypass mode in the IMP software that Cohen had used, just forwarded the underlying datagrams to the user application. The resulting protocol suite was collectively known as TCP/IP and was published as a set of four specifications, edited by Jon Postel, in 1980 and 1981,[91] and the ARPANET transitioned to it at the beginning of 1983.[92] This is the same protocol suite, with some updates, that the Internet is running today. In fact, their creation, TCP/IP, (see Figure 1.4) which marked the first use of the term "Internet," allowed vastly different computers and networks to

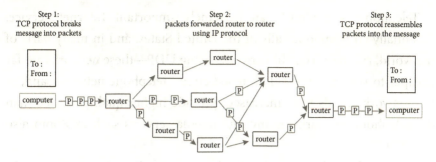

Figure 1.4. How TCP/IP Works

communicate for the first time, though it would take several more years for their idea to be realized, as is discussed in Chapter 2.[93]

UDP became the transport protocol used for interactive voice and video, audio and video streaming, interactive gaming, network management, stock tickers, and many other real-time applications.

WHAT IF CERF HAD NOT BEEN PERSUADED TO SPLIT TCP AND IP?

If Cerf and Kahn's original—reliable transfer only—protocol had not been modified to enable a non-error-corrected transfer mode, the Internet of today would be far less important than it is since it enables some of the most important Internet applications, particularly where Internet bandwidth is scarce, causing congestion. Packet loss is rare in the absence of congestion, so TCP could be used for voice in areas of plentiful bandwidth because there will be few cases where TCP's error correction will cause gaps in transmission. But scarce bandwidth was ubiquitous online for more than a decade after TCP/IP was first rolled out, and is still the case in many parts of the world, including significant parts of the United States. Thus, congestion and the resulting packet loss meant that voice and other real-time interactive services would not have been feasible without the adoption of UDP.

Telephony is obviously an extremely important Internet service. Essentially all telephone calls in the United States, and in many parts of the world, run over TCP/IP networks using UDP—these networks are far cheaper to run than the old switched circuit telephone networks and, as the network speeds have increased, provide higher quality service than did telephone networks. Many multimedia services such as Zoom also use UDP.[94]

UDP further allows for the development of alternative Internet reliable information transport services by passing the underlying datagrams to the end system applications, including applications that implement reliable information transfer in ways different than does TCP. The Quick User Datagram Protocol Internet Connections (QUIC) protocol, originally developed by Google and standardized by the Internet Engineering Task Force (IETF),[95] is an example of such a protocol. QUIC has far less overhead than TCP does while providing much better security.[96] Without UDP, the TCP/IP protocol suite, and thus the Internet, would not have become what it has, essentially the underlying transport for the entire world's telecommunications.

WRAP UP

The four decisions covered in the chapter laid the technical foundation for the Internet. The decision to use packet switching meant that the Internet can support a wide variety of applications running at very different speeds over the same physical network. The decision to make use of an external device to perform most of the calculations needed to direct packets to their proper destinations meant that devices of all sizes and power from door cameras to smartphones, and laptops to room-sized super computers, can communicate over the Internet without spending too much of their computing power doing so. The decision to use datagrams meant that carriers and ISPs are not gatekeepers that can dictate what applications can and cannot be run. And, finally, the decision to support an unreliable communications option meant that the Internet could support a wide variety of real-time interactive applications even where there might be bandwidth constraints.

The next chapter moves up a few levels and discusses a number of nontechnical policy decisions that, in hindsight, were key to creating what has become an almost ubiquitous communications infrastructure.

2

"Layer 9"—Core Policy Decisions That Gave Us the Internet We Have

> Technology and politics are conceptually inseparable because the rules under which technological enterprise is undertaken is essentially political in nature. Politics is precisely about what the rules are and who is favored by them, but most important, it is about who gets to make them. Where there is technology, there is embedded politic.
>
> —GERALD SUSSMAN, author[1]

Chapter 1 focused on the key technical decisions that got us the Internet of today. This chapter discusses some of the nontechnical decisions that were important along this digital road. Additional policy decisions will be covered in Part II.

When we say "nontechnical," we are referring to decisions that were not driven by purely technical criteria. Instead, the decisions were driven, at least in part, by real-world economic or political criteria, by a desire to achieve some future technical dominance, and by government dictate.

The six nontechnical forks we will discuss in this chapter are:

Forks in the Digital Road. Scott J. Shackelford and Scott O. Bradner, Oxford University Press. © Oxford University Press 2024.
DOI: 10.1093/oso/9780197617762.003.0002

1. *International standardization:* Should the international technical standards development organizations adopt TCP/IP as the network technology of the future?
2. *Free code:* Should the U.S. government ensure that the source code for TCP/IP is available for free?
3. *Access to government-sponsored networks:* Since the U.S. government is not supposed to compete with the private sector, who should be able to make use of the Advanced Research Projects Agency Network (ARPANET)?
4. *Access to government-sponsored networks take 2:* Same question as above, but for the National Science Foundation Network (NSFNET)? The answer need not be the same.
5. *NSFNET protocol support:* In a multiprotocol world, what protocols should the NSFNET support?
6. *Government Open Systems Interconnection Profile (GOSIP):* Should the U.S. government mandate what protocols can be used on the Internet?

Each of these forks, some of which may seem quite insignificant, underscores a key topic with many wider implications that continue to ripple into the 21st century. Several of these forks are explored further in Part II, particularly their wider implications.

2.1. CCITT TURN DOWN TCP/IP

Threat to the Status Quo

To the casual reader, the characteristics of this new paradigm may seem innocent enough, almost too philosophical to have any bearing on hardnosed product development and business issues. To IBM and the PTTs, however, each characteristic represented a sharp object pointed directly at their hearts, and more importantly at their bottom lines. This was not at all what IBM and the PTTs had in mind. In fact, it invalidated their business models. . . .

The researchers' perfectly reasonable, but radical new networking model was counter to the traditional model of telephony and data communications of both IBM and the PTTs. They had angered not one but many 500 pound gorillas!

—JOHN DAY, who was there.[2]

Fork 5: Will the Telephone World Accept TCP/IP?

By the late 1970s, many in the telecommunications business had concluded that the transport of data over networks was going to grow in importance, perhaps not to the level of voice transport, but still quite crucial. But there was a deep disagreement over just what kind of data transport, a difference of opinion rooted in various architectural and business models. The Internet of today is just what the big players in the telecommunications industry, the telephone companies, and IBM, feared, but they were not able to stop that future, although they tried.

THE TELEPHONE BUSINESS AND IBM

Throughout the 1970s, traditional telephone companies, such as AT&T in the United States and the postal, telegraph, and telephone services (PTTs) in Europe and most of the rest of the world, provided essentially all of the telecommunications services available for use. The telephone business was quite large, to put it mildly. For example, the annual revenue for U.S. telephone carriers in 1975 was $31.3 billion ($165.3 billion in 2022 dollars).[3] The total had grown to $49.8 billion ($262.8 billion) by 1979, while the total number of people employed by U.S. telephone carriers was 840,000 in 1975 and had grown to 928,000 by 1979.[4] Big business, indeed; it does help to be a legal monopoly.

Although the FCC Carterfone decision in June 1968 had theoretically made it possible to attach non–telephone company equipment to the telephone network,[5] it was not until 1977 that the FCC specifications for devices to directly attach to the telephone network were finally approved by the courts.[6] So, in the mid-1970s, the huge revenue the telephone carriers were receiving came from a telephone network where the telephone companies owned and controlled everything end to end: the telephones at each end, the telephone switches along the way between the source and destination, and the wires interconnecting everything. All telephone services, such as call forwarding, answering machines, etcetera, could legally be provided only by the telephone companies themselves through a legally sanctioned monopoly.

Thus, when it came time to develop standards for the transport of computer data over networks, the telephone companies had an operating model that they were used to in the telephone world and wanted to continue to exploit in the digital world—a model in which everything was in the realm of the carrier. Because of Carterfone, the phone companies knew their days were numbered for carrier control at the customer premises, but they had hopes of blocking any additional erosion of their territory. Pouzin's datagram model (see Section 1.3) was a direct attack on the telephone world's model, and Pouzin's was an attack that the telephone world tried its best to deflect.

It was not just the telephone companies that were under attack by the Pouzin's datagram model—IBM was as well. In the 1970s and 1980s, IBM was the king of corporate data networking. The IBM networking technology was different from the telephone networking technology, but the philosophy was the same—IBM assumed that all of a corporation's networking ran IBM's centrally-controlled networking technology. A world of distributed networks and devices owned and operated by untold numbers of firms and individuals was, as a result, science fiction.

Telephone Standards Development

The primary venue for standards development for the telephone industry in the 1970s was the Consultative Committee for International Telephony and Telegraphy (CCITT), which at that time was part of the International Telegraph Union (ITU) (now the International Telecommunication Union).[7] The history of the ITU goes back to the original international telegraph standardization meeting in 1865, which is the world's oldest international organization.[8] ITU members are countries. The CCITT was created by the ITU in 1956 to work on telecommunications standards.[9] Membership in the CCITT was open to the national telephone companies (PTTs) of ITU Member States.[10]

In 1968 the CCITT created a Working Party on New Data Networks. By 1972, the working party had published 11 recommendations (CCITT term for standards) that specified interfaces between telephone circuit-switched networks and private data networks. They had also dipped a toe into the concept of packet-switched networks by mentioning the concept in one of 23 topics that the working party planned to take a look at over the next four years.[11]

Another standards development organization that was working on standards for data networking in the 1970s was the International Organization for Standardization (ISO). The ISO's membership consists of the national standards bodies of a large number of countries.[12] The ISO's work is quite broad and is not limited to data networking. Indeed, it has published standards covering topics as wide ranging as "calibration of thermometers, food safety regulations, and the manufacturing of wine glasses, shoe sizes, musical pitches, security management, and environmental management."[13] A part of the ISO, known as subcommittee 6 (SC6), was working on networking standards in the mid-1970s and still did as of 2022.[14]

INTERNET STANDARDS DEVELOPMENT

Shortly before the deployment of the first ARPANET sites in 1969, a small group of Advanced Projects Research Agency (ARPA)-connected researchers formed an ad hoc technical group to develop the specifications of the protocols to be used over the ARPANET. The group called itself the "Network Working Group" and was coordinated by UCLA graduate student Steve Crocker. Born in 1944 and having grown up in Pasadena, California, Crocker earned his Ph.D. in computer science from UCLA and studied artificial intelligence at MIT.[15]

The Network Working Group published its notes—both proposed and technical specifications—with Crocker's help, in a documentation series labeled Request for Comments (RFCs). A decade and a half later,

"Layer 9"—Core Policy Decisions

the Network Working Group evolved into the Internet Engineering Task Force (IETF), which is today the primary Internet technology standards development organization.[16] The IETF took over the publication of RFCs, which now number more than 9,000.[17] The organization is discussed further in Chapter 7.

INTERNATIONAL NETWORK WORKING GROUP (INWG)

Encouraged by Larry Roberts, about a dozen network researchers got together with Vint Cerf, Louis Pouzin, and Donald Davies in October 1972 to talk about the future of packet data networking.[18] They named their group the International Network Working Group (INWG). The INWG discussed the requirements for a future packet data networking protocol, particularly at a meeting in New York in June 1973.[19] Cerf and Kahn published the first version of their new Internet Protocol in September 1973 as INWG document #39. They said the document was "an attempt to collect and integrate the ideas uncovered at the June 1973 INWG meeting in New York, as well as some ideas which have been worked out since that time by various other people."[20]

Other researchers in the INWG published their own proposals, which the group considered along with INWG 39, which resulted in agreement on a new specification published in early 1976 as INWG 96.[21] In early 1976, the INWG voted to submit INWG 96 to CCITT.[22]

CONSULTATIVE COMMITTEE FOR INTERNATIONAL TELEPHONY AND TELEGRAPHY (CCITT)

From the start of its 1972 work plan, CCITT, as Donald Davies noted at the time, had focused almost exclusively on circuit-switched technology.[23] But by the mid 1970s, packet-switched network technologies had begun to get significant deployment around the world: not only the ARPANET in the United States and the Cyclades network in France, but also commercial networking standards, including Systems Network Architecture (SNA) from IBM, DECnet from Digital Equipment Corporation, and XNS from Xerox.[24] CCITT reacted by developing X.25, a packet-switched networking standard that was designed to implement virtual circuits and that emulated a switched circuit network.[25] X.25 was finalized in 1976 but had already been widely deployed by that point in the telephone world.[26]

It is not surprising that the CCITT decided that its packet-switched standard should be one that emulated a switched circuit network since CCITT members, the national postal, telegraph, and telephone services (PTTs), had a very strong economic interest in preserving the carrier-controlled business model of telecommunications. It is also not surprising that the CCITT turned down the INWG's offer of INWG 96 to be the basis for the future data network since the datagram network model in INWG 96 threatened that very business model.[27] Vint Cerf noted that even a representative from the U.S. Defense Communications Agency, the people that were soon to be running the ARPANET, "actively lobbied in the CCITT AGAINST the offer on the grounds that X.25 was all they needed."[28]

After CCITT turned down the offer of INWG 96, it was offered to the ISO, which was also developing a standard for packet-switched networking. INWG 96 fared a bit better in the ISO, where it influenced the design of one of the five optional transport protocols in the Open System Interconnection (OSI) protocol suite[29] (see Section 2.6.). CCITT turning down INWG 96 meant that the Internet Protocol was not adopted as the future data networking protocol by the primary telephone standards organization. Instead, TCP/IP development and standardization was left to the ARPANET technical community, which after 1983 became the Internet technical community.

What if CCITT Had Said Yes?

If the CCITT had accepted INWG 96 and switched its standardization efforts to it rather than to X.25, it is likely that CCITT would have taken over all future development of TCP/IP. CCITT's standardization efforts were focused on what was good for the PTTs because the PTTs made up the membership of CCITT. Thus, the CCITT would not have been all that interested in supporting the datagram concept that underlay INWG 96 and TCP/IP in general. For example, while, after much lobbying by the INWG, the first version of X.25 as produced by CCITT included a datagram mode, that option was dropped in subsequent versions when it became clear that no telephone company wanted to deploy such a technology.[30]

TCP/IP as developed by CCITT would have been a very different protocol. It would have been a protocol designed to preserve carrier (PTT) control of all data transmissions rather than the protocol the Internet technical community developed—one that specifically excluded the carrier from controlling the communications. TCP/IP as developed by CCITT would have ensured that the carriers controlled what applications were allowed on the network and ensured that the carriers were able to charge whatever they could for individual applications.

The ISO did adopt some of INWG 96, but not much. As noted earlier, all that remained after the ISO had done its work was that one of the five transport protocols was a datagram connectionless transport whose design was strongly influenced by INWG 96. But as was the case with the X.25 datagram mode, carriers were not all that enthusiastic about offering the connectionless transport option to their customers.

Perhaps the most important factor as to why it was critical that the telecommunications standards bodies, both CCITT and the ISO SC6, turned down the offer to take over the development of TCP/IP is that both of those bodies assumed they were developing standards for telephone companies to run (CCITT more than the ISO, but still both). TCP/IP, as designed by the INWG, was meant to be run by independent organizations over telephone networks rather than as the telephone networks themselves. In other words, TCP/IP as developed by CCITT or the ISO would not have had enabling permissionless innovation as its core goal, and permissionless innovation is the core strength of the Internet of today.

2.2. DARPA FUNDS BERKELEY TO ADD TCP/IP SUPPORT TO UNIX

DARPA was also recognizing reality. Prominent researchers, hungering for the magnetic tapes carrying Berkeley's latest distributions like so many desperate junkies, demanded that DARPA adopt Berkeley Unix because that's what they were already using.

—ANDREW LEONARD, author[31]

Fork 6: Should the U.S. Government Fund Easy Access to Internet Protocol Software?

The TCP/IP technical specifications were finalized in the late 1970s and published in 1980 and 1981 (see Section 2.5). In 1980, the U.S. Department of Defense (DoD) mandated that all packet-oriented DoD networks use TCP/IP.[32] Concurrent with the mandate, in 1980, the Defense Advanced Research Projects Agency (DARPA) contracted with the University of California, Berkeley, to add TCP/IP support to the Unix operating system. The result of the effort was a very low-cost full implementation of the full TCP/IP protocol suite and of many Internet applications that could be used with Unix or integrated into other computer operating systems.

UNIX

The Unix operating system was developed by Ken Thompson and Dennis Richie at AT&T Bell Labs in the late 1960s and early 1970s, ostensibly as a platform to support word processing.[33] But Unix was much more than that—it was an easy-to-use but very powerful full-fledged computer operating system that many users saw as superior to the vendor-specific operating systems then available.

Unix quickly became the operating system of choice for scientific computing and engineering workstations because of its power and because it was, let's face it, very cheap. Unix was so affordable because AT&T was not permitted to sell any products not directly related to telephones or telecommunications under a 1956 consent agreement with the U.S. government. AT&T instead licensed Unix very inexpensively.[34] A Unix source code license was only $200 for educational institutions, and $20,000 for for-profit corporations.[35]

Unix at Berkeley

One of the educational institutions that licensed Unix in the early days was the University of California, Berkeley. Soon after they got the source code, some Berkeley graduate students began to modify and extend it. In 1977, the students packaged up their add-ons to the AT&T Unix distribution into a mag tape and called it the "Berkeley Software Distribution" (BSD) and started sending copies on demand to other educational institutions. A later BSD version included the sources for the full Unix operating system and all the applications.[36]

One needed a Unix source license from AT&T to be able to get the BSDs from Berkeley, but, as noted earlier, that did not cost all that much.

DARPA

Around the same time, DARPA (the name had been changed from ARPA in 1972[37]) had concluded that the continued expansion of the ARPANET depended on establishing a common operating system for ARPANET-connected computers because it was not practical to standardize computer hardware itself. DARPA chose Unix as the common operating system because it had proven to be portable to new hardware.[38]

In 1979, Berkeley proposed that DARPA fund Berkeley to add TCP/IP support to its Unix distributions. DARPA agreed and signed an 18-month contract to accomplish the task.[39] It took a little longer but, by 1983, Berkeley had shipped tapes with the full source code for Unix, including source code for the full TCP/IP protocol suite.

Berkeley Networking Release

After the breakup of the AT&T system in 1983, AT&T was released from its earlier restrictions and started treating Unix as a product, raising the cost of Unix source licenses to as much as $100,000.[40] In response, Berkeley developed a release that contained only the Berkeley-created TCP/IP networking code in mid-1989. This code was made freely available over the Internet.

The Result

The result of the DARPA contract with Berkeley was that companies developing new computers could get source code for the full TCP/IP stack and Internet applications for a very low cost before 1989, or for free after 1989. This meant that these companies could adopt what was quickly becoming the standard networking protocol for far less than it would cost for the company to develop its own networking protocol. Over time, the low cost of TCP/IP implementations coupled with the increasing scope of the Internet, which by now only used TCP/IP, meant that vendors who had developed their own protocols had to add TCP/IP support to their systems to drop their own networking protocols altogether. In doing so, the companies increased the importance of TCP/IP and of the Internet.

What if DARPA Had Not Funded the Berkeley TCP/IP Development??

If DARPA had not decided to focus on Unix and had not decided to fund the Berkeley TCP/IP efforts, there would have been much less reason for companies to abandon their own protocols, and an Internet united by the common use of TCP/IP might never have happened.

There was another effort that mirrored the DARPA/Berkeley TCP/IP endeavor at around the same time. In 1983, the larger European computer manufacturer requested funding from the Research Open System for Europe (ROSE) project as part of the European Strategic Programme on Research in Information Technology (ESPRIT). This project had the intention of developing support for the complete OSI protocol suite to run on the manufacturers computer systems, including the connectionless protocols.[41] Dennis Jennings, who was later the initial NSFNET director, was one of the reviewers of the project and got the European Commission to agree that the resulting code would be distributed for free to all academic or research institutions in Europe. But when Jennings attended a ROSE Project review meeting in October 1985, he was told that the ROSE consortium participants had decided that it was not in their commercial interest to make the code available under free license to academic institutions.[42] If the ROSE Project had gone ahead

"Layer 9"—Core Policy Decisions

with the original idea, OSI might have been on an equal footing with TCP/IP, at least costwise. As Jennings recently said, that was the day that ISO/OSI died.[43]

2.3. ENABLING STUDENTS TO USE THE ARPANET

> There was a strong current of concern among CS departments about the widening gap between the "haves"—the few universities with ARPAnet access—and the great majority of "have nots." At the time the ARPAnet was restricted to about 150 DoD contractors and there was no way that the DoD was going let another 120 universities join. So the dead cows were the gap between the ARPAnet-connecting the remaining universities, and the threats to survival and well-being that we all felt in our guts.
>
> —PETE DENNING, computer scientist[44]

Fork 7: Should All Students Be Able to Use the ARPANET?

The initial host computers were connected to the ARPANET at three universities and one research center on the U.S. West Coast in 1969. The network grew rapidly—by mid-1971, there were 23 hosts, and by 1981, that figure had grown to 213 hosts.[45] The majority of the hosts were at universities, generally in the universities' computer science departments, but most universities had no ARPANET connection. Thus, they could not engage in easy collaboration with researchers at the "haves"—those universities with ARPANET connectivity. Many researchers at the unconnected universities saw the lack of connectivity as a threat to the very existence of their research programs. Even at the universities that were connected to the ARPANET, almost none of the students, faculty, or staff were permitted to use it. Indeed, ARPANET access remained limited until the early 1980s when a new network, and a political decision, changed everything.

The ARPANET

As described in Chapter 1, the ARPANET was a creation of the Advanced Research Projects Agency in the U.S. DoD. From the very beginning, the DoD said that use of the ARPANET was for U.S. government business only. As the *ARPANET Resource Handbook* put it,

> The ARPANET is intended to be used solely for the conduct of, or in support of, official U. S. Government business.[46]

The above statement essentially defined an acceptable use policy (AUP) for the ARPANET. If the only legitimate use of the ARPANET was to conduct or support official U.S. government business, then any other use was prohibited, even by an otherwise legitimate user. At Harvard, and many other universities at the time, this rule was interpreted to mean that only researchers who were directly supported by U.S. government grants could have access to the ARPANET. And even when such a person could have access, what they could do was limited by the scope of their funding. That meant access was limited to a small percentage of the faculty and staff and an even smaller percentage of the students at a university, and even then for only certain closely monitored activities. At Harvard, some university staff, including one of the writers, were permitted to use the ARPANET under the "in support of" clause.

Computer Science Network (CSNET)

ARPANET connections were very expensive, at over $100,000 per year, and so few universities could afford them on their own.[47] Partially because of the cost and partially because of the ARPANET requirement that only sites doing "official U.S. Government business" could be connected, not all that many universities had joined the ARPANET. In mid-1977, there were only 113 hosts connected to the ARPANET, and a number of those were nonuniversity research sites.[48]

The idea of another, cheaper research network to provide connectivity to far more universities started in May 1979 with a meeting arranged by Larry Landweber, a professor and chair of the University of Wisconsin computer science department.[49] After earning his Ph.D. from Purdue University in 1967, Landweber joined the faculty at the University of Wisconsin, where he stayed until his retirement in 2000.[50] It was there while in Madison, then, that Larry crafted a proposal to the National Science Foundation (NSF) that would "change his life" and in many ways shape the future trajectory of the Internet.[51]

After a lot of discussion and a few iterations of rejected proposals, in November 1980 Landweber, along with Dave Farber from the University of Delaware, Tony Hearn from the RAND Corporation, and Peter Denning from Purdue University, submitted a proposal to the U.S. NSF for a new Computer Science Research Network (CSNET) to be interconnected with the ARPANET. To Larry's amazement NSF funded the project in January 1981 with the requirement that CSNET be operational within three years and be able to stand on its own within five years.[52]

CSNET, as envisioned by Landweber et al., was "to introduce networking into all of the computer science departments at universities, and also computer research groups in industry and government, throughout the United States."[53] The NSF proposal for CSNET assumed that the new network would run the TCP/IP protocol suite that the ARPANET was in the process of adopting, so all CSNET sites would have the full complement of services that ARPANET users had: email, file transfer, and remote login, although CSNET was focused on email. It also assumed that the ARPANET would be one of the multiple transport networks that CSNET would interconnect with and would utilize for transport and that "the existing ARPANET university community would be a component of CSNET at no cost to DARPA."[54] The last point meant that existing ARPANET sites, such as Harvard, could become CSNET sites, assuming they also paid the CSNET dues, which were relatively cheap at the time ($5,000 per year/university).

The CSNET AUP did not limit which people at a university or other CSNET site could make use of CSNET services.[55] Once a university was connected to CSNET, then, depending on local university policies, in theory every student, faculty member, and staff member could communicate with people at any other CSNET site. This openness initially caused a problem for CSNET because it conflicted with the ARPANET access restrictions.

The issue was solved at a meeting in early 1981 when Bob Kahn, then the ARPANET program director, agreed to develop a memorandum of understanding that would permit CSNET sites to have email access to ARPANET sites and vice versa.[56,57]

THE RESULT

As soon as Harvard joined CSNET (using the ARPANET for CSNET connectivity), they were able to remove the restrictions that were in place to restrict ARPANET email to those at the university with direct federal grant support. The university was then able to expose thousands of students and staff members and hundreds of faculty members to the power (and travails) of email.

Of course, and even more importantly, CSNET also enabled countless staff, faculty, and students at non-ARPANET CSNET universities to email's potential. CSNET was the reason that generations of students graduated from Harvard and the other 180 CSNET universities as Internet users.[58] Wherever these students went, they took with them an understanding of the advantages of widespread digital connectivity, and in many cases demanded their new employers join the revolution. Thousands of companies and other organizations did just that, placing added pressure on those firms that provided goods and services to similarly join up, or be left behind.

Thus, the creation of CSNET was instrumental in exponentially growing the demand for the Internet during its pre–web growth phase.

WHAT IF ARPANET ACCESS HAD REMAINED EXTREMELY LIMITED??

If CSNET had not been created, the Internet as we know it today may never have happened, or if it did, it could have been significantly delayed. When CSNET was established, the whole concept of packet data networks was almost unknown to the general public and little known or understood even in the telecommunications industry. The only regular users of packet data networks were the relatively few researchers getting direct

"Layer 9"—Core Policy Decisions

U.S. government support and those few users of Donald Davies's National Physical Laboratory network in the U.K. Telecommunications Office. Everyone else had to use whatever the telephone companies wanted to offer as transportation services.

In addition, without the lessons learned from CSNET, NSF might never have created NSFNET as a wide area general purpose TCP/IP network.[59] NSFNET vastly increased the number of people in the United States who learned the power of this type of communication. NSFNET was also how the European Organization for Nuclear Research (CERN) got its Internet connectivity in the early 1990s[60] when Tim Berners-Lee published the World Wide Web concept and protocols, as is discussed in Chapter 4.[61] Without CSNET, NSF might not have been able to justify creating NSFNET, and without NSFNET, Berners-Lee might never have developed the World Wide Web and the future of telecommunications might have been left to the telephone companies.

2.4. NO COMMERCIAL TRAFFIC ON NSFNET

> Scott Bradner: How can I tell a commercial packet from a non-commercial packet?
> Steve Wolf: Be ready to survive an audit.
> —SCOTT BRADNER AND STEVE WOLF (NSFNET MANAGER)[62]

Fork 8: Should the U.S. Government Subsidize a Commercial Internet?

The U.S. NSF has been supporting data networking for quite a while,[63] not quite as long as ARPA, but still quite a while. One early example of NSF support was the 1981 NSF grant that helped establish CSNET (see Section 2.3). In 1985, the NSF established supercomputer centers at Cornell University; the University of Illinois; University of California, San Diego; and Princeton University.[64] Harvard was a member of the John Von Neumann Consortium for Scientific Computing, a 12-member consortium that was the corporate parent for the NSF supercomputer located at Princeton University.[65] As part of the awards, NSF also paid for data lines from the supercomputer centers to the consortium members. For example, Harvard had a data line to MIT, which in turn, had a data line to Princeton.[66]

A year later, the NSF linked the supercomputer centers together with a "backbone" network.[67] This network was connected to the ARPANET, ensuring worldwide connectivity.[68] Dennis Jennings, the manager of the networking project at the NSF, decided that the backbone network as well as the links between the supercomputer centers and their users would run TCP/IP (see Section 2.6). Later, starting later in 1986, the NSF sponsored the creation of "regional networks," many of which were expansions of the supercomputer-to-user connections.[69] Jennings also decided that the regional networks would not be limited to supporting only NSF-sponsored connections but, instead, were open to all academic users.[70] The backbone network was referred to as the "NSFNET backbone" or simply "NSFNET" and the regional networks as "NSF regional networks."[71] Harvard, like other research institutions, used the arrival of the link to the NSFNET to justify building out a campus network. The NSFNET and the NSF regional networks, along with the campus networks, created a three-level design that Jennings had described to the National Science Board back in 1985,[72] which also happened to be just the kind TCP/IP was designed to support. The NSFNET supplanted the ARPANET by 1990 when the ARPANET was closed down for good.[73]

NSFNET BACKBONE ACCEPTABLE USE POLICY (AUP)

Because the NSFNET was funded by the U.S. government, it was important that it not look like the government was competing with the private sector. Thus, the NSFNET published an "NSFNET Backbone Acceptable Use Policy" that stated the purpose of the network and what was and was not acceptable use of the network.[74] The AUP said that the NSFNET backbone services were "provided to support open research and education in and among US research and instructional institutions, plus research arms of for-profit firms when engaged in open scholarly communication and research."[75] The AUP also stated that "use for for-profit activities" or "use by for-profit institutions" was unacceptable.[76] Finally, the AUP maintained that the AUP applied only to the NSFNET backbone, and it did not apply to the regional networks, which were expected to formulate their own AUPs.[77]

As can be seen from the quote at the start of this section, determining if a particular communication was acceptable or not was not an easy task and involved a very nuanced evaluation of the purpose of the communication.

IMPACT OF THE NSFNET BACKBONE AUP

The NSFNET backbone AUP meant that for-profit companies could not use the NSFNET as their Internet backbone, even though they might have many recent university graduates that were demanding Internet connectivity (see Section 2.3) or had realized that there were good business reasons to be part of the Internet in-crowd. This provided a business opportunity for the creation of Internet Service Providers (ISPs) who could provide the connectivity instead.

By the late 1980s, new backbone ISPs—ISPs with nationwide coverage—were formed in response to the opportunity, including Performance Systems International (PSINET) and Alternet/UUNET (Unix to Unix NETwork).[78] If the NSFNET had not had the restrictive AUP, then there would have been little reason to establish commercial ISPs because the U.S. government would carry traffic at a far lower cost.

The very restrictive NSFNET backbone AUP did not last all that long. In late 1992, the U.S. Congress passed an amendment (the Boucher Amendment) offered by Congressman Rick Boucher to a bill establishing a national technician training program.[79] As is explored further in Chapter 6, the amendment said that the NSF was authorized "to foster and support access by the research and education communities to computer networks which may be used substantially for purposes in addition to research and education in the sciences and engineering."[80]

Steve Wolfe, then NSFNET program director at NSF, used the Boucher Amendment to open up the NSFNET backbone AUP to permit commercial traffic.[81] In other words, he saw its potential and so is credited with helping move the Internet from a government-funded science project to a global phenomenon. Earning his Ph.D. in Electrical Engineering at Princeton in 1961, he taught at Johns Hopkins and later worked for the U.S. Army, where he introduced UNIX, among other innovations. The NSFNET did not last all that long; the NSFNET backbone was decommissioned in April 1995.[82] But the NSFNET had proven the workability and usefulness of very wide spread packet network availability.

What if NSFNET Had Accepted Commercial Traffic from the Beginning?

The restrictive NSFNET backbone AUP only lasted a few years, but they were critical years for packet-switched data networking. Between the mid-1980s when the NSFNET backbone was first deployed and 1992 when the AUP was revised in response to the Boucher Amendment, the number of computers connected to the TCP/IP Internet grew from about 2,000 to over 1,000,000.[83]

The establishment and expansion of the commercial ISPs is what enabled this rate of growth and enabled the NSF to decommission the NSFNET backbone when it did. If the NSFNET had supported commercial use from the beginning, the incentive to invest in building commercial ISPs would have been far less, and the Internet expansion would have been delayed, perhaps significantly, as a result. In addition, what U.S. Internet there was would have been more dependent on the NSFNET, requiring the U.S. government to invest much more money in growing the capacity of the NSF to keep up with the demand.

The strict NSFNET backbone AUP is one of the factors that enabled the building of a U.S. Internet infrastructure capable of expanding to meet the exponentially increasing demand for Internet connectivity.

2.5. ONLY INTERNET PROTOCOLS PERMITTED ON NSFNET

You cannot build a corporate data network with TCP/IP.

—IBM network engineer, ca. 1992[84]

Fork 9: Should the NSFNET Support the Common Vendor Network Protocols?

The NSFNET was established in 1985 to interconnect supercomputer centers and to provide connectivity to the users of those centers (see Section 2.4). At that time, there were a lot of different vendor-specific networking protocols in use. One of those protocols was the Digital Equipment Corporation (DEC) protocol they called DECnet. The computers that provided access to the supercomputers at the supercomputer centers were DEC VAX computers that ran DECnet. Many of the supercomputer users also used VAX computers back at their home institutions. It would seem logical for NSFNET to directly support DECnet so that the connections between the user's own computers and the supercomputer centers would "just work." But, as we'll see, that is not what was done, which made a major difference.

It Was a Multiprotocol World

Before the easy availability of TCP/IP software (see Section 2.2), many computer vendors had created their own networking protocols. This author's course in networking technology in the early 1990s covered AppleTalk from Apple computer, DECnet from Digital Equipment Corporation, SNA from IBM, the OSI protocols, TCP/IP, Xerox Network Systems (XNS) from Xerox, and Internetwork Packet Exchange (IPX) from Novel.[85] There were still other network protocols in use at that time, including Virtual Integrated NEtwork Service (VINES) from Banyan, and Chaosnet from MIT. Major router vendors at the time, such as Cisco Systems, supported most of these protocols in what they called "multiprotocol routers."[86]

Each of the vendors thought, or at least said, that their protocol was the best, at least for some applications. One example is in the quote at the start of this section. IBM had developed SNA as its networking protocol. SNA had a large number of features designed to let network managers control every aspect of its operation. With SNA, network managers could control the performance of every node on the network very precisely. TCP/IP had none of the same kind of controls, so IBM maintained that, by definition,

TCP/IP could not be used for an enterprise network. That was because IBM had defined what an enterprise network needed to be based on SNA's features. DEC had done the same with DECnet. These vendor protocols were "better than TCP/IP," at least in the vendors' minds and often in the minds of the users of the networks.[87]

The Harvard network in that time period supported TCP/IP, DECnet, AppleTalk, and IPX, along with a separate SNA network.

Supercomputer Centers and Their Users

All the NSFNET supercomputer centers had similar architectures, consisting of one or more supercomputers with front-end computers that were used to schedule computing tasks and move data. For example, the John von Neuman Center (JvNC) at Princeton University, the center that Harvard was connected to, had two CDC Cyber 205 supercomputers and a cluster of DEC VAX 8600s as the front-end systems. Some of the VAXs ran VMS, and some ran Unix.[88] At Harvard, many of the major users of the JvNC supercomputers were in the physics department. The department had its own DEC VAX computer that the users accessed through terminals in their offices.[89]

When Harvard first brought up the connection to the JvNC, it only ran TCP/IP, which frustrated the physics folks, who knew that they could have a far more seamless interaction with the supercomputer if their VAX could communicate directly with the JvNC VAXs using DECnet. The physics department chair asked one of the authors, as the Harvard JvNC liaison, to get DECnet enabled. Even though the author knew the answer from previous discussions with Dennis Jennings, then the NSFNET manager, he asked anyway.

NSFNET

As discussed in Section 2.4, Jennings decided that the NSFNET would support TCP/IP. But Jennings had decided to support TCP/IP. In what he called "the key decision," he had determined that "all the computers on the NSFnet would be required to run the TCP/IP protocol suite."[90] This policy covered not only the NSFNET backbone but also the NSF-sponsored links between the users and the NSF-sponsored supercomputer centers. So, of course, the answer from Jennings to Harvard "no." Physics interactions had to be over TCP/IP.

The Result

The result of Jennings's decision was that everyone who wanted to use the NSFNET, whether interacting with a supercomputer or someone at another university across the country, had to be using a computer that supported TCP/IP. It also meant that the campus network that the person was connected to had to support TCP/IP, even if the campus was an all-DEC/VMS campus that ran on DECnet, or an all-Novel campus that ran on Internetwork Packet Exchange (IPX).

This provided yet another incentive to support TCP/IP that applied to campus network managers and computer purchasers. It also applied to equipment manufactures—if they wanted to sell their computers to people who used the NSFNET, the computers would have to support TCP/IP. Jennings's decision also meant that the management of the NSFNET was far simpler than it would have been if it had to support multiple transport protocols.

What if NSFNET Had Been Multiprotocol?

Without the TCP/IP decision, the management of NSFNET and the NSF-sponsored regional networks would have been harder and more complex. It would also have significantly reduced the pressure on equipment manufacturers to support TCP/IP, some of whom, for example, Microsoft, took a long time to roll out the support anyway. Microsoft's delay was a great business opportunity for a number of companies who made fortunes selling add-on TCP/IP software for Microsoft PC operating systems, mostly based on the Berkeley Networking Release.

Without Jennings's TCP/IP decision, the networking world would have taken longer, perhaps much longer, to get to where it is today, which is almost universally a TCP/IP-only world.

2.6. THE DEATH OF GOSIP

> [In 1989], it appeared to many experts in the field that the OSI model and its protocols were going to take over the world and push everything else out of their way. This did not happen . . . [the reasons] can be summarized as 1. Bad timing. 2. Bad technology. 3. Bad implementations. 4. Bad politics.
>
> —ANDREW TANENBAUM, computer scientist[91]

Fork 10: Should the Government Mandate the OSI Protocol Suite?

Starting in the late 1970s, the OSI protocol suite was touted by many telecommunications experts as *the* future of data networking, and, as the above quote put it, OSI was going to take over the [data networking] world and push everything else out of its way—in particular, supplanting TCP/IP as the protocol of the future Internet. Well, things did not turn out that way, but it took a long time before the U.S. government was willing to admit that it was backing the wrong horse.

THE OSI STANDARDS

In 1977, after the CCITT rejection of the INWG and Vint Cerf's offer of INWG 96 as the basis for an international data networking standard, and the CCITT's subsequent adoption of the X.25 standard (discussed in Section 2.1), a number of the participants in the failed INWG effort joined in the work of the newly formed ISO Subcommittee 16 (SC16). SC16 was established to focus on OSI.[92]

SC16 proceeded to work in as orderly a fashion as could be expected considering the widespread interest in the topic, and by December 1983, the work was far enough along for the Institute of Electrical and Electronics Engineers (IEEE) to publish a special issue of its proceedings mostly devoted to OSI.[93] Other than the OSI reference model, which had been published earlier in 1983, the articles in this issue described specifications that predated the OSI effort or work in process. The common attitude about the OSI protocols among the formal standards organizations and many of the regulatory agencies in various governments around the world was summarized by Richard desjardins in his afterword for the IEEE issue:

> OSI has come of age. Beginning in March 1978, OSI in six action-packed years has defined a Reference Model, services protocols for seven layers of interconnection. Due to the unprecedented cooperation among manufacturers, network providers, governments, and users, OSI implementations will begin to appear in 1985. By the end of the decade, most existing and new information systems will evolve into an OSI capability to exchange information easily and thus create the world information society.[94]

The political push for the OSI protocols started early and, at its peak, was quite strong and concerted. In March 1983, long before the actual specifications for the OSI protocols were published, the British and French governments had announced plans for adopting the OSI protocols, and in the United States, the American National Standards Institute (ANSI) required that the OSI reference model be used in future standards efforts and that "[e]very standards project must identify its approach to maintaining consistency with OSI."[95]

Government OSI Profile (GOSIP)

Over the next few years, many governments worldwide announced OSI mandates of one sort or another. In the United States, the National Institute of Standards and Technology (NIST) developed and published GOSIP in mid-1988 as Federal Information Processing Standard (FIPS) 146. GOSIP defined "the details of an OSI configuration for use in the Government so that interoperable OS products can be procured from commercial vendors."[96] It was needed "because OSI standards allow many potential options and choices, some of which are incompatible."[97] Support for OSI following GOSIP became mandatory for any computing equipment purchased by the U.S. federal government starting on August 15, 1990.[98]

The adoption of GOSIP by the U.S. government in 1989 was just a reflection of what Andrew Tanenbaum, the author of the most popular textbook on computer networking at the time, was talking about in the quote at the start of this section—that "experts" around the world strongly believed that OSI protocols were going to "take over the world and push everything else out of their way."[99]

Even IETF, the maintainer of the TCP/IP protocol suite, had succumbed to the belief. The ISO (OSI) conversion was seen as an "area of concern," and specific technical issues with such a conversion were discussed during the first meeting of the IETF in January 1986.[100] The ISO (OSI) protocols and transition continued to be discussed during successive IETF meetings.[101] When the IETF created formal working groups in 1987, an OSI-related working group was among the first ones created.[102] Finally, when the IETF established Areas for better management of working groups in 1989, it included an "OSI Interoperability" community.

As it turned out, final OSI specifications took a long time to appear—one analyst said in 1988 that the OSI specifications were being finalized "about as swiftly as molasses climbing uphill during a cold wave."[103] The same analyst noted that "TCP/IP already exists as a proven network standard supported by more than 100 vendors."[104] But even this analyst seems to have been a believer in the inevitability of an OSI takeover because he quotes another analyst as saying "[b]ut down the road looms OSI, which will ultimately replace TCP/IP. This is not a question of if, but when."[105] But, as Andrew Tanenbaum noted a decade later, the OSI implementations were "huge, unwieldy and slow"[106] when they did finally appear.

Meanwhile, back in the real world, the use of the TCP/IP protocol suite grew rapidly in the years after the ARPANET switched to TCP/IP in January 1983. By 1990, the date the U.S. government's OSI mandate went into effect, there were over 300,000 computers running TCP/IP connected to the Internet and located in more than a dozen countries.[107] At the same time, there were likely fewer than 1,000 computers running a full OSI suite. In addition, there were just as many other computers running TCP/IP in educational institutions, research organizations, and private companies around the world that were not connected to the Internet. Within a year, the number of computers running TCP/IP on the Internet had doubled, and the Internet was in use across more than 100 countries.[108] In 1990, there was no international network running the OSI protocols and few interorganizational production networks running those protocols. And by the end of 1993, the number of Internet-connected computers running TCP/IP had reached 2,000,000.[109] But still the U.S. government, and many other governments around the world, insisted that OSI was the way of the future.

The end of 1993 was also an important time for the U.S. government's view of the OSI protocol suite. Faced with the rapid expansion of the use of TCP/IP and the lagging adoption of the OSI protocols, the belief in the inevitability of an OSI takeover started to fade a few years after the U.S. government's GOSIP mandate went into effect in 1990. For example, Milo Medin, a researcher at NASA, was quoted in 1992 as saying "NASA is going to OSI, Mars & Pluto, not necessarily in that order."[110] The IETF had the same doubts and had closed its OSI-related area in early 1993.[111]

The doubts about the inevitability of an OSI takeover and the recognition of the very rapid spread of TCP/IP were also becoming present elsewhere in the U.S. government. In October 1993, NIST, the organization that had defined the U.S. version of GOSIP, established the Federal Internetworking Requirements Panel "to study and recommend policies on the use of networking standards by the Federal government."[112] One of the panelists was Milo Medin.

After about a year of deliberation, the Federal Internetworking Requirements Panel concluded that GOSIP needed to be opened up to include TCP/IP in addition to the OSI protocols. Following the panel's advice, NIST published a draft revision of GOSIP and asked for comments on it in September 1994.[113] After receiving and evaluating comments, NIST published GOSIP Version 2.[114]

After reiterating that the OSI protocols could be used for U.S. government applications, GOSIP Version 2 said in paragraph 10, "In addition, other specifications based on open, voluntary standards such as those cited in paragraph 7 may be used" while paragraph 7 said, "such as those developed by the Internet Engineering Task Force (IETF), the International Telecommunication Union, Telecommunication Standardization Sector (ITU-T; formerly the Consultative Committee on International Telegraph and Telephone [CCITT]), and the International Organization for Standardization (ISO)."[115] Thus, the revised standard said that other standards could be used, specifically including those developed by the IETF—that is, TCP/IP. This simple act of recognizing that there was a legitimate alternative to the OSI protocols turned out to be the death knell for OSI. There continued to be pockets of OSI use for a few years, but it did not take long for everyone in the business to understand that TCP/IP had won and there was no reason to even think about OSI. The Internet finally had one protocol to rule them all.

The NIST decision recognized the reality of the exploding availability and use of the TCP/IP protocols compared with the lack of availability and use of OSI products. To be clear, this decision was not based on which set of protocols was "better," and the decision did not say that OSI should not be used. Arguments over which protocol was superior are still going on today.

The NIST decision cleared the way for TCP/IP to take over the networking world (to paraphrase Andrew Tanenbaum). The decision also led to the phaseout of the standards activity related to the OSI protocol suite. It took a number of years, but after a while, the hugely expensive (in both time and money) and duplicative effort of standardizing both TCP/IP-related technology and OSI-related technology at the same time died out.

Andrew Tanenbaum said that OSI failed because of 1. Bad timing. 2. Bad technology. 3 Bad implementations. 4. Bad politics. Bad timing in that the OSI standards took a very long time to get done, which gave TCP/IP a significant head start because it could be implemented long before it was even possible to implement OSI; bad technology in that the fundamental

"Layer 9"—Core Policy Decisions

model of the protocol suite was flawed and the standards were extraordinarily complex, thus "difficult to implement and inefficient in operation;" bad implementations in that the "extraordinarily complex" specifications led to buggy implementations; and bad politics in that OSI was seen as a product of European telecommunications bureaucracies whereas TCP/IP was part of U.S.-developed Unix.[116]

Two other factors that Tanenbaum did not mention were cost and access to specifications. As discussed in Section 2.2, the full source code for the TCP/IP suite of protocols and applications was included in Berkeley Unix for little or no cost, and source code for just parts of the OSI suite was very expensive—hundreds of thousands of dollars in many cases.[117] The full TCP/IP specifications were made available electronically for free by ARPA and could be reproduced by anyone in any format, whereas the specifications for the OSI technologies were only available in paper form at a high cost from CCITT and ISO and could not be reproduced without specific permission.[118] Thus, it was easy and cheap for educational institutions to obtain and distribute the standards for TCP/IP to students but hard and expensive to do so for OSI.

It might be that OSI would have muddled through on its own, considering the vast resources of the monopoly telecommunications companies, who tried very hard to make OSI succeed, but OSI was not dying in a vacuum. TCP/IP had become a runaway success by the time the OSI specs were being adopted,[119] so, by all logic, OSI should have been doomed.

WHAT IF THE U.S. GOVERNMENT HAD PERSISTED IN MANDATING GOSIP?

What if the NIST decision had gone the other way and NIST had doubled down on an OSI future?

The Internet of today would likely not be much different if NIST had not enabled a TCP/IP future. It would still be a TCP/IP Internet, largely because of the relative cost and maturity of the TCP/IP products—they were essentially free and had been subject to many years of real-world use. In contrast, the OSI implementations were very expensive, complex, and buggy.

But that said, the path to today's Internet would likely have been far more expensive and confusing. If NIST had doubled down on an OSI future, the U.S. government, as well as other governments around the world, would have continued their requirements for government systems to use the OSI protocols. Standards bodies would have continued their duplicative efforts. Vendors would have been forced to support protocols that few customers wanted to run. And where government regulations required that OSI be implemented, costs would have been much higher and thus innovation slower.

Wrap Up

While they did not directly change the technology of the Internet, the six decisions covered in this chapter shaped the economic environment that wound up facilitating the rapid growth of the Internet and the policy environment in which it was allowed to flourish. The decision by the CCITT to not adopt TCP/IP meant that TCP/IP development was not only focused on what was good for the telephone companies. The decision to fund the Berkeley implementation of the TCP/IP protocol suite for Unix meant that computer manufacturers could get inexpensive source code for a very powerful networking suite of protocols and applications rather than having to pay a premium to develop their own. The decision to let all faculty, students, and staff of ARPANET sites use the ARPANET for email led to generations of students who understood the power of data networking and demanded access to that power when they joined the workforce. NSFnet's decision to not permit the use of commercial traffic on the early NSFnet network provided the key incentive for the development of commercial Internet service providers. Further, NSFNET's decision to only support TCP/IP on the NSFNET caused many computer companies to implement TCP/IP on their products so that their customers could make use of the NSFNET. Finally, the U.S. government's decision to abandon the GOSIP mandate and let government-funded sites use whatever protocols that could support the site's mission freed those sites to make use of TCP/IP, which unlike GOSIP actually worked.

Part II delves more deeply into some of these choices and their wider policy implications, while also breaking new ground on the history of cybersecurity, development of the World Wide Web, regulation of online speech, emergence of ISPs, and the evolution of what passed for Internet governance.

PART II

A Play in Five Acts

3

A Flaw in the Design?

It's not that we didn't think about security. . . . We knew that there were untrustworthy people out there, and we thought we could exclude them.[1]

—ALBUS DUMBLEDORE, *aka MIT Researcher David D. Clark*

Early Internet pioneers, in some ways, were remarkably farsighted. In 1973, a group of high school students reportedly gained access to the Advanced Research Projects Agency Network (ARPANET), which was supposed to be a closed network managed by Bolt Beranek Newman Inc. (BBN) under contract to Defense Advanced Research Projects Agency (DARPA).[2] Computer scientists and Internet forefathers Vinton Cerf and Robert Kahn suggested building encryption into the Internet's core protocols, which would have made it far more difficult for hackers to launch certain types of cyberattacks by compromising systems attached to the Internet.[3] But the U.S. intelligence community objected at the time, though officials didn't publicly say why. The only reason their intervention is widely known today is that Cerf hinted at it in a 1983 paper he coauthored.[4]

Starting with the Morris worm in 1988 and continuing through Stuxnet and the Snowden revelations of NSA monitoring of Internet communications, the history of cybersecurity is a complex one that in many ways dates back to far before the Internet itself existed. This chapter tells this backstory, including why security was not built in from the beginning (if indeed

Forks in the Digital Road. Scott J. Shackelford and Scott O. Bradner, Oxford University Press. © Oxford University Press 2024. DOI: 10.1093/oso/9780197617762.003.0003

it was ever possible) and how that animates many of today's cybersecurity policy headaches from ransomware to government monitoring of Internet communications and law enforcement's desire for "backdoors" into devices such as smartphones. Moreover, Stuxnet arguably bought the United States valuable time to let the diplomatic process play out, leading to the Iran nuclear deal. Yet at the same time it demonstrated to allies and adversaries around the world what was possible, and we are still just beginning to understand all the ramifications. Can Pandora's box be closed? What if it was never opened? And can we re-engineer the Internet to improve cybersecurity, and even if we could, what would we lose? This chapter attempts to grapple with these questions, and more.

CYBERSECURITY PRIMER

Recall the last time you logged on to check your personal email. The way you did so is probably very similar to the way someone halfway across the world would do so. We tend to access the Internet in similar ways; we request IP addresses through the same sorts of servers and send messages along the same types of routers. This means that we all use the same Internet protocols, or standards, which are written and published by bodies such as the Internet Engineering Task Force (IETF) and World Wide Web Consortium (W3C), as discussed in Chapter 7. We use the same sorts of devices, operating systems, applications, and programs to create documents, open attachments, and send emails. And we are all human, which means we have common experiences while using this hardware and software. Shared vulnerabilities exist at each of these levels, contributing to the cyber threat, beginning with the Internet's physical infrastructure.

At its most basic level, the Internet is composed of a series of cables, computers, and routers.[5] Innocent or malicious hardware flaws, along with design decisions, in this physical infrastructure can give rise to myriad vulnerabilities. These take many forms, including spyware, viruses, worms, Trojan horses, and Distributed Denial of Service (DDoS) attacks.[6] Before delving into a brief history of cyber insecurity, it is important to note that encryption, which is at the heart of this chapter, is only one aspect of understanding a "secure" Internet. What security means for the average Internet user likely denotes ensuring the confidentiality, availability, and integrity of their data as it transits cyberspace.

Thus, it is important to note at the outset that the decisions made in and around 1978, which form an integral part of this chapter, could not then and cannot now secure vulnerable Internet infrastructure along with end nodes (such as your smartphone). One need only consider the near ubiquitous presence of end-to-end encryption used on many websites today to understand that this has not ended cybercrime—the best encryption in the world still won't stop a run-of-the-mill email phishing attack. Similarly, a different fork taken—such as encrypting IP or including monitoring software that would have made the Internet into a type of distributed firewall, only letting "good/verified" content through—would have had dramatic effects on the evolution of cyberspace, including the pace of innovation. These trade-offs will be considered further below. First, though, we turn to a (very) brief history of cybersecurity, highlighting the types of attacks that could, and could not, have been prevented by different decisions being made by Cerf, Kahn, and others in 1978 and thereafter.

A BRIEF HISTORY OF BUGS AND CYBER ATTACKS

David Clark, a senior research scientist at the MIT Computer Science and Artificial Intelligence Laboratory commonly known by the nickname "Dumbledore," given for his wisdom and not his impressive beard or fashion sense, recalled when he first grasped the "dark side" of the Internet. He remembers a day in 1988 when he was chairing a meeting of network engineers, and a computer worm began to spread out of control.[7] "Damn," David recalls saying in response to learning of the worm. "I thought I had fixed that bug."[8]

MORRIS WORM

In fact, it turned out that a different bug was causing problems, one that came to be known as the Morris worm.[9] Back in November 1988, Robert Tappan Morris, son of the famous cryptographer Robert Morris Sr., was a 20-something graduate student at Cornell who wanted to know how big the Internet was—that is, how many devices were connected to it.[10] So he wrote a program to show that he could get a program running on every machine on the ARPANET without the program being detected, which would also keep count.[11]

The program worked well—too well, in fact. Morris was concerned about someone spoofing his program, so he decided that 1 in 7 times he would let a second copy run, a figure that should have been closer to 1 in 700.[12] This seemingly small change wound up making a big difference, leading to the worm copying itself to new machines at an exponential rate.[13] When he realized what was happening, even his messages warning system administrators about the problem couldn't get through.[14]

Worms and viruses are similar, but different in one key way: a virus needs an external command, from a user or a hacker, to run its program. A worm, by contrast, hits the ground running all on its own. For example, even if you never open your email program, a worm that gets onto your computer might email a copy of itself to everyone in your address book. In this era, few people were concerned about malicious software. It took 72 hours for researchers at Purdue and Berkeley to halt the worm.[15] In that time, it infected tens of thousands of systems.[16] Estimates for the overall cost of cleaning up in the aftermath of the Morris worm vary widely, from hundreds or thousands of dollars for each affected machine when factoring in system downtime, but the fact that it was arguably the "first significant cyber attack" is clear.[17]

In the clamor of media attention about this first-of-its-kind event, confusion was rampant. Some reporters even asked whether people could catch the computer infection.[18] Sadly, the lack of cybersecurity literacy continues to be a topic of concern, though there is a new generation of reporters holding the powerful to account, including the likes of Nicole Perlroth, Andy Greenberg, and Kim Zetter.[19] Morris wasn't trying to destroy the Internet, but the worm's widespread effects resulted in him being prosecuted under the then-new Computer Fraud and Abuse Act, previewing the myriad controversies that have swirled around that law since it was enacted.[20] He was convicted of a felony and sentenced to three years of probation and a fine of roughly $10,000. In the late 1990s, though, he became a dot-com millionaire and is now a professor at MIT. As such, things didn't work out so poorly for the world's first cyberattacker. However, it is important to note that even if a few decisions in the late 1970s and early 1980s went another way, the Morris worm or something like it would likely have happened anyway, underscoring the wide array of cyber threats we face. After all, Morris took advantage of lax password security and a software bug to help the worm proliferate. To better understand this episode and its meaning, we first provide some additional historical cybersecurity context.

Figure 3.1. Robert Tappan Morris in 2008, Courtesy of Wikimedia

PUTTING THE MORRIS WORM IN CONTEXT: A LOOK BACK AND AHEAD

Before diving into the decision of whether or not to encrypt TCP/IP—which itself would not have been a panacea, as we will see—it is first helpful to better understand the bugs and problems framing this debate. This is by no means a comprehensive accounting of the history of cybersecurity in the 20th century leading up to our critical fork in 1978, which is the focus of this chapter; such histories have been written, and they should be read and commended.[21] Often, though, the focus is on the period extending from 1980 to the present, in part due to the security vulnerabilities made possible by the decision not to encrypt IP in 1978.[22] As such, we focus here on the earlier epoch, which set the stage for both what happened in 1978 and thereafter.

Consider one of the first successful hacks on record, in the way that we normally use the term. In 1903, the British inventor and magician Nevil Maskelyne had an idea. He decided to target a public demonstration of a new technology—Morse code—that was meant to showcase its utility and dependability over a distance of some 300 miles.[23] In a feat with modern parallels, such as Stuxnet, given the lengths he went to in order to undertake the hack, Maskelyne took it upon himself to build a 50-meter radio mast that would overpower the message.[24] The radio enabled him to unleash a barrage of insults—including the word "Rats" repeated ad nauseum—against the Italian radio pioneer Guglielmo Marconi, who Maskelyne likened to "a young fellow of Italy, who diddled the public quite prettily."[25] It turned out that Maskelyne was frustrated at Marconi's patent monopoly on Morse code, but he defended his actions as being in the "public good," given that it highlighted the security flaws in wireless technology.[26] Similar arguments pervade the ethical hacking movement to this day, making Maskelyne a precursor to many 21st-century white and gray hat hackers.[27]

Fast forward nearly four decades to 1940 with World War II underway. The French comptroller general of the Vichy French Army, René Carmille, was an early "punch card computer expert."[28] Among other things,

Figure 3.2. Nevil Maskelyne in 1903, Courtesy of Wikimedia

Carmille was in charge of undertaking a census for the Nazi officials ruling France at the time, helping them target vulnerable Jewish populations still living in France. Carmille took it upon himself to reprogram the punch card machines to slow down the processing, delaying the Nazis' plans and saving countless lives in the process. Although Carmille was eventually found out, dying in a Nazi concentration camp before it could be liberated, both his bravery and status as a pioneer of ethical hacking—along with showcasing the potential of insider threats to undermine systems—are valuable lessons that continue to resonate.[29]

Just a few years later, in 1949, the Hungarian scientist and early cybersecurity pioneer Jon von Neumann published *The Theory of Self Reproducing Automata*.[30] This seminal work inspired a generation of researchers to develop self-replicating software of the kind that eventually led to the Morris worm. Key insights were gleaned along the way, though not from computers, but from another communications breakthrough—telephones.

Joe Engressia loved to whistle. And he was good at it. So good, thanks to his knack for absolute pitch (which let him replicate any pitch perfectly), in fact, that he became one of the first people to use "phreaking" in 1957.[31] By whistling at a certain pitch—it turned out, 2,600 hertz—Joe found that he was able to fool AT&T's payment modules, allowing him to bypass its payment process and thus make unlimited free phone calls.[32] Making use of this backdoor into AT&T systems, which its engineers used to remotely work on the network, an entire generation of "phreaks" were inspired to learn about, and exploit, technology—including Apple cofounders Steve Wozniak and Steve Jobs. Although the phreaks had moved on by the 1980s, following the breakup of the AT&T monopoly, the realization that there were workarounds and backdoors in technology that hackers could exploit motivated a generation of hackers as the Internet developed.

It's fitting, then, that the term "hack" also did not originate in the computer context but, rather, may be traced to MIT's fabled Tech Model Railroad Club circa 1961 when members hacked their high-tech train sets in order to modify their functions.[33] As Walter Isaacson noted in *The Innovators*, the members "embraced the term *hacker* with pride. It connoted both technical virtuosity and playfulness."[34] They later moved on from toy trains to computers, using a new nearly 10-ton behemoth school computer, the IBM 704, to innovate, explore, create new paradigms, and try to expand the tasks that computers could accomplish. IBM, to its credit, embraced this mindset, inviting high-school-aged students to probe its new computers in 1967, who managed to "bomb the system," resulting in more resilient systems and becoming one of the first examples of a hacking competition.[35]

The stage was nearly set for the Internet. All that was missing was a way to break up and transmit data across diverse networks and permit multiple users to access shared data sets. These problems were solved thanks to the efforts of many researchers, including the RAND engineer Paul Baran, who developed packet-switching technology,[36] and Donald Davies from Britain's National Physical Laboratory, who made the case for breaking up data into small pieces to make transmission easier, as was explored in Chapter 1.[37] A passage from Baran's 1960 paper on the topic is telling of his motivations: "The cloud-of-doom attitude that nuclear war spells the end of the earth is slowly lifting . . . the possibility of war exists but there is much that can be done to minimize the consequences."[38] Davies, on the other hand, had a "placid vision" about the benefits of breaking up data into manageable pieces, which could then move around the distributed network architecture envisioned by Baran, helping to move the Internet from theory to practice.[39]

With these technologies, it became possible for the Pentagon's Advanced Research Projects Agency (ARPA) to set up a dedicated network (ARPANET), which, as was explored in Part I, is commonly considered to be the precursor to the Internet. On Oct. 29, 1969, Professor Leonard Kleinrock and Charley Kline sent Stanford University researcher Bill Duval a two-letter message: "LO." As was mentioned in the Preface, the message, the full word "login," was truncated, perhaps appropriately, by a bug.[40] Although considered at first to be somewhat uninspiring, especially in the immediate aftermath of Neil Armstrong's recent words upon setting foot upon the moon, Kleinrock did like that the message could be considered shorthand for "Lo and behold"—somewhat fitting given that this computer crash heralded the digital era.[41]

With the nascent Internet up and running, the first computer virus—called Creeper—was not far behind. It was born in 1971, infecting the network of the Digital Equipment Corporation, and precipitating the first antivirus product—Reaper—to delete the malware from its system. Creeper was the brainchild of researcher Bob Thomas, who wrote the program for ARPANET to say, "I'm the creeper, catch me if you can."[42] Ray Tomilson—the inventor of email—wrote Reaper, which stopped Creeper but also was self-replicating, making it the first real-world example of a computer worm.[43]

Alarm bells began to go off, though not universally, in the early 1970s about how easy it was for the still nascent Internet to be accessed from the outside. Among those who were most concerned by the trend toward early cyber insecurity was Robert Metcalfe, an engineer who would go on to coinvent Ethernet tech as well as found the digital electronics manufacturer 3Com in 1979.[44] During a 1972 demonstration of the networking technology for a variety of telecommunications insiders, including AT&T executives, the system crashed, which reportedly caused some of the AT&T executives to laugh: according to Metcalfe, "They were happy. They were chuckling. . . . They didn't realize how threatening it was. . . . [The crash] seemed to confirm that it was a toy."[45] This underscored who the enemy was to Metcalfe, who remained largely a voice in the wilderness, with most early cybersecurity issues being confined to telecommunications fraud, phreaking, and other attempts to circumvent phone network protocols.

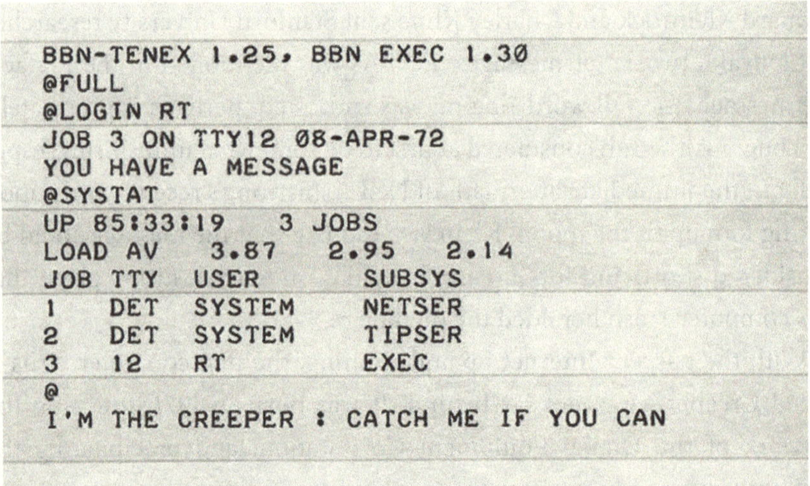

```
BBN-TENEX 1.25, BBN EXEC 1.30
@FULL
@LOGIN RT
JOB 3 ON TTY12 08-APR-72
YOU HAVE A MESSAGE
@SYSTAT
UP 85:33:19    3 JOBS
LOAD AV   3.87    2.95    2.14
JOB TTY   USER        SUBSYS
 1   DET   SYSTEM      NETSER
 2   DET   SYSTEM      TIPSER
 3   12    RT          EXEC
@
I'M THE CREEPER : CATCH ME IF YOU CAN
```

Figure 3.3. Creeper, the World's First Internet Worm

A Flaw in the Design? 77

That laissez-faire attitude, though, began to change by the mid-1970s thanks to the work of numerous security academics, which was summarized in a 1976 report to the Air Force cataloging the potential national security implications of unauthorized computer access.[46] Indeed, by 1976, it was a commonly-held view that "Security has become an important and challenging goal in the design of computer systems."[47] Still, significant gaps persisted, allowing 16-year-old Kevin Mitnick to famously hack The Ark, a computer system at the Digital Equipment Corporation that was used for developing operating systems, which resulted in jail time for the first of a series of cyberattacks he would launch over the coming decades.[48]

This, then, sets the stage for 1978 when cyberspace, and the world, could have taken a very different course when it came to incorporating encryption into the TCP/IP protocol. It is considering that vital fork in the digital road that we turn to next.

THE FORK: WHAT IF IP HAD BEEN ENCRYPTED?

A common criticism of the Internet, which has been frequently repeated, is that security was not built in and, as a result, computers keep getting hacked and people have to either live with the consequences or do their best to rely on workarounds and patches, such as virtual private networks to encrypt their traffic or specialized privacy software to protect their identity. To understand the choice that was made back then, consider the wider context. At that time, the early online community was limited to a few dozen researchers, not the billions now using the Internet, which is why Clark's comment that "we thought we could exclude" untrusted outsiders did not seem as impossibly naive then as the sentiment does today.[49] The focus, as Cerf has stated, at the time was not "on how you could wreck this system intentionally" but, rather, on "getting this thing to work at all."[50] This also made sense since there was, frankly, relatively little of value to steal on the ARPANET of the late 1970s. As the author Janet Abbate stated in *Inventing the Internet*, "People don't break into banks because they're not secure. They break into banks because that's where the money is. . . . They thought they were building a classroom, and it turned into a bank."[51]

It is also worth keeping in mind that these engineers were reacting to the legacy of a powerful monopoly in the form of AT&T as they were thinking about building a new network that was not as rigid, centralized, expensive, or heavily regulated.[52] After all, AT&T telephone networks had no built-in security, other than isolation. Still, it was on AT&T's wires that ARPANET sparked to life in 1969 with the "LO" message, described earlier. Soon to follow was email traffic, the original "killer app" responsible for some 75% of ARPANET traffic by 1972 and presaging the future cyber insecurity that email would introduce, such as through phishing campaigns.[53] Still, the debate between the rigid, centralized "Bellheads" and the more decentralized, anarchic "Netheads" continued throughout the 1970s and reflected the reality of the different network architectures being developed.[54] Both Cerf and Kahn, it should come as no surprise, were passionate Netheads, as was discussed in Chapter 1.

Why, though, did Kahn and Cerf not encrypt their invention—after all, Kahn was coming from an environment steeped in Defense Department needs and national security concerns. Well, it was not for lack of trying.[55] A few years earlier in 1975, Cerf began working with the NSA to design a secure data communications protocol. At that point, though, specific encryption algorithms remained a closely guarded national security secret, particularly the classified symmetric key systems used to encrypt data packets.[56] Encryption protects data by scrambling it with a randomly generated passcode, called an encryption key. Several of Cerf's colleagues at Stanford, including Marty Hellman and Whitfield Diffie, were working on such a public, nonclassified alternative—what came to be known as Rivest-Shamir-Adleman (RSA), which is a key exchange mechanism used to support encryption—but at the time it remained speculative. The underlying algorithms had not yet been developed, so it came out just a tad too late to help.[57] Still, even if it had been available, key exchange mechanisms do not, by themselves, protect anything. Encryption would have aided a number of topics that would come to bedevil future cybersecurity and privacy practitioners, including user authentication. However, there are other versions of this tale. In one, Cerf admits to just being impatient: "It would not have aided my sense of urgency to have to, have to stop for a minute and integrate the public-key crypto into the system. And so we didn't."[58]

Thus, the simple version of the story that the U.S. intelligence community objected to encryption within TCP/IP, though officials didn't publicly say why, thus leading to today's cyberinsecurity, is not the whole story—and is also overly simplistic about what really happened.[59] Plus, even if encryption had been built into TCP/IP, there's a school of thought that the drawbacks would have been substantial. For example, the processing power available on the nascent Internet could have been mismatched with the number crunching needed to decode encrypted packets, potentially inhibiting the spectacular growth of the global Internet described in the next chapter.[60] Further, even if that problem were overcome, such security may not have boosted personal privacy but, rather, made the anonymity long possible on the public Internet much harder to realize. In essence, a "secure" Internet could well resemble one with Chinese characteristics, as will be explored further in wider implications, for human rights, innovation, and much more.

On New Year's Day 1983, TCP/IP became the core Internet protocol for ARPANET.[61] This coincided with the University of Wisconsin creating the domain name system explored further in Chapter 4. That same year, Cerf touted in a paper his belief that TCP/IP should continue to evolve "in cooperation with our NATO allies" and not "remain static," showcasing the extent to which Cold War decision-making still suffused cybersecurity decision-making.[62] Indeed, as Cerf later admitted, "We were well aware of the importance of security . . . but from a military standpoint, operating in a hostile environment . . . I was not so much thinking about it in terms of the public and commercial setting as in the military setting."[63] Further, the reliance on updating, or the idea that "security is retrofittable," as Cerf would later lament,[64] also underscores "the move fast and break things mentality" that pervaded Silicon Valley and contributed to the "Patch Tuesday" mentality that gave tech firms like Microsoft such an atrocious reputation for cybersecurity through the early 2000s.[65]

WIDER IMPLICATIONS

As Cerf has lamented, "Four decades ago, when Bob Kahn and I were creating the TCP/IP networking protocol for the internet, we did not know that we were laying the tracks for what would become the digital superhighway that powers everything in society from modern business to interpersonal relationships."[66] This insight is telling since the stakes for the prevalent cybersecurity about which we are far too familiar could not be higher and now extend to real-world damage, and even injury and death, as seen in the spate of ransomware attacks targeting hospitals during the Covid-19 pandemic.[67] This section traces several of the wider implications resulting from the development of TCP/IP in the 1970s and early 1980s, including: (1) cybersecurity and cyber conflict, (2) Internet of Things (IoT), (3) backdoors, and (4) the potential to re-engineer the Internet and its implications.

CYBERSECURITY AND CYBER CONFLICT

The near ubiquitous cybersecurity vulnerabilities that plague the 21st-century digital economy have contributed to the rapid growth of cybercrime networks and the use by nation-states of cyber weapons to further their national security goals. In early 2022, for example, it was widely reported that Russia used cyberattacks as a prelude to invading Ukraine; indeed, cyberattacks are an integral part of blended 21st-century hybrid warfare.[68] The blurry lines between the public and private sectors, and critical versus noncritical infrastructure in cyberspace, have put small businesses and families in the crosshairs, even as such techniques have also provided an off-ramp to military escalation, thus buying time for diplomacy, as is frequently argued in the case of

Stuxnet.[69] Although estimates vary widely, it is not atypical to discuss trillions being lost annually to identity and trade secrets theft, with the likes of North Korea relying increasingly on cyberattacks to fund its despotic regime.[70]

It is too simplistic to say that, had TCP/IP been encrypted, all this damage and harm could have been avoided. Yet it is also true, as Cerf maintained: "We didn't focus on how you could wreck this system intentionally."[71] The Morris worm discussed earlier, for example, reportedly "sparked both rage that a member of their community would harm the Internet and alarm that the network was so vulnerable to misdeeds by an insider."[72] If he, Kahn, and other researchers had assumed the worst of human nature, then perhaps they could have proactively addressed systemic insecurity, though it is also true that "crime and aggression are the inevitable manifestation of basic human failings, beyond easy technological solutions."[73] Still, encrypting IP would not have stopped the Morris worm, or many other similar—and quite distinct—cyberattacks over the ensuing decades.

Regardless, the results of not building in security at the protocol level should not be overstated. Even if this had been done, today's Internet users would still have to remember or otherwise manage complex passwords and multifactor authentication systems to ensure secure communications since security is still needed at the local computer level; encrypting IP only ensures that the endpoints of communication are correct, and that the communication could not be copied (or seen). As the Nobel Laureate Elinor Ostrom famously said, there are "no panaceas."[74] People with more advanced security needs often use virtual private networks or specialized privacy software like Tor to encrypt their online activity, though the risks have lessened over time due to the increasing use of encryption through e-commerce and otherwise.[75] But technological tools alone are not enough, and neither are laws and regulations about online activity—including the law under which Morris was charged. The dozens of state and federal cybercrime statutes on the books have not yet seemed to reduce the overall number or severity of attacks, in part because of the global nature of the collective action problem.

There is cause for hope, though. In the wake of the Morris worm, Carnegie Mellon University established the world's first Cyber Emergency Response Team partly as a clearinghouse for bug reports, which has been replicated in the federal government and around the world. Some policymakers are talking about establishing a national cybersecurity safety board to investigate digital weaknesses and issue recommendations, much as the National Transportation Safety Board does with airplane disasters.[76] More organizations are also taking preventative action, adopting best practices in cybersecurity as they build their systems, rather than waiting for a problem to happen and trying to clean up afterward. If more organizations considered cybersecurity as an important element of corporate social responsibility, they—and their staff, customers, and partners—would be safer.[77]

INTERNET OF THINGS

The IoT was envisioned by Cerf, Kahn, and others decades before it was a near mundane, everyday reality. Many of us are surrounded by smart appliances, speakers, and other devices from the moment we awake. Unfortunately, these Internet-connected devices suffer from the same security vulnerabilities as their personal computer brethren. For example, as is described in *The Internet of Things: What Everyone Needs to Know*,[78]

> Consider October 2016, when a distributed denial of service (DDoS) attack emanating from a vast network of small, cheap Internet-connected devices, which collectively came to be known as the Mirai botnet, paralyzed Internet servers run by a tech firm called Dyn. That, in and of itself, might not have been a big deal, but the results certainly were. Because Dyn managed (and continues to operate) a significant part of Internet infrastructure, access to a number of important Internet services was slowed, or even stopped entirely, for much of the eastern United States during the attack. The Mirai botnet was so successful, and noteworthy, because it took advantage

of security weaknesses in Internet-connected devices such as security cameras and home routers. Initially, some thought that the attack was politically motivated, but investigators determined that, in fact, it was not a shadowy criminal group or nation state behind the botnet; instead, it was three college students, trying to get an edge on the *Minecraft* computer game. "They didn't realize the power they were unleashing," said FBI agent Bill Walton. "This was the Manhattan Project."[79]

Cerf attested that there were at least two basic flaws built into the Internet—a lack of security in TCP/IP and lack of IP address space to connect all the stuff that would eventually be connected to it, embodying the Internet of Things.[80] It turns out that the second issue has been easier to correct than the first, given the rollout of Internet Protocol version 6 (IPv6).[81] Yet other issues pertaining to the first remain pressing, including the ongoing debates over backdoors in encryption technologies.

BACKDOORS

Simply put, a backdoor in computing "is a method of bypassing the normal method of authentication[82] but is ultimately a device issue. The topic became noteworthy in the 1990s as cryptography technology spread, even as the government tried to maintain tight controls in an episode known to history as the Clipper Chip saga.[83] The idea then, as now, was to give law enforcement backdoor access to encrypted keys (that only they could access) so they could decrypt communications.[84] Yet the extreme challenges of safeguarding the access key and the larger issues with mandating backdoors have so far meant the idea has not progressed in the United States, despite increased pressure such as in the aftermath of the 2015 San Bernardino shooting.[85] Cerf has called such backdoors "super risky," elaborating that "The Internet has numerous security challenges, and it needs more users and ISPs to adopt strong measures like encryption, two-factor authentication and HTTP over SSL."[86] That has not stopped other governments, though, including Australia, from requiring them.[87] And the fact that the United States is a close intelligence-sharing partner with Australia through the Five Eyes means that the U.S. government enjoys many of the benefits of such a policy without having to mandate it and face a fierce domestic backlash threatening the broader global privacy movement.[88]

RE-ENGINEERING THE INTERNET

As Kahn noted in 2011, "Various characteristics of the existing Internet make it especially vulnerable to harmful interference. One is the lack of overt security, which makes communications vulnerable to interference. Second is lack of identity management, which makes verification less secure than perhaps may be desired or necessary."[89] Although calls to "re-engineer" the Internet are popular and are often viewed as a way to rein in the worst abuses of both Silicon Valley and the intelligence community,[90] in reality, TCP/IP is regularly updated. But starting again is another story. After all, consider the migration to IPv6, which started in 1995, did not require any relearning on the part of users, but is still in progress as of this writing. Telling English drivers, for example, to switch one day and start driving on the other side of the road would result in calamities, as would rethinking the global flow of data and underlying packet switching.

Yet we need not look at a fictional alternative universe or timeline to envision what the Internet would look like with aggressive identity management and encryption, and with it a lack of anonymity—and privacy. The online experience in China today, in many ways, resembles the types of controls that the global community of Internet users could have experienced if decisions were made differently in 1978 and 1983. The International Telecommunication Union (ITU), discussed further in Chapter 4, could have had a larger role in regulating IP, and potentially identifying who sent it, a form of deep packet inspection that remains more the exception than the rule globally. Similarly, the identity management that makes it possible for the Chinese government to control its population through draconian censorship and monitoring could be more the norm, which could benefit cybersecurity by improving attribution and accountability, even as it risks human rights, particularly privacy. In lieu of re-engineering the Internet, more should be done to encourage basic cyber hygiene, along with incentivizing the uptake of IPv6 given that it is able to support encryption, meaning that we will have the tool to see what can (and indeed could have) changed if IP had supported encryption from the beginning.[91] Other possibilities based on exciting new technologies also beckon. For example, Kahn has even posited using various blockchain-enabled technologies to establish trust through strong cryptography.[92] Regardless of the question, blockchain seems to be the answer.

WRAP UP

Cerf and Kahn are at the center of this story, but as with any key fork in the history of cybersecurity and Internet governance, there is an entire cast of characters who contributed to the decision itself and its aftermath. The story presented here is meant to help illustrate some of the reasons why this fork was taken and TCP/IP was left unencrypted, along with highlighting a few of the many implications of that decision and asking the perennial "what if?" question that is integral to this exercise. On the one hand, there is cause for hope with IPv6 uptake expanding and encryption increasing even as cyberattacks continue to surge; the future of the Internet seems secure, even if it may never expand to the rest of the solar system and become an Interplanetary Internet, as some advocates have argued.[93] Yet the underlying issues of insecurity, anonymity, and privacy remain unresolved, both online and offline. Before the next iteration of the Morris worm or Mirai does untold damage to the modern information society, it is incumbent on all of us—governments, companies, and individuals alike—to set up rules and programs that support widespread cybersecurity, without waiting another 30 years.

4

The Web for Free

> The ultimate goal of the web is to support and improve our web-like existence in the world. We all have to ensure that the society we build with the web is the sort we intend.[1]
>
> —TIM BERNERS-LEE

The early Internet of the 1980s and early 1990s was exploding in connectivity, and potential. The number of hosts grew 500-fold in the 1980s, for example, from approximately 200 in 1980 to more than 100,000 by 1989.[2] By 1990, fully 42% of U.S. adults had used a computer.[3] But the Internet was still tough for many people to navigate, even though many of the underlying technologies—such as "hyperlinks," a term coined by Ted Nelson in 1965[4]—had already been developed. The trick, as is so often the case, was to take advantage of the growing ubiquity of these technologies and combine them in a novel way to make it so that *anyone* could create and find information online.

Innovation is a team sport, but as we have seen, individuals can still play key—even outsized—roles in creating and combining the technologies that have made the Internet possible.[5] There is a strong case to be made that Tim Berners-Lee, and his creation—the World Wide Web—is just such an individual, and story.

As a kid, Tim always loved to tinker. This passion continued during his university days. While at Oxford in 1976, he built his first computer,

Forks in the Digital Road. Scott J. Shackelford and Scott O. Bradner, Oxford University Press. © Oxford University Press 2024.
DOI: 10.1093/oso/9780197617762.003.0004

before starting his career at a U.K.-based telecom manufacturer that focused on distributed transaction systems, and message relays.[6] Starting in 1978, though, he decided to leave his stable job and take a chance as an independent consultant, including a six-month stint—in a move that would change the world—as a software engineer at CERN (Conseil Européen pour la Recherche Nucléaire, or European Council for Nuclear Research) in Switzerland.[7] While at CERN in 1980, Berners-Lee wrote a notebook program called ENQUIRE ("Enquire-Within-Upon-Everything"), which allowed "links to be made between arbitrary nodes."[8] This humble program would serve as a foundation nearly a decade later to birth what later would become the World Wide Web.

Indeed, Berners-Lee came up with the original idea of what became the World Wide Web in 1989, based on his earlier ENQUIRE project, which was similarly designed to "allow people to work together by combining their knowledge in a web of hypertext documents."[9] Begun in October 1990, Berners-Lee wrote the original web server, and client (web browser), making its debut within CERN that December, and on the Internet publicly in the summer of 1991 in the form of the first website as seen in Figure 4.1.[10] As he later noted,

The world wide web went live, on my physical desktop in Geneva, Switzerland, in December 1990. It consisted of one Web site and one browser, which happened to be on the same computer. The simple

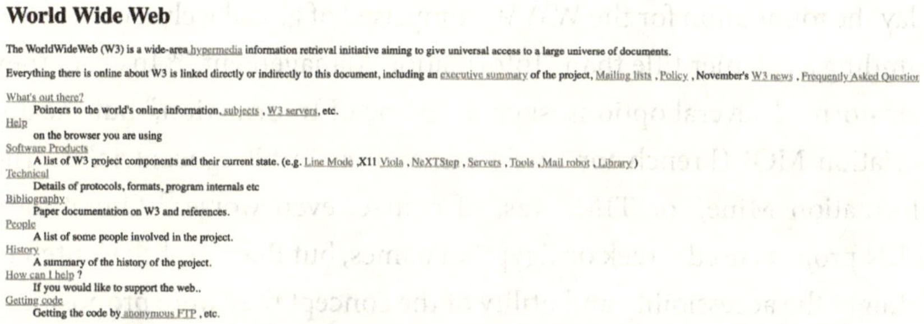

World Wide Web

The WorldWideWeb (W3) is a wide-area hypermedia information retrieval initiative aiming to give universal access to a large universe of documents.

Everything there is online about W3 is linked directly or indirectly to this document, including an executive summary of the project, Mailing lists , Policy , November's W3 news , Frequently Asked Question

What's out there?
    Pointers to the world's online information, subjects , W3 servers, etc.
Help
    on the browser you are using
Software Products
    A list of W3 project components and their current state. (e.g. Line Mode ,X11 Viola , NeXTStep , Servers , Tools , Mail robot , Library)
Technical
    Details of protocols, formats, program internals etc
Bibliography
    Paper documentation on W3 and references.
People
    A list of some people involved in the project.
History
    A summary of the history of the project.
How can I help ?
    If you would like to support the web..
Getting code
    Getting the code by anonymous FTP , etc.

Figure 4.1. First World Wide Website
World Wide Web, http://info.cern.ch/hypertext/WWW/TheProject.html (last visited Sept. 17, 2021).

setup demonstrated a profound concept: that any person could share information with anyone else, anywhere. In this spirit, the Web spread quickly from the grassroots up.[11]

In a presentation to the Internet Engineering Task Force (IETF), Berners-Lee used his original name—the universal document identifier (UDI)—in describing the innovation, which has been discussed and built on the work of numerous others, including Nelson.[12] In his book *Weaving the Web*, Berners-Lee confessed that there was a strong, adverse reaction to this approach. Many thought that it was arrogant, to say the least, in calling his creation "universal."[13] It seemed that he was only a step away from proposing an *Encyclopedia Galactica* à la Isaac Asimov's *Foundation* series.[14] Taking the criticism on board, he consented that "*uniform* document identifiers" would suffice.[15] In time, this notion evolved into the more general uniform resource identifier (URI),[16] but Berners-Lee never gave up on his notion that the records should be as persistent as possible to reinforce the universality of cyberspace to create "an interconnected information space."[17]

Of course, Berners-Lee did not accomplish any of this on his own. For example, he had a deep and fruitful partnership with a Belgian engineer named Robert Cailliau. As reported by Walter Isaacson, "In the marriage of hypertext and the Internet, Robert was best man."[18] Cailliau's methodical attention to detail was matched by Tim's vision.[19] This partnership played out in Berner-Lee's original submission to CERN seeking funding to lay the foundation for the WWW comprised of global web servers, such as finding a catchier title than "Information Management."[20] Instead, they brainstormed several options, such as "Mine of Information," but the abbreviation MOI (French for "me") came off as "a bit egocentric."[21] "The Information Mine," or TIM, was, of course, even worse.[22] Oftentimes, CERN projects used Greek or Egyptian names, but Berners-Lee wanted to highlight the accessibility and utility of the concept they were proposing.[23] Finally, he suggested they "Call it the World Wide Web."[24] Despite some protests from Cailliau given how long it took to say "WWW," Berners-Lee stuck to his guns, and the project became: "WorldWideWeb: Proposal for a HyperText Project."[25]

On August 6, 1991, Berners-Lee saw a post on the Internet's alt.hypertext newsgroup with the question: "Is anyone aware of research or development efforts in . . . hypertext links enabling retrieval from multiple heterogeneous sources?"[26] His answer "became the first public announcement of the Web": "The WorldWideWeb project aims to allow links to be made to any information anywhere . . . [i]f you're interested in using the code, mail me."[27]

The hallmarks of the Web—universality, decentralization—have made such rapid scaling possible by simply using three technologies: "a page in the HTML (hypertext markup language) format, name it with the URI naming convention, and serve it up on the Internet using HTTP (hypertext transfer protocol)."[28] We are all still dealing with the torrent of innovation that Tim unleashed on that day; if anything, Tim was more successful in promoting his vision than he ever could have imagined, saying at one point, "I had no idea that people would put literally everything on it [the Web]."[29] But that is the topic of Chapter 5. Here, we consider the question of "What if Tim was a member of a different church?," to which many aspiring billionaire founders of unicorns aspire: the worship of getting big, and breaking things?

THE FORK: TO PATENT, OR NOT TO PATENT, THAT WAS THE MULTIBILLION-DOLLAR QUESTION

Somewhat to their surprise, the CERN management team embraced Tim and Robert's concept, so much so that they sought to patent it to protect the innovation. Cailliau thought the idea was worth considering,[30] but Berners-Lee immediately resisted. If the WWW was patented, its growth would be impeded. Keeping the web free, and open, would be the best— and fastest—way, Tim reasoned, to ensure that their proposal would become what it promised, a true "Worldwide Web." As Robert recalled, "Tim's not in it for the money."[31]

Instead, Tim was driven more by his beliefs that stemmed from his membership in the Unitarian Universalist Church centered on "peer sharing and respect."[32] Further, the 1953 CERN Convention included language that its "experimental and theoretical work shall be published or otherwise made generally available."[33] As a result, CERN eventually published a document that relinquished "all intellectual property rights to this code, both source and binary form" and granted permission "for anyone to use, duplicate, modify, and redistribute it."[34] This resulted, according to Isaacson, in "one of the grandest free and open-source projects in history."[35] As Tim once reflected, drawing parallels to the structure and meaning of the Internet Engineering Task Force, "The design of the Internet and the Web is a search for a set of rules which will allow computers to work together in harmony, and our spiritual and social quest is for a set of rules which allow people to work together in harmony."[36] In this way, his work intersects with that of the economist Elinor Ostrom and her work on commons governance, which will be explored further; if data were considered as a type of common property, or public good, the implications on Internet governance would be profound.[37]

The decision to keep the web in the public domain changed history and put the Internet on course for the explosive growth that it experienced in the 1990s, and thereafter. This, in turn, set the stage for a sequence of events set off by a decision from the University of Minnesota to ask for a license fee for certain classes of for-profit users who wanted to use the Gopher protocol that preceded the WWW (at the time, the service was free to universities, but not to companies).[38] This move was met with calls of "treason" and led to industry dropping its use of Gopher for fear of IP rights violations.[39]

By March 1993, at an IETF meeting in Columbus, Ohio, Berners-Lee was being "accosted" in the hallways with concerns from members that CERN would follow suit and charge for WWW access.[40] Berners-Lee pushed for the opposite approach, convincing CERN to issue a statement that it would be offered free of charge or constraints in its next release of the WWW software scheduled for April 30, 1993.[41] As Tim said at the time, "Philosophically, if the web was to be a universal resource, it had

The Web for Free   91

to be able to grow in an unlimited way."[42] As CERN argued at the time, "Through these actions, making the software required to run a web server freely available, along with a basic browser and a library of code, the web was allowed to flourish."[43]

The free availability of the web led to the successful release, and rapid uptake, of several pioneering web browsers, including NCSA Mosaic and, by December 1993, Netscape's Mozilla browser.[44] Not only were the browsers revolutionary at the time given that they made use of Berners-Lee's WorldWideWeb tech, but they were also released as a download, for free, on the Internet. In short order, this led to the majority of Internet users using these browsers, contributing to the further rapid expansion of the web. Thirty years later in 2021, more than 4.6 billion people were actively using Tim's invention.[45]

WHAT WOULD HAVE BEEN THE RESULTS OF BERNERS-LEE PATENTING THE WWW?

If Tim Berner-Lee's philosophy and personal code of ethics had been different, there is a good chance that the Internet would have evolved in a very different manner, and rate, since the early 1990s. If CERN had patented the underlying technology, for example, it would likely have stalled or blocked the growth of not only the web itself, but also all the companies that have come to rely on it, including browsers such as Yahoo! and later Google, and more recently social media networks including Facebook and X, formerly Twitter. In a world, for example, in which website owners and operators along with software creators would have to pay a license fee to CERN, not only would that centralize control and make CERN both a de jure and de facto Internet gatekeeper impacting the content and services available online worldwide, but it could also have undermined the experimentation (and associated speculation) of the dot-com boom. If you have to get permission or pay a fee before doing things online like creating a new website, it is far less likely that a student, such as Mark Zuckerberg, would (for better or worse) be able to experiment and create Facebook.[46] It is possible that an ancillary result of such a system would have been Swiss law, and perhaps eventually the EU, having an even larger impact on cyber norms, including free speech debates as discussed further in Chapter 5 involving Section 230. Regardless, the Internet would have evolved with governments and government-backed organizations like CERN at the beating heart of the web, a state of affairs that advocates of cyber sovereignty would prefer, as will be discussed further.[47]

To understand a larger implication of making the World Wide Web free, let us consider an analogy. National parks used to be completely free with no entrance fees.[48] Similarly, much of the U.S. interstate system is toll free, outside of certain states like Florida.[49] The difference between completely free versus *mostly* free is magnified when it comes to technology. If any fee is involved, transaction costs are dramatically raised and open-source software is rendered obsolete, and it becomes necessary to justify investments in advance, potentially forestalling myriad innovations. Permission isn't needed to innovate in an end-to-end network such as that which the WWW became. In contrast, no one confused AT&T with an innovator during its long monopoly on U.S. telephone services, with the decades it took to roll out touch-tone phones being a case in point.[50] Yet such issues are merely the tip of the proverbial iceberg when considering the wider implications of the key decision to keep the WWW free, open, and interoperable, with the British telecom effort to claim a patent on URLs being a case in point.[51]

WIDER IMPLICATIONS

The fork taken by Tim and his colleagues at CERN has resulted in a slew of impacts for business, society, and even human rights. Indeed, issues of equality, fairness, and equity seem to have been driving forces behind Tim's decision-making throughout the period. He remarked, for example, that "[g]etting people online is a very important part of addressing inequality in general."[52] The United Nations General Assembly, along with a growing number of leading nations, civil society groups, and even tech firms, now recognize Tim's ultimate vision in the form of treating Internet access itself as a human right.[53] The notion of Internet access as a human right, though, is not without controversy. Vinton Cerf, another "father of the internet," for example, has argued that technology itself is not a right, but a means through which rights can be exercised.[54] Yet more and more nations have declared their citizens' right to Internet access.[55] Spain, France, Costa Rica, Estonia, and Greece have codified this right in a variety of ways, including in their constitutions, laws, and judicial rulings.[56] In October 2010, Finland made broadband access a legal right for all its citizens.[57] A former head of the International Telecommunication Union has argued that governments must "regard the internet as basic infrastructure—just like roads, waste and water."[58] Global public opinion seems to overwhelmingly agree.[59] Further, during the Covid-19 pandemic, there were growing calls for promoting—and enforcing—this right, as an increasing amount of our personal and professional lives are being lived online.[60]

But, despite Tim's efforts, access to the web isn't free. As of this writing, more than three billion people still are not online, and those who are online may not have access to the bandwidth and services they need to thrive in an increasingly knowledge-driven global economy. Through the Web Foundation, Berners-Lee wants users to change that by making it possible for anyone to purchase a gigabyte of data on their phone for less than 2% of their monthly income.[61] Thus, access costs continue to be a concern decades after Berners-Lee first made his stand against charging for the web. This theme continues to echo throughout his life, as seen in Tim's founding of the World Wide Web Foundation in 2009 to "defend the Open Web and further its potential to benefit humanity."[62]

These same philosophies are echoed in ongoing cyber norm building efforts, such as the Paris Call for Trust and Security in Cyberspace, which affirms a vision for cyberspace that is "open, secure, stable, accessible, and peaceful."[63] This sentiment, in turn, echoes decades of diplomatic efforts led by the U.S. government and allied democracies to, in many ways, realize the vision for the web that Berners-Lee laid out in 1991. Standard setting, being fueled by a multistakeholder process, is a key component of this effort.[64] This is key to such efforts as transparency in government data sharing, and the serendipitous creation of novel programs, and content.[65] As Rolf Heuer, CERN Director-General, has said,

> There is no sector of society that has not been transformed by the invention (the web). . . . From research to business and education, the web has been reshaping the way we communicate, work, innovate and live. The web is a powerful example of the way that basic research benefits humankind.[66]

Yet, this shared vision, and the multistakeholder process of Internet governance more generally, is under perhaps the greatest threat since it crystallized more than 30 years ago.

Looking ahead to the next 30 years of the web's development, the future is not necessarily as open and free as the first 30 years of the web's existence. These threats come in many forms and have many implications for the future of cyberspace. As Berners-Lee has noted on the 20th anniversary of the web's founding in 2010,

> The Web as we know it . . . is being threatened in different ways. Some of its most successful inhabitants have begun to chip away at its principles. Large social-networking sites are walling off information posted by their users from the rest of the Web. Wireless Internet providers are being tempted to slow traffic to sites with which they have not made deals. Governments—totalitarian and democratic alike—are monitoring people's online habits, endangering important human rights.[67]

Let us consider several of these issues here that are of particular interest to Berners-Lee: (1) net neutrality, (2) social networks, (3) anticompetitive behavior, as well as (4) cyber sovereignty and digital fragmentation.

NET NEUTRALITY

A term first proposed by Columbia Professor Tim Wu, "net neutrality" refers to the idea that Internet service providers such as Comcast and AT&T do not know what applications are being used and make no effort to handle traffic differently based on the application or who is sending or receiving the traffic in question.[68] Ensuring that the Internet remains "an open playing field is crucial for innovation," as suggested by many advocates including Berners-Lee.[69] He has argued, for example, that "Although the Internet and Web generally thrive on lack of regulation, some basic values have to be legally preserved."[70] This is an area of growing global convergence with at least 12 nations recognizing, and enforcing, the right.[71] The United States has made net neutrality into a partisan tennis ball with the right being recognized by the Federal Trade Commission in a sweeping ruling in 2015, while in 2017 it was repealed during the Trump administration.[72] The future of net neutrality in the United States, as of this writing, remains unresolved.

SOCIAL NETWORKS

Facebook. Instagram. Twitter, now X. LinkedIn. TikTok. What all these sites and the many new niche social media sites that are regularly being created have in common is that they are, in essence, walled digital gardens separate from the rest of the World Wide Web.[73] This has major implications for media and publishers,[74] but at a higher level for every Internet user. For example, the monopolistic power that such social media sites can wield raises serious concerns about limiting competition, and stalling innovation, as will be explored.[75] As Berners-Lee has stated, "Each site is a silo, walled off from the others. Yes, your site's pages are on the Web, but your data are not."[76] In essence, because of the growth in popularity of these services, the web as an open, interconnected beehive of innovation and largely uninhibited peer-to-peer production may not be dead,[77] but it is under threat in tandem with the rise in nation-states exerting increasing control over the web's functions as will be explored. The rise in social networks has also made their community norms and content moderation practices even more central to fostering—and manipulating—democratic dialogue, which is a key theme of Chapter 5.

ANTICOMPETITIVE BEHAVIOR

As of September 2021, Facebook was worth more than $1 trillion, Amazon nearly $1.7 trillion, Alphabet (the parent company of Google) $1.85 trillion, Microsoft $2.2 trillion, and Apple $2.35 trillion for a combined value of over $9 trillion.[78] That figure is so large that it is nearly double the GDP of Japan (the third largest economy in the world), and not too far off from that of China.[79] Such accumulated economic power—built in part from the success of the digital walled gardens that many of these firms have helped to nourish—has naturally led to concerns of anticompetitive behavior. Antitrust regulators in the United States, European Union, and China are actively investigating the practices of these firms as part of a global crackdown on big tech, but many of the laws that are being used (especially in the United States) remain antiquated, designed to deal with railroad and oil monopolies, not Instagram.[80] Plus, even successful antitrust attempts in the past, such as with IBM in 1969 and Microsoft in 1998, actually "left both companies not only intact, but also on trajectories to increase their market power."[81] There are projects with which Berners-Lee and others remain engaged that can bridge these walled gardens—such as Diaspora and Status.net—but their uptake remains limited.[82]

CYBER SOVEREIGNTY

Former Obama White House Cybersecurity Coordinator Rob Joyce has said, "If we go to the lowest common denominator, where everyone builds their walled garden and data must be localized and data is exploited by totalitarian regimes, then it really cuts against the core of the fundamental internet that the U.S. envisioned . . . "[83] To this sentiment could be added a challenge to the vision of the web that Berners-Lee helped to pioneer. Russia, for example, has made it an established state policy to isolate itself from the World Wide Web, such as a 2019 "sovereign Internet" law that "requires internet service providers (ISPs) to install equipment that allows authorities to circumvent providers and automatically block content the government has banned and reroute internet traffic themselves."[84] Whereas China, for example, similarly embraces cyber sovereignty (Wangluo Zhuquan) to control how its citizens, along with residents in other nations participating in its Belt and Road Initiative, use the web and experience cyberspace.[85] Yet it is not just Russia and China but a growing number of nations that are practicing some form of cyber sovereignty; indeed, it has been reported that "two-thirds of all internet users [are] currently subjected to some degree of censorship of criticism aimed at the government, military, or ruling families."[86]

Adam Segal from the Council on Foreign Relations makes the broader point that the success of cyber sovereignty rests on "widespread disillusionment with the spread of disinformation, threats to privacy, and concentration of economic and political power by big technology firms"—in other words, the very implications that similarly concern Berners-Lee for decades years and have been introduced earlier.[87] As Tim has said, "walled gardens," no matter how pleasing, can never compete in diversity, richness, and innovation with the mad, throbbing web market outside their gates."[88] Such a series of "fragmented islands" would inhibit the freedom to connect that has been so instrumental in creating the modern knowledge economy, along with a vibrant democratic tradition, given its ability to promote free speech.[89] Indeed, the universality aspect of what made the web so attractive in the first place is what's at stake in this moment of growing cyber sovereignty.

LOOKING AHEAD

Through the World Wide Web Consortium, which added artificial intelligence to its mission, becoming the Computer Science and Artificial Intelligence Laboratory (CSAIL) in 2003, Berners-Lee has long remained engaged in these issues. For example, he joined Oxford's faculty in 2016 but is still active in the Decentralized Information Group, which seeks "to give people control of their data and to de-centralize the Web."[90] The accolades for Tim's pioneering work and vision have continued unabated, such as in 2016 when he was awarded the ACM A.M. Turing Prize—also known as the "Nobel Prize of Computing"—"for inventing the World Wide Web, the first web browser, and the fundamental protocols and algorithms allowing the Web to scale."[91] In 2020, he cofounded a new startup with the cybersecurity guru Bruce Schneier called Inrupt, which is "designed to bring Tim Berners-Lee's distributed data ownership model . . . into the mainstream."[92] Although challenges mount to Tim's original vision for the web, through such initiatives and grassroots organizations, there is still time to keep the web free for the next generation.

5

Regulating Online Speech

No experiment can be more interesting than that we are now trying, and which we trust will end in establishing the fact, that man may be governed by reason and truth. Our first object should therefore be, to leave open to him all the avenues to truth. The most effectual hitherto found, is the freedom of the press.

—BENJAMIN FRANKLIN (PRINTER)[1]

We were in this position before, when printing presses broke the existing system of information management. A new system emerged and I believe we have the motivation and capability to do it again.

—JOHATHAN GRUDIN (MICROSOFT)[2]

By 1996, the Internet boasted more than 73,000 servers, and 22% of surveyed Americans were going online.[3] What they found there, though, worried some members of Congress and their constituents—particularly the rapidly growing amount of pornography targeting kids. In response, Congress passed the CDA, which sought to regulate indecency and obscenity in cyberspace. The U.S. Supreme Court struck down portions of the law on free-speech grounds shortly thereafter, but it left in place a little-known provision that has come to be known as Section 230, which was designed to limit the liability of Internet platforms for the information

Forks in the Digital Road. Scott J. Shackelford and Scott O. Bradner, Oxford University Press. © Oxford University Press 2024.
DOI: 10.1093/oso/9780197617762.003.0005

posted by individual users. Section 230 reads in part, "No provider or user of an interactive computer service shall be treated as the publisher or speaker of any information provided by another information content provider."[4] Those 26 words, as various observers have noted, released Internet service providers and web-hosting companies from legal responsibility for information their customers posted or shared online, while also providing protections to websites that decided to moderate their communities. In other words, they "created the Internet" as we know it today.[5]

This single sentence provided legal security that allowed the U.S. online technology firms to flourish, which in turn conquered much of the digital world. That protection let companies feel comfortable creating a consumer-focused Internet filled with grassroots media outlets, bloggers, customer reviews, and user-generated content. Yet critics note that Section 230 also allows social media sites like Facebook and Twitter to operate largely without regulation. This, in turn, has fueled a wave of disinformation and hate speech that proliferates on these platforms, which has challenged key pillars of U.S. society and those of other advanced and emerging democracies around the world.

Looking back now more than 25 years after its passage, what can we learn from the history of Section 230 as we seek to rein in the worst abuses of large social media firms? What are the global implications of Section 230 and the U.S. approach to regulating online speech that it embodies, and what if we had taken a different fork along the way?

A BRIEF HISTORY OF SPEECH REGULATION IN THE UNITED STATES

The common-law rules that have provided a foundation for regulating online speech came mostly from First Amendment cases dealing with the liability of bookstores and newsstands for the material that they sold.[6] An early, and important, example of such rulings was the 1959 U.S. Supreme Court case *Smith v. California*, which involved an LA-based bookstore owner named Elazar Smith who was convicted for selling an "obscene" book in contravention of a local ordinance.[7] Smith won in the Supreme Court, arguing that imposing strict liability on bookstore owners violated the First Amendment since the law did not require any specific knowledge of the book in question, unduly chilling protected speech.[8] Otherwise, Smith—and other LA bookstore owners—would effectively only be allowed to sell books that they have personally inspected, which, needless to say, would be quite a burden for even the most well-read bookseller.[9]

The Supreme Court kept grappling with how best to approach the responsibility for booksellers over the following decade, such as in the 1968 case *Ginsberg v. United States*, in which the court upheld a New York law penalizing the sale of pornography to minors with a "reason to know" requirement.[10] Other cases, such as the 1975 *Hamling v. United States*, involving the mailing of obscene materials, brought further clarity that the defendants in the case should be found guilty if they "had knowledge of the character of the materials."[11] This scienter (knowledge) requirement is also in defamation law, permitting liability only if the defendant "knows or has reason to know of its defamatory character."[12]

This was the state of play through the 1980s, but things became a bit more complicated by the 1990s with the rise of the World Wide Web discussed in Chapter 4. As online bulletin boards and forums proliferated, questions quickly arose about the liability of platform owners for policing so much suspect or illegal content.[13] The first seminal case to test how distributor liability should apply online was *Cubby v. CompuServe*, a 1991 dispute involving a CompuServe contractor who posted allegedly defamatory statements on a CompuServe forum.[14] The judge used the distributor liability framework from *Smith* and granted summary judgment for CompuServe.[15] Critically though, the judge noted that the greater the degree of "editorial control," in the words of Professor Allen S. Hammond, the "greater its potential liability to users and third parties for damage caused by the information's content."[16]

The next waystation in this legal odyssey came four years later when another judge was faced with a dispute involving posts on a financial forum on CompuServe competitor Prodigy.[17] Critically, unlike CompuServe, Prodigy "had implemented user content guidelines, automatically screened user posts for offensive terms, and contracted with 'Board Leaders' who enforced the user guidelines."[18] These policy differences wound up being integral to the judge deciding in *Stratton Oakmont v. Prodigy* that Prodigy was not acting as a distributor like CompuServe, but as a publisher with the same liability as the author. In the process, this created a perverse incentive for such services to not moderate user content lest they similarly be faced with legal consequences.

These rulings, while only persuasive and not binding in many U.S. courts, were the only games in town as Congress began considering the issue of content moderation in earnest. In particular, there was growing concern about encouraging a hands-off approach to moderating user content.[19] *Prodigy* became particularly animating for Representative Chris Cox, who read a *Wall Street Journal* article about the case on a flight back from California in 1995, leading him to rough out a legislative proposal to overturn the case.[20]

THE ROAD TO SECTION 230

In 1995, Congress was doing something that it had not attempted in nearly 60 years—overhauling federal telecommunications law.[21] At that point in history, the Internet was largely a sideshow, with the exception of concerns over the widespread availability of pornographic material online, especially to minors.[22] This concern wound up animating the CDA, authored by Senator James Exon, which, among other things, would have imposed criminal penalties for posting indecent material that might be seen by minors.[23] His overriding goal was "to provide much-needed protection for children."[24] Constitutional free speech concerns were front of mind, though, including among Republican House leadership. Newt Gingrich, for example, said the CDA was "a violation of the right of adults to communicate with each other."[25]

As an alternative to the CDA, Representatives Chris Cox and Ron Wyden decided to fashion a proposal that would reverse *Stratton Oakmont v. Prodigy* and still reduce minors' access to online pornographic material, while also promoting the growth of the commercial Internet.[26] Chris Cox was born in St. Paul, Minnesota, in 1952, an academic all-star from an early age who would eventually attend both Harvard Law School and Business School before working in the Reagan Administration and being elected to Congress, serving from 1989 to his resignation in 2005.[27] Ron Wyden was also born in the heartland before making his way west, in his case in Wichita, Kansas, in 1949. A basketball star who grew up largely in Palo Alto, California, he has degrees from Stanford and the University of Oregon School of Law. Wyden and his wife raised five children in their adopted hometown of Portland, Oregon. He was elected as a congressman in 1980 and as a senator in 1996.[28] Both men shared an interest in emerging tech issues, including the burgeoning Internet, along with free speech. Although they formed an unlikely duo, they made "a pact to think about cutting edge issues where people haven't thought through it fully. They'd have to approach it without a knee-jerk response."[29]

Their common curiosities germinated into an idea that became the Internet Freedom and Family Empowerment Act,[30] which was introduced in June 1995, just a month after *Stratton Oakmont*. It included language that would eventually become known as Section 230.[31] The key terms in Section 230, including "interactive computer service," were defined broadly and later interpreted by courts to "mean that platforms are not responsible for the content that their users post, whether or not they moderated user content,"[32] although exceptions did exist for criminal law, intellectual property, and privacy violations.[33]

To further underscore the governmental hands-off approach to content regulation on the commercial Internet memorialized by Section 230, there were findings statements attached to the bill highlighting the authors' belief that cyberspace had "flourished, to the benefit of all Americans, with a minimum of government regulation."[34] This viewpoint was informed by a 1995 report from the Center for Democracy and Technology, which warned against criminalizing "indecent content" and recommended instead "user empowerment," particularly by encouraging the private sector to develop tools to protect kids online, such as Net Nanny.[35] In considering and eventually passing Section 230 on a vote of 420-4 as an amendment to the larger telecommunications overhaul, Congress was explicitly trying to "ensure that platforms did *not* have an incentive to be neutral" and ensure that the federal government would not be thrust in the role of policing online content.[36]

Eventually, both Section 230 and the CDA were included in the final telecommunications bill that was finally signed into law in 1996.[37] At the time of its passage, only 52% of senators had an Internet connection, and only 26% had email addresses.[38] Within a year, the CDA would be struck down by the Supreme Court as being an "unnecessarily broad suppression of speech,"[39] though, as was noted, the Court left Section 230 intact.[40] But how could things have turned out differently, and what have been the wider implications of these 26 words globally?

THE FORK: WHAT IF SECTION 230 HAD BEEN DRAFTED, OR INTERPRETED, DIFFERENTLY?

Congress passed Section 230 in 1996 "at the dawn of the modern, commercial Internet" to, according to Kosseff, "fill the gaps in the common law that govern the liability of companies that distribute content created by others."[41] Yet debates over the meaning and impact of Section 230 are far reaching, with some arguing that the act has made it too easy for Internet platforms to shirk their responsibility to take down harmful content. Others assert that the law allows these same platforms to moderate too freely, permitting harmful and biased discrimination of opposing viewpoints.[42] As Kosseff has argued, "Section 230 is responsible for the open Internet that Americans know today, as platforms are free to allow— or moderate—user content without fearing company-ending litigation."[43]

It took years for Section 230's sweeping liability protections to be made clear by the courts.[44] As is frequently the case with statutory interpretation, though, there is more than one way to read the law. For example, a more limited interpretation could be that "interactive computer service providers" such as the likes of eventually Facebook and Twitter are not publishers, but distributors.[45] This reading would still make the platforms liable if they "knew or had reason to know of the defamatory or otherwise illegal content" of posts.[46] A second, broader reading of Section 230 would require "courts to consider a distributor as a type of publisher."[47] This interpretation wound up being the one adopted by the courts in a case involving Ken Zeran, who was being targeted on America Online (AOL) for allegedly selling tasteless T-shirts about the Oklahoma City bombing.[48] The court sided with AOL, deciding that "distributor liability, or more precisely, liability or knowingly or negligently distributing defamatory material, is merely a species or type of liability for publishing defamatory material."[49] The cause of "open and free discourse" on the Internet,[50] thus, had seemed to win the day, and, indeed, the debate arguably became "the most important court ruling in Internet law."[51] Few could have foreseen the wider implications of this ruling, which continue to shape the 21st century.[52]

What if the court in *Zeran* had adopted the first reading listed above: that AOL was a distributor that had reason to know about the defamatory posts targeting Zeran, given that he had proactively reached out to the firm? The scope of Section 230 as we know it today would have been curtailed, to be sure, leading AOL to more strictly police content. As will be discussed, there can be myriad unintended consequences to such seeming improvements over the status quo, with firms being overly expansive in taking down content lest it be deemed objectionable to one group or another. There is also a case to be made that it would have been harder for the next generation of social media firms, such as Facebook, to scale up as fast as they did without the certainty the broad reading of Section 230 afforded. But would that have been such a bad thing? Certainly it would be for Meta stockholders and the many users and businesses that rely on the Facebook ecosystem, but might competitors have been given more space to innovate and flourish, resulting in greater consumer choice and a richer digital social ecosystem? Such questions are impossible to answer with any certainty, but it seems likely that the concerns over social media firms doing too little—such as during the 2016 U.S. election cycle—to identify and take down misinformation and disinformation might have been more readily assuaged.

It should be noted, though, that there are limits to Section 230's immunity, including in situations where the platform helped create the content in question.[53] Further, Congress has made reforms to Section 230 over the years, such as in 2018 when it amended the law to provide an "exception for certain sex trafficking-and prostitution-related claims."[54] As Professor Kosseff argued in congressional testimony,

> The *Zeran* reading of Section 230 eliminates the *Stratton Oakmont v. Prodigy* problem by preventing platforms from becoming liable for user content they are unaware of simply because they have moderated some other content. But it goes much further than that; it also allows platforms to decide whether to keep up or take down content that they are aware of without facing potential liability for that content. And that is how Section 230 has created the legal framework for the Internet that we know today.[55]

Section 230, though, is but one of a slew of federal and state laws, industry norms, and constitutional protections impacting content moderation, and one that is often misunderstood.[56] One example is a 2019 story in the *New York Times* entitled "Why Hate Speech on the Internet Is a Never-Ending Problem," which prominently featured Section 230 as "the law that shields it," prompting a later retraction that it was, in fact, the First Amendment that was most pertinent.[57] Before the retraction was issued, though, a federal judge had already cited the article as evidence for "Section 230's grant of immunity for speech-based harms such as hate speech or libel."[58] This confusion has, in part, animated efforts to reform the law, along with bipartisan frustration over its real and perceived impacts on content moderation in cyberspace.

REFORMING SECTION 230

As of this writing, more than 25 bills have been introduced to repeal or revise Section 230, along with pending action by the Supreme Court.

The approaches envisioned run the gambit from imposing a duty of care requirement on platforms to a requirement to block harmful content, along with offering further exceptions to Section 230, including for civil rights violations.[59] As Professor Kosseff has argued, though, none of these changes can "address every problem with the Internet," and many will come with "unintended consequences."[60] For example, even with outright appeal of Section 230, Congress could neither "pass a law that holds platforms liable for online hate speech"[61] nor prohibit the online spreading of disinformation, given all the ways in which the First Amendment has been interpreted to protect lies.[62] It could also lead to a return of the same perverse incentives that were brought up in the wake of *Stratton Oakmont*; as Ron Wyden has argued, "without Section 230, sites would have strong incentives to go one of two ways: either sharply limit what users can post, so as to avoid being sued, or to stop moderating entirely."[63] So long as platforms act "independently and voluntarily," there is no state action, so the First Amendment does not apply, permitting these platforms to regulate and even ban constitutionally protected speech including disinformation.[64]

On the other hand, adopting a distributor liability system would encourage Internet platforms to block not only harmful or illegal content, but potentially also other speech deemed damaging to avoid liability resulting from a renewed "reason to know" standard. Given the lack of bipartisan consensus among those who are concerned about platforms blocking too much—or too little—"harmful" speech, another way forward may be to add to the list of Section 230 exceptions, such as for claims involving "civil rights, antitrust, stalking, harassment, intimidation, international human rights law, and wrongful death."[65] The trick lies in managing the wider implications of even such targeted revisions, as seen in the 2018 decision by Craigslist to take down its entire personal ad section after the sex trafficking prohibition was passed, potentially making life more dangerous for sex workers in the process.[66] And the same goes for so-called neutrality reforms to Section 230—would the Internet be a safer and better place, for example, if Facebook were not permitted to ban hate speech?[67]

Absent congressional action, there also are growing calls among the judiciary for a narrower reading of Section 230, including from U.S. Supreme Court Justice Clarence Thomas, who has seemed to favor a reinterpretation of *Zeran*. In particular, he has argued that paring back the sweeping Section 230 immunity would not necessarily guarantee platform liability for content but would, rather, "give plaintiffs a chance to raise their claims in the first place."[68] As of this writing, it was unclear how Thomas and the other justices would rule in the pair of Section 230 cases before the Supreme Court in 2023.[69]

A final opportunity for U.S. reform—aside from self-regulation, as will discussed—lies with the executive. Although former President Donald Trump and President Joe Biden agree on very little from a policy perspective, one area of alignment during the 2020 presidential campaign was undermining, and promising to reform or repeal, Section 230. Both administrations issued executive orders designed to further this goal, including the 2020 Executive Order 13925: Preventing Online Censorship, which tasked the Secretary of Commerce and the Attorney General to work through the National Telecommunications and Information Administration (NTIA) to clarify FCC rule-making power vis-à-vis Section 230.[70] The Department of Justice suggested four areas for reform shortly before the 2020 election, which unsurprisingly were shelved in its aftermath. The Biden Administration, though, also issued an executive order in May 2021, which among other things revoked Trump Administration executive actions on the topic.[71] The ping pong match continues.

GLOBAL PERSPECTIVES

It is important to note that the U.S. approach to regulating online speech, as with free speech generally, is an outlier. Most advanced democracies— to say nothing of authoritarian regimes—permit a wide range of speech restrictions. Even in Western democracies, it is not uncommon for otherwise liberal governments that promote an Internet freedom agenda to ban the sale of Nazi memorabilia online as in France and Germany, for example. Other regimes, such as Thailand, have made it a crime to spread disinformation. It is thus important to recall that no nation is an island in cyberspace, and as important as the Section 230 debate is to understanding the U.S. context and the extent to which it has influenced how major Internet platforms perceive the protection of free speech online, we are not operating in a vacuum. In fact, the regulatory ripple effects in how other nations are managing content online are shaping the Internet arguably more than the seemingly circular policy debates happening in Washington.

Consider the 2018 "Code of Practice on Disinformation," which resulted from the European Commission pressuring Facebook, Google, and Twitter to boost "transparency around political and issue-based advertising."[72] This initiative was groundbreaking in many ways, including the technology industry agreeing "to self-regulatory standards to fight disinformation."[73] Among other provisions, the code requires signatories to cull fake accounts and create safeguards against misrepresentation and the misuse of automated bots, along with empowering consumers and the broader research community.[74] In response, these firms have set up "searchable political-ad databases," begun to take down "disruptive, misleading or false" information from their platforms, and rejected ads that are inconsistent with election integrity policies.[75] Unfortunately, this did not seem to have the desired impact, as several organizations reported that EU election hashtags, such as #EUElections2019, still "received a high level of suspiciously inorganic engagement."[76] Similarly, an activist group called Avaaz found that, despite these efforts, there were more than "500 far-right and anti-EU Facebook pages and groups" being followed by some 32 million people.[77]

Other countries have taken a different approach to developing codes for disinformation, such as Australia investing in efforts to guard its citizens against information warfare using microtargeting.[78] It has also invested in regional alliances, such as the Pacific Cyber Security Operational Network (PaCSON),[79] which is intended to foster cooperation among South Pacific island nations by providing a mechanism to share cybersecurity threat information and defensive tools, techniques, and ideas. New Zealand has also been proactive in developing norms around the spreading of harmful content online, particularly in the aftermath of the terrorist attack on Christchurch, New Zealand, on March 15, 2019. Following the attack, the prime minister of New Zealand and the president of France brought together heads of state and leaders from the tech sector to adopt the Christchurch Call to Eliminate Terrorist and Violent Extremist Content Online, which is a commitment by government and tech companies to "eliminate terrorist and violent extremist content online."[80] Although broadly focused on extremist content in particular, the 18 original signatories were joined by more than 30 nations and tech firms, including Microsoft, Twitter, and Facebook, in their pledge to, among other things: ensure commitment to human rights law, encourage media outlets "to adopt ethical standards," and work together to prohibit the dissemination of terrorist content, such as by committing to regular and transparent reporting.[81]

Unlike efforts in the United States, European Union, or Australia, Asian democracies have been willing to criminalize the spreading of misinformation. Malaysia, for example, has criminalized the sharing of misinformation.[82] Myanmar and Thailand have leaned on law enforcement actions, which have been abused in some cases to silence critics of public corruption, to rein in misinformation.[83] While in Indonesia, for example, President Joko Widodo spearheaded the creation of the new National Cyber and Encryption Agency to combat disinformation in their elections.[84] One example was in June 2019, when a member of the Muslim Cyber Army was arrested in Java for posting misinformation to the effect that the Indonesian government was being controlled by China.[85]

It is apparent that more nations are using increasingly heavy-handed tactics to clamp down on Internet freedoms in the name of fighting disinformation. The problem of disinformation in India, for example, is so severe that it has been likened to a public health crisis.[86] One Microsoft study, for example, found that 64% of Indians encountered disinformation online in 2019, which was the highest proportion among 22 surveyed countries.[87] Not only have these incidents affected elections by spreading false information about candidates on WhatsApp, but they have also led to real-world harms, including at least 33 deaths and 69 instances of mob violence.[88] In response, the Indian government has shut down Internet access for certain groups more than 100 times in 2018–19 and has proposed laws that would give it largely unchecked surveillance powers, mirroring Chinese-style Internet censorship.[89]

These global responses to disinformation highlight the stakes and the wide implications of such diverse approaches to content moderation, with Section 230 being but one example among many.

WIDER IMPLICATIONS

Chris Cox and Ron Wyden—the authors of Section 230—have similarly been proactive in dismissing claims that the law requires, or should require, websites to adopt content moderation policies, and they think that importing negligence concepts that would require new agency rulemaking is not a good idea.[90] Rather, they maintain that a key goal of Section 230 was to incentivize websites to experiment with filtering techniques while protecting free speech and privacy online.[91] Cox makes no bones about his position, affirming that

> [r]epealing the law entirely would return us to the legal no man's land that necessitated 230 in the first place. We hear a lot about Big Tech, but there are over 200 million websites available to every American—all of which are governed by Section 230. So taking 230 away really would wreck the internet.[92]

Indeed, since Section 230 was passed, the FCC has been largely sidelined with a consultative role in determining standards without any authority to enforce them.[93] This fact underscores the extent to which the private sector has become, as designed, the gatekeeper for online content moderation. The rise of such digital walled gardens is but one of the wider implications of Section 230, along with the spread of misinformation and disinformation.

PRIVATE SECTOR AS GATEKEEPER

As Wyden has said, "Clearly, to guard the portals of cyberspace, the private sector is in a far better position than the federal government."[94] The result has been, as predicted, a diverse range of content moderation policies that have resulted in divergent sanctions for similar conduct, such as Twitter permanently banning former President Donald Trump following a series of tweets calling into question the legitimacy of the 2020 election, leading to the January 6 insurrection on the U.S. Capitol while Facebook merely suspended his account.[95] Such self-regulation has the flexibility "to adapt to rapid technological progress"[96] better than black-letter law like Section 230, which often changes incrementally. Self-regulation also has the potential to be more efficient and cost-effective than command-and-control-style regulation while also instilling civic virtue, though it is not a panacea. Yet the rise of seemingly all-powerful tech monopolies has resulted in calls to rein them in, such as through antitrust. Active investigations are underway in the United States, Europe, and even China, which is seemingly cracking down on any remaining independence of its domestic tech industry.[97]

The end result, though, is giving major Western and Chinese tech firms that much more power to influence the online experience for billions of people. Such technocapitalism has its benefits, including the creation of what are now many of the most valuable businesses in the world as measured by market capitalization—after all, it would have been hard, if not impossible, for the likes of Twitter or even Google to emerge in Europe, given its widely divergent approach to data governance. However, as we have seen, the problems proliferating from these platforms are manifest, from disinformation threatening electoral integrity—the lifeblood of democratic systems—to misinformation about life-saving vaccines to fight the Covid-19 pandemic, resulting in untold suffering and deaths.

ONLINE MISINFORMATION AND DISINFORMATION

It is no secret that misinformation and disinformation spread via social media has undermined trust in public health authorities during a global pandemic. Fueled by algorithms that favor the spreading of controversial, attention-grabbing personalities, it is impossible to fully measure the scope, meaning, and impacts for such practices. One project that has tried is Indiana University's Observatory on Social Media, which has developed an array of tools, including Hoaxy, to track the spread of misinformation on Twitter.[98]

Similarly, studies have been done tracking attempts to use information warfare to undermine trust in elections around the world. A prime sponsor is Russia, which has been developing its disinformation capabilities for decades, long before the first packet of information was sent on a fiber optic cable. Pre Soviet Union, the Tsarist secret police (the Komitet Gosudarstvennoy Bezopasnosti (KGB), now Federalnaya Sluzhba Bezopasnosti (FSB), which is the Federal Security Service predecessor, used disinformation.[99] Joseph Stalin created an independent agency for dezinformatsiya designed to undermine political opponents and mislead Soviet citizens and foreigners alike as to the USSR's intentions.[100] During the Cold War, for example, Russian agents helped plant "hundreds of bogus headlines around the world," such as the claim that the U.S. government created the autoimmune disease AIDS, a false claim that was first mentioned in an Indian newspaper in the 1980s after being planted by a KGB agent. That story eventually circled the world and was even mentioned by a famous American newsperson, Dan Rather, on the *CBS Evening News* in 1987.[101]

Russia has been linked with "confidence attacks" aimed at destabilizing democracies (especially those in bordering countries, such as Ukraine) and undermining trust in elections, a practice that, as we have seen, dates back centuries. However, this practice now makes use of modern technologies along with the implicit trust and openness in democratic societies. Russia, of course, is not alone in such efforts, nor is it the only nation practicing an assertive form of cyber sovereignty, which is discussed further in Chapters 7 and 8.

WRAP UP

This chapter has told the story of why we regulate online content the way we do and how things might have turned out differently. If Cox and

Figure 5.1. Tim Berners-Lee (2014)

Wyden, for example, had not taken such an interest in *Stratton Oakmont*, it's quite possible that the CDA would have been the only (if very limited) game in town. Without a Section 230 backstop, the perverse incentives in *Stratton Oakmont* would have continued and likely deepened with more companies being fearful of exercising editorial control lest they be held accountable for the content on their platforms. The content moderation policies that we *deserve*, rather than those that we have, are the topic for Part III, after we finish telling the story about how we got here. Our next stop is an aspect of the commercialized web, namely, the so-called ISPWars of the 1990s.

6

Why We're Still Living in 1995

ISP Wars and Net Neutrality

> Allowing a handful of broadband carriers to determine what people see and do online would fundamentally undermine the features that have made the Internet such a success, and could permanently compromise the Internet as a platform for the free exchange of information, commerce, and ideas.[1]
>
> —VINTON CERF

How should consumers use the Internet? Is an Internet service that only allows access to Facebook actually "Internet access?" How many connection options should consumers have? Should the government be in the business of guaranteeing Internet access as a public utility? Is there a human right to Internet access? Though these questions have enjoyed newfound resonance during the Covid-19 pandemic, they date back decades. The first major Internet service providers (ISPs) were, after all, in the business of delivering the Internet to their customers and aimed to make a profit from doing so. Over time, these ISPs were taken over by carriers—traditional telephone and cable TV companies (the likes of Comcast, which has been commonly cited as one of America's most-hated brands).[2] These carriers were in the content business, including telephone calls and TV distribution. Thus, there was a fundamental disconnect

---

Forks in the Digital Road. Scott J. Shackelford and Scott O. Bradner, Oxford University Press. © Oxford University Press 2024.
DOI: 10.1093/oso/9780197617762.003.0006

between the historic ISP business model and the vision of the new owners of these ISPs. This disconnect can be seen in the statement by former AT&T CEO Edward Whitacre Jr., who complained that Google was using AT&T's network for free.[3] Such sentiments are at the heart of the larger net neutrality debate that continues to rage in the United States, even as it becomes more settled globally.[4]

This chapter explores the maturing commercialized web of the 1990s, how the policy decisions made about ISPs have changed the basic philosophy of the Internet during this period, and how that has led to the bitter and continuing fight over net neutrality today. We focus on 1995, when the ISP market in the United States became more competitive, launching a wave of mergers and consolidation leading to the so-called ISP Wars. At the heart of this chapter is how economic considerations have impacted the content—and price point—available to Internet users and what role government should play in ensuring a competitive and level playing field.

HOW WE GOT HERE: FOLLOWING THE MONEY AND TRACKING THE TURNING POINTS

The ISP Wars that came to a head in the late 1990s, along with the larger issue of net neutrality, cannot be understood without a brief survey of the preceding history. It's a long and complex tale that we endeavor to present here in abbreviated form, knowing that much of the nuance and historical context is necessarily omitted. In brief, before the interconnection made possible by Transmission Control Protocol (TCP) / Internet Protocol (IP) and the World Wide Web, as was discussed in Chapters 4 and 5, it was common for each burgeoning online community to operate separately.

Consider the story of CompuServe, which was founded by electrical engineering students Dr. John R. Goltz and Jeffrey Wilkins in 1969 as a subsidiary of Golden United Life Insurance. Based in Columbus, Ohio, the company's purpose was to support in-house computer processing for the life insurance company as well as to become an independent business in computer time-sharing for professionals—useful tasks, in other words, but not exactly world-shattering stuff. But CompuServe Information Service (CIS)—the official name of the subscriber-based on-line service—opened its network to folks at home on September 24, 1979. Originally marketed through Radio Shack under the name MicroNET, the service was pricey and limited. And it didn't stop there; in many ways, CompuServe popularized email (it filed for trademark protection on the term "email" in 1983 but abandoned its claim a year later) and with it on-line social media.

Thus, by the 1980s, as we have seen, change was in the air with Advanced Projects Research Agency Network (ARPANET) members, for example, also being able to access Usenet servers.[5] Yet a key factor in the 1980s remained the prohibition by the federal government of commercial traffic on government-sponsored backbones under the National Science Foundation's (NSF's) Acceptable Use Policy, which came into effect in 1986, as is discussed in Chapters 2 and 3.[6] Yet this lack of commercial in-vestment also meant that "[f]ederal agencies shared the cost of supporting this common Internet infrastructure, such as trans-oceanic circuits."[7] The growing number of governmental cooks in the kitchen, though, necessitated the creation of a coordinating committee, which became the Federal Networking Council (FNC).[8] The FNC also helped to work with international partners such as Réseaux Associés pour la Recherche Européenne (RARE) in Europe to support the global research commu-nity.[9] Such a shared governance approach to core Internet infrastructure had a long history, dating back to intermixed traffic on ARPANET, such as from the Computer Science Network (CSNET) beginning in 1981, which was itself a "major step along the path to the Internet."[10]

Gradually, though, the commercial dam began to break. Vint Cerf, for example, went to the FNC for permission to connect MCI Mail (a com-mercial email service) as a year-long test starting in 1989.[11] Other email providers soon followed suit. According to Cerf, "As soon as they did that, they suddenly discovered that everyone in each of those previously private email services could talk to everybody else through the Internet."[12] This, though, had an unintended consequence in "that interconnection single-handedly destroyed the commercial email business because Internet mail was free."[13] In other words, just as new avenues were opening up to carry commercial traffic, the business case for doing so evaporated.

The stage was set for a new era of commercial web traffic enabled by the rapid scaling of TCP/IP and the World Wide Web, as was discussed in Chapters 3 and 4, along with other milestones along the way, including a 1988 UN meeting to define a regulatory framework for data networks.[14] Thus, by the 1990s—particularly with the end of NSF's Acceptable Use Policy in 1992—the Internet was available to the general public via commercial ISPs and to myriad commercial services. Bulletin board systems, Usenet servers, and various databases migrated to the Internet, setting the scene for the 1990s dot-com boom. Key players in this boom were the new breed of ISPs, led by Delphi, Prodigy, CompuServe, and America Online (AOL) in 1995. The following section digs into the history of AOL as a lens through which to tee up our digital fork.

YOU'VE GOT MAIL

Growing up and getting online in the 1990s, it's hard to overstate the importance of AOL in shaping the online experience for millions of users. From the likes of Tom Hanks and Meg Ryan falling in love over the service in the 1998 romantic comedy *You've Got Mail* to parodies of 500-hour AOL CDs seeming to rain down from the sky, in many ways the firm defined the era. But its beginnings were far humbler.

From a young age, Steve Case—along with his brother Dan—were on the lookout for business opportunities as they grew up in Honolulu, Hawaii. A political science graduate from Williams College, Case held a variety of marketing roles for companies like Procter & Gamble, Pizza Hut, and Control Video Group.[15] The last had an ahead-of-its-time business plan to offer downloadable video game software via phone lines. The plan flopped, but Case convinced the firm to reorganize itself in 1983 as Quantum Computer Services. According to *Time*, "His idea was to create an online bulletin board for owners of Commodore 64 computers. It wasn't a sexy niche, but he thought it might have potential. From 1985 onward, Case nurtured Quantum from a few thousand members to more than 100,000."[16] By 1989, Quantum Computer Services launched its first instant messaging service, and by 1991 it got a new name—AOL.

By the time Case became CEO in 1993, AOL had introduced its own email system along with chat rooms and curated access to the rest of the exploding World Wide Web. The driving philosophy was "simplicity over gadgetry."[17] The equation worked, with user growth exploding so much that by 1995, NSF decided to sunset National Science Foundation Network (NSFNET), which was a major step in the privatization of the Internet.[18] Preceding this development, though, in 1995 was the Conseil Européen pour la Recherche Nucléaire (CERN) decision discussed in Chapter 4 that kept the web in the public domain. By its peak in 2000, AOL would be the largest ISP in the world up to that time.[19]

In essence, then, the larger commercialized Internet in the 1980s and 1990s is a tale of the U.S. government enabling commercial ISPs to interconnect with the NSFNET, then closing the NSFNET itself, leaving commercial ISPs like AOL as the only games in town. By 1996, there were some 1,400 ISPs spread across the nation, a number that ballooned to over 4,500 ISPs by 1998, coming back down to 2,854 by 2022.[20] The market was ripe for consolidation, which played out at an increasing clip with larger ISPs gobbling up the competition and major telecommunication firms acquiring ever-larger segments of the Internet backbones. Billions were soon changing hands, coming to a head in the ISP Wars. Although no one entity "owned" the Internet, large conglomerates were able to leverage their control of key Internet infrastructure to effectively charge a fee to small ISPs for access to their networks. Further, bigger firms like AOL were able to negotiate more favorable terms, putting smaller players at a distinct disadvantage.

The end results of all this consolidation were a host of commercial innovations and waves of investment in networking and broadband connections. But issues abounded, including a lack of competition, leading large ISPs to block services like virtual private networks (VPNs) and Voice over Internet Protocol (VoIP) (as happened with Madison River).[21] More generally, there are concerns about consolidation driving up prices for

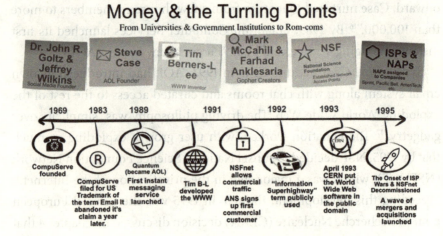

Figure 6.1. Turning Points in an Increasingly Commercialized Web
Phone Icon: This photo by an unknown author is licensed under CC BY-NC.

consumers, limiting their choices, and feeding continued concerns over net neutrality. Before turning to such wider implications, though, we first consider the fork: What if commercial traffic on the nascent Internet had been welcomed from the beginning? And conversely, what if the FNC turned down Cerf's request and the government continued to exercise greater control over the Internet through NSFNET not only until 1995, but perhaps even to this day? Clearly, under such a scenario, the U.S. government would realistically not be the only ISP, given the expense and inefficiency involved, but there is also the related question: what if NSF and Congress had permitted nonneutral ISPs? See Figure 6.1 for a timeline summarizing some of these key turning points.

THE FORK: WHAT IF COMMERCIAL TRAFFIC HAD BEEN WELCOMED EARLIER OR WAS BANNED FOR LONGER?

If the FNC had been more welcoming to commercial traffic—and indeed never would have created the Acceptable Use Policy to begin with—then the government-subsidized Internet backbone upon which so much of what became the Internet was built would have required greater private sector support from a much earlier period, as was discussed in Chapter 2. This likely would have been beneficial to the likes of Vint Cerf and MCI Mail, who would have been able to enjoy the benefits of interconnection in the early instead of late 1980s, perhaps moving the subsequent dot-com boom up by years.

Yet it is also true that the impacts of the NSFNET Backbone's Acceptable Use Policy on prohibiting traffic "not in support of Research and Education" meant that local and regional commercial traffic flowing on parallel networks was encouraged, even as publicly supported nation-scale transport was discouraged, leading to the rapid development of long-haul private carriers.[22] The privately financed augmentation of long-haul traffic would not have been necessary if NSFNET had allowed commercial traffic earlier, which could have either pushed back or perhaps entirely avoided the ISP Wars to follow. Similarly, if the government had more closely scrutinized all the mergers and acquisitions that made up the ISP Wars from 1995 forward, as happened later with the barring of the 2015 Comcast $45 billion bid for Time Warner, then consumers could have been left with greater choice and lower connection costs.

WIDER IMPLICATIONS

Decisions made in 1995, but also throughout the 1980s and 1990s, have fueled a wave of concerns and implications with which we continue to grapple in the 21st century. This includes, first and foremost, ongoing discussions about the proper role of government in regulating ISPs as part of the broader "net neutrality" debate. Related issues, including the evolution of cyber sovereignty and the human right to Internet access, were addressed in Chapters 3, 4, 5, and 6 and will be returned to in Part III.

WHAT DOES ALL THIS HAVE TO DO WITH NET NEUTRALITY?

According to Professor Tim Wu, who coined the term, "Network neutrality is best defined as a network design principle. The idea is that a maximally useful public information network aspires to treat all content, sites, and platforms equally. This allows the network to carry every form of information and support every kind of application."[23] As applied to this common carrier context in particular, net neutrality may be understood as "a series of rules centered on the idea that ISPs must service customer requests in a way that is agnostic to data being provided."[24]

Nations around the world interpret net neutrality in different ways. The global debate was kicked off in 2002 following a decision by the U.S. Federal Communications Commission (FCC) to reclassify broadband services as an "information" service rather than a "telecommunication" service.[25] Although seemingly a minor and amorphous distinction, this reclassification had major impacts, including that "ISPs would be able to prioritize or block certain types of traffic."[26] In other words, the FCC did not regulate information services and carriers, meaning that they were largely free to proceed unfettered. The U.S. Supreme Court upheld the FCC process leading to the reclassification in 2005,[27] though that did not end the debate. In fact, more than 27,000 comments were received by the FCC as the agency considered net neutrality rules.[28] Former FCC Chairman Michael Powell also influentially called for four "Net Freedom" principles to help guide the agency's efforts, along with the overall ISP industry, including: (1) freedom to access (legal) content, (2) freedom to use applications, (3) freedom to attach personal devices to their home networks, and (4) freedom to obtain information about their service plans.[29]

After a flurry of proposed bills and false starts, in 2010, the FCC adopted "three basic rules for preserving the Internet as an open platform for innovation, investment, job creation, economic growth, competition, and freedom of expression," including: (1) transparency, (2) no blocking, and (3) no *unreasonable* discrimination.[30] Ultimately, a court of appeals struck down the process the FCC followed that culminated in the nonblocking component of the rule, and a letter was sent by 122 tech investors and financial institutions to then-FCC Chairman Tom Wheeler describing how current FCC rules did not do all that could be done to promote a free and open Internet.[31] Then, in 2015 the FCC reclassified broadband once again as "telecommunication services"[32] and noted that the open Internet rules had led to some $212 billion in investments over three years and helped to prevent "ISPs from blocking, prioritizing, degrading or establishing fast/slow lanes for legal content."[33]

The U.S. telecom industry fought back hard against the new rules with another round of proposed bills by sympathetic lawmakers, but it ultimately took until a new FCC Commissioner came into office—Ajit Pai in 2017—who worked with the new conservative majority, to roll back the new open Internet rules.[34] Once the Biden administration came into office, new FCC Chairman Nathan Simington has argued strongly for congressional action to forestall further instability rather than playing another round of regulatory ping pong.[35] Although Congress has not acted as of this writing, other states, including California, have codified net neutrality protections.[36] Plus, once the Senate confirmation process plays out, there is every indication that the FCC will reinstate net neutrality rules through its regulatory powers as well.

Even as the regulatory playing field with regard to net neutrality remains unsettled in the U.S. context, it is increasingly well settled globally, with more than 50 nations taking a mix of reactive and proactive approaches to ensuring protections, including limiting traffic management to what is "reasonable."[37] Most of these regulations—with the notable exception of Japan's—forbid the type of traffic differentiation (including blocking and throttling content) that is at the heart of many net neutrality concerns, though many of these jurisdictions still do not deal with zero-rating[38] and specialized services.

An array of controversial topics has arisen as part of this larger debate due to both regulatory and technological developments, such as content delivery networks (CDNs) in which a content provider "pays a CDN to place its content closer to the users," constituting a backdoor means to prioritize its data, though this concern may be mitigated if the ISP lets any content owner—or CDN—do the same thing for the same fee.[39] At the same time, as has been discussed, Internet traffic flows are global, and thus packets are transiting networks with divergent regulatory environments, making it both important—and challenging—to detect traffic differentiation wherever it exists.[40] Plus, new technologies, including 5G, which is further powering the evolution toward an Internet of Everything, also raise net neutrality issues. For example, a feature of 5G networks is so-called network slicing, "which consists of creating virtual networks that support specific Quality of Service (QoS) requirements for different customers and applications."[41]

As a result, from both a technological and regulatory perspective, the future of ISP regulation that is at the heart of this chapter—including to what extent governments, such as for emergency services, or private firms should be able to determine both the content and speed at which data is delivered—remains unsettled, particularly in the United States, even as there is a growing convergence globally. If the private market for ISPs had evolved differently, for instance, because commercial traffic had been allowed on NSFNET earlier, it's quite possible that these concerns would have manifested in different ways at different times. Yet, save for the wholesale ownership and regulation of key Internet infrastructure by state-owned enterprises, it is likely that net neutrality concerns would still have manifested. Still, it is worth noting that support for local, publicly backed municipal broadband networks remains high, particularly in the United States, with more than half of adults surveyed in a 2021 *Morning Consult* poll backing a public option for home broadband.[42] However, this support is not driven by net neutrality concerns so much as a lack of affordable, high-speed Internet access, particularly in underserved rural areas.[43]

WRAP UP

A poster child of the later stages of the ISP Wars was WorldCom, with high-profile corporate governance and business ethics failings that led to important statutory reforms, including Sarbanes-Oxley Act.[44] The WorldCom bankruptcy cost some 300,000 jobs and more than $180 million in investor losses; there were even allegations that in addition to puffing up profits, it undermined consumer confidence in the broader Internet ecosystem.[45] The bad taste that the scandal left in the mouths of many investors and consumers alike is an ongoing concern. In some ways, such scandals were made possible by the decisions from the 1980s and 1990s, including the termination of NSFNET in 1995, but it's important to note that corporate wrongdoing is untethered from such forks in the digital road. Similar tales could be told in the wake of any change in government policy, such as deregulating the airline industry. Still, the anticompetitive behaviors exhibited by tech firms, including ISPs discussed in Chapter 4, are an ongoing concern, including in the context of net neutrality. The next chapter discusses some key decision points in the history of Internet governance, focusing just a few years later on 1998 and with the decision to create ICANN (Internet Corporation for Assigned Names and Numbers).

7

What Passed
for Internet Governance

Architecture is politics.

— Electronic Frontier Foundation (EFF)

cofounder Mitchell Kapor[1]

Much of this book has focused on some of the key technologies and moments that have given rise to the Internet as we know it today. So far, we've been less focused on the bigger questions, including who should govern these capabilities that so easily span sectors and borders. Consider the Transmission Control Protocol / Internet Protocol (TCP/IP) addressing scheme explored in Chapters 2 and 6, which is required for every computer or device connected to the Internet from your laptop to your smart doorbell. These are a string of numbers such as 132.9.107.14, which are hard for people to remember—imagine if our physical addresses were as abstract. The parts of this number are used like a mailing address to identify specific subnetworks and nodes, just as certain lines of a mailing address correspond to a street, city, or state.[2] These values are used in network protocols to identify nodes, differentiate applications, and even data types. It's much easier to recall something like "www.indiana.edu." As a result, there had to be a distributed database of which names were associated with which addresses, so people didn't get confused or end up visiting

Forks in the Digital Road. Scott J. Shackelford and Scott O. Bradner, Oxford University Press. © Oxford University Press 2024.
DOI: 10.1093/oso/9780197617762.003.0007

What Passed for Internet Governance

a site that they did not intend. But how to create such a registry—and who should help run it?

For years, a graduate student—turned Internet forefather—Jon Postel held the reins to the Internet's address system. Originally, starting in the late 1960s, that record was kept on a floppy disk by Jon. By 1998, though, he and others were pointing out that such an important bookkeeping process shouldn't be handled by just one person or a few. He proposed forming an independent self-governing organization to perform the functions he had been doing under a U.S. government contract, which eventually came to be known as the Internet Corporation for Assigned Names and Numbers (ICANN). But it took until 2016 for ICANN to enjoy the independence that Jon envisioned, once the U.S. Department of Commerce let its contract with ICANN lapse.

For nearly 20 years, ICANN did that work, though objections particularly from developing nations and emerging cyber powers over the perceived U.S. government control grew steadily. Finally in 2016, following a political fight, the Department of Commerce let the contract expire, and ICANN's governance shifted toward a broader, more globalized structure. But that's not the end of the tale. In fact, it's hardly the beginning. How should this saga inform the next phase of global Internet governance? How else can support for multistakeholder Internet governance be strengthened at a time of increasing cyber sovereignty? And how might things have turned out very differently?

A BRIEF HISTORY OF INTERNET GOVERNANCE

The sci-fi author William Gibson coined the term "cyberspace" in his novel *Neuromancer* in 1984, in which he described "a consensual hallucination experienced daily by billions."[3] One need only view pedestrians staring at their smartphones while walking down the street, often with headphones in, to know that Gibson was on to something. But what exactly is Internet governance? Many scholars and policymakers perceived the Internet, and cyberspace generally, as a borderless and self-governing space in the 1990s devoid of the authority of territorial states.[4] The term has evolved with the changing conceptions of cyberspace itself. For example, in 2005, the World Summit on the Information Society defined Internet governance as "the development and application by governments, the private sector, and civil society, in their respective roles, of shared principles, norms, rules, decision-making procedures, and programs that shape the evolution and use of the internet."[5] Although a helpful starting point, the term remains confusing given the extent to which technical standard setting is conflated with the emergent behaviors of Internet users. There is also no foreordained requirement that Internet governance must be multistakeholder in nature (i.e., involving representatives from governments, the private sector, and civil society). What is clear, though, is that an integral component of Internet governance is the development of norms for Internet operators and increasingly content providers, along with technical standards underpinning internetworked systems.

The story of Internet governance may be broken down into three phases. Phase 1 encompassed influential network engineers and the ad hoc organizations that they developed, such as the Internet Engineering Task Force (IETF), extending from roughly 1969 to the birth of ICANN in 1998. Phase 2 coincided with the commercial success of the Internet and the first global "digital divide" represented by the economic divergence of information and communication technology resources between developed and developing nations, which is the focus of this chapter. It also marked the emergence of so-called Web 2.0, which was first suggested in 1999 to describe the emergence of collaborative tools and online communities that generate content as opposed to the passive viewing of material online (i.e., Web 1.0). Finally, Phase 3 has been defined to date by the extent to which nations have begun to assert a greater role in Internet governance, at least in their own countries, underscoring the potential for a "new 'digital divide'" to emerge not between the "haves and have-nots," but between "the open and the closed."[6] Yet, at the same time there are growing calls to focus on the emergence of a decentralized Web 3.0 built on distributed architectures that enable users to "control their own data, identity, and destiny."[7] Needless to say, such a techno-utopian vision is at odds with the increasing degree of cyber sovereignty being practiced by many nations.

As so many things do, it all started with a working group. Larry Roberts, as the chief scientist at the Advanced Projects Research Agency (ARPA) in 1967,[8] received approval to build what would become the ARPANET and issued an RFP in 1968. As was discussed in Chapters 2 and 3, the goals of the new project were first "to develop techniques and obtain experience on interconnecting computers in such a way that a very broad class of interactions are possible," and second "to improve and increase computer research productivity through resource sharing."[9] Many of the big names in technology did not bid for the contract, perhaps because traditional networking theory indicated that packet-switched networking was likely to be useless because of the lack of any performance or quality guarantees. Finally, Bolt Beranek Newman Inc. (BBN), based in Cambridge, Massachusetts, was awarded a contract to start building the ARPANET in January 1969.[10]

The ARPANET was not the Internet, even though the term started to be used around this time. The early ARPANET was a test bed for many experiments such as email, as was discussed in Chapter 6 though it was a production network where experiments could be run at the application level but not a network where experiments could be run on networking itself. To help create and run these experiments, Requests for Comments (RFCs) were written starting with RFC 1 by Steve Crocker, as was discussed in Chapter 2.[11] The series quickly caught on, expanding to more than 150 offerings by 1973, a number that was flagged until the IETF took over the series in the 1980s.[12] Crocker was the initial coordinator for the RFC series but handed that task to fellow graduate student Jon Postel in June 1971.

If machines are connected on the Internet via a name and address index akin to a phone book, then its editor was Jon Postel, whom techies call the "God" of the Internet.[13] Jon was never comfortable with this framing, though—he responded, "Of course, there isn't any 'God the Internet.' The Internet works because a lot of people cooperate to do things together."[14]

As a kid Jon was interested in technology, which he pursued as a computer science student earning both his BS and MS from UCLA in the late 1960s. As a doctoral student in the 1970s, Postel was enlisted as the caretaker of the master copy of the "hosts.txt" file, which listed the ARPANET's computer names and corresponding IP addresses.[15]

Starting in 1972, Jon began keeping lists: first, of ARPANET socket numbers, which in time expanded to the more general term "protocol parameters," and then, with the deployment of TCP/IP, of Internet protocol address assignments. The set of bookkeeping functions that Jon took on voluntarily, and which he performed manually, was titled Internet Assigned Numbers Authority (IANA).[16] According to the Internet Hall of Fame, his efforts "provided the stability the Internet's numbering and protocol management systems needed for it to grow and scale."[17] As the Internet grew, however, the system became unmanageable.

Enter the DNS, which translates domain names into IP addresses so people do not have to remember complex strings of digits, and which both simplified and further complicated Jon's job and was created in 1983 to spread the work across many coordinating files and servers.[18] Each domain name holds a uniquely coded name. For example, www.rotary.org is a three-part name located in three separate database files. The end of each domain name (i.e., dot-org or dot-com) indicates the top-level domain (TLD) of which there are two types (country code and generic).[19] As of 2021, there were more than 300 country code TLDs (such as dot-uk), while the list of generic TLDs was expanding from 22 "to possibly 1,400 new names."[20] The files are located on one or more "DNS servers," or name servers, which are "queried," or asked, to resolve the question of which IP address corresponds to a given domain name.[21] There are nearly a million DNS servers on the Internet resolving billions of queries daily.[22] Each of these DNS servers is independent for each name in the hierarchy.[23]

Despite the multiple steps involved in the DNS, this system is fast. With its hierarchical structure and ability to resolve queries by caching, the DNS effectively scaled the Internet's address system so much that the fundamental operation of the DNS has hardly changed since 1983.[24] The same is not true for governance. Postel, who had been responsible for updating the TLD server addresses of the hosts.txt file, otherwise known as the "authoritative root zone file," or root, manually updated the DNS for years, which is still how updates happen to this day.[25] When Postel was its manager, if someone erased the root, then the TLDs would have disappeared and DNS servers would not have known how to resolve queries and direct Internet traffic, a scenario that could still play out today.[26] In short, the Internet's naming system would have crashed. Computers would still be connected to other machines on the network, but there would be no way to find them—just like the previously mentioned example, phones would still exist without a phone book, but no one would know how to place a call.

All the parts were in place for IANA by 1984, with funding from the U.S. government through a Defense Advanced Research Projects Agency (DARPA) contract in 1988, which was then extended to 1997. Between 1984 and 1995, the U.S. government maintained a remarkably hands-off approach to the DNS root servers, leaving the task to IANA and volunteers. IANA's responsibilities included IP addresses' domain names, root domains, and protocol parameters. For IP addresses, the actual assignments were performed by regional registries, which are non-profit geographically based organizations. Occasionally, it may have had to help resolve disputes between competing organizations but generally encouraged the parties to "settle it themselves." IANA was comprised of different committees for protocols, along with an Industry and User Committee including advocacy groups, with a nine-member board. Similarly, the IETF also evolved naturally from technical communities to deal with particular problems, and as a result, it has enjoyed greater legitimacy than artificial constructs such as ICANN as will be discussed, though it, too, is not without its critics.[27]

In the beginning, as with Postel's IANA, the IETF was a means for U.S. government-funded researchers to coordinate with one another.[28] No one was obligated to attend IETF meetings, but it seemed to be in everyone's best interest to do so.[29] In a sign of the IETF's growing importance, its first meeting in January 1986 consisted of 21 researchers.[30] The basic administrative framework of IETF was settled by the early 1990s. It is comprised of working groups and area directors of functional areas, including applications, routing, and security.[31] There is also a general area director who functions as IETF's chair.[32] These structures developed organically, and IETF has a reputation for being a relatively flat organization, adopting ideas when justified by results rather than rank.[33] Indeed, an early IETF mantra coined in 1992 survives: "We reject: kings, presidents, and voting. We believe in: rough consensus and running code."[34] By 2022, IETF meetings regularly attracted more than 1,000 participants in 2019.[35] A growing number of nations, including China, are seeking to influence if not supplant the IETF outright by replacing its role in the development of Internet technical standards with the International Telecommunication Union (ITU).[36]

Postel, pictured in Figure 7.1, and his small team were funded by a series of contracts from the U.S. government to aid in this bookkeeping function, but, starting in about 1998, Postel began developing a plan to create a stand-alone IANA organization.

Figure 7.1. Jon Postel with Map of Internet Top-Level Domains (1994)

1998 DNS WARS: THE U.S. GOVERNMENT STRIKES BACK

Because the TCP/IP network was not yet geopolitically or economically important in the 1980s and early 1990s, few challenged Postel's authority over the root.[37] Similarly, the U.S. government paid a small start-up called Network Solutions, Inc. (NSI) in 1992 to edit the root zone under U.S. government direction and to take over registering subdomains in dot-com, dot-net, and dot-org, which (no real surprise) went largely unreported in the mainstream news.[38] Given the rapidity with which the Internet was expanding, soon it was costing NSI more to manage the registrations of subdomains (because of the growth of subdomains) than the government was paying NSI—the government authorized NSI to charge registrants so that the service could continue after the government money ran out. In 1995, NSF went along with this plan (initially at $100 for two years). With more than 100,000 dot-coms registered by 1995, and over a million by 1999, the stakes were quickly growing, and NSI got to have the growing pie all to itself in collaboration with the government. However, that apathy soon ended. By the mid-1990s, fortunes were at stake, and people became more concerned with DNS issues,[39] foreshadowing larger debates about governance and cybersecurity to follow.

The context from which ICANN has evolved is similar to a dramatized version of dialing 4-1-1 for information. Imagine that the sole means of communicating is by telephone and that there is no way to memorize a phone number. To get in touch with anyone for anything, you must consult the phone book—of which there is only one copy that is managed by one person. Naturally, you are hesitant to trust this person because he could remove or change a number in the phone book on a whim and without any legal consequences. Not long ago, this is not unlike how the Internet functioned.

Because vesting authority had not been a key concern when TCP/IP was still experimental, most Internet engineering and policy projects were simply contracted out by the U.S. government. Cerf, the "father" of the Internet and cocreator of TCP/IP,[40] has said that those contracted with were mostly graduate students who went about developing the Internet's architecture as they saw fit.[41] As the Internet grew, research positions of "the ARPANET elite"—including Kahn, Cerf, and Postel—began to blur into management roles.[42] These managers tried to institutionalize their duties through an alphabet soup of new organizations, including: the Internet Activities Board, which became the Internet Architecture Board (IAB) in 1983; the IETF in 1986; IANA in 1988; the Internet Research Task Force (IRTF) in 1989; the Internet Society (ISOC) in 1992; and the World Wide Web Consortium (W3C) in 1994.[43] Whereas IANA was headed by Postel and was in charge of maintaining the root and recording IP address allocation,[44] ISOC was created in part to protect IETF from lawsuits and solicit funding for the other organizations.[45] But then, as the DNS Wars broke out in the late 1990s, ISOC asserted itself as an appropriate body for determining the "highest questions of Internet policy"—putting it at odds with the U.S. government.[46]

By March 1994, Postel was arguing that it was "extremely unlikely" that any new TLDs would be created, and he suggested that the Internet Society take over the function of deciding on new TLDs. In 1996, ISOC and IANA organized an ad hoc committee to resolve DNS issues, enlisting in their cause other governments, the World Intellectual Property Organization, and the ITU, among other institutions.[47] Then, in February 1997, IANA was sued (naming Postel) by Image Online Design over an alleged deal that would have allowed the firm to sell dot-web web addresses, which further ratcheted up tensions over the status quo.[48] At an ITU conference in London in January 1998, Clinton Administration Science Advisor Ira Magaziner foreshadowed the U.S. government approach. Scott Bradner gave a presentation in John Postel's place at the meeting, entitled "Institutionalizing the IANA Functions to Deliver a Stable and Accessible Global Internet for Mission Critical Business Traffic and Transactions."[49] It did not come as a major surprise then when the committee laid out a proposal for a new Internet governance structure. The U.S. government then started a public process to decide how to manage the DNS TLDs and the other bookkeeping functions in January 1998, prompting, some suggest, Postel's "test."[50]

On January 28, 1998, Postel began a test of eight of the Internet's root nameservers, instructing them to divide control over domain naming between public and private entities. Although Internet usage was not interrupted, the U.S. government quickly responded by ordering Jon to undo these changes, which he did the same day.[51] Before the week was out, the U.S. National Telecommunications and Information Administration had issued a new proposed rule that would have created what we now call ICANN.

The U.S. government's decision to ignore the ad hoc committee's proposal was a turning point, although it ultimately accepted Jon's proposal a few days after he passed. Despite this, critics continued to voice their opposition, including IBM, AT&T, and U.S. civil society groups, citing concerns about power grabbing.[52] The U.S. government began bargaining with corporate interests and significant international stakeholders; still, many developing countries were only involved at the periphery.[53] Throughout the summer of 1998, negotiators crafted a plan that had originally been proposed by Jon in response to the white paper and was ultimately backed by the U.S. government and a powerful coalition of stakeholders.[54] The result of this process was ICANN, a nonprofit corporation headquartered in the United States with a board of directors from the private and public sectors drawn from around the world, but without a significant role for foreign governments, which was chartered in particular to: record protocol parameter, assign blocks of IP addresses to regional registries, and manage the root zone file.[55] The global reaction to this state of affairs hastened Phase 2 of Internet governance, which included efforts aimed at globalizing Internet policymaking.

Due to this coalition building, ICANN had many supporters when the U.S. government formally signed a contract with it in February 1999 including EU and non-EU governments along with the ITU, since, by then, many nations were clamoring for a greater role in Internet governance.[56] This increased attention grew partly from rapid increases in cybercrime and espionage, as well as the potential of cyber warfare, illustrating the link between cyber insecurity and the evolution of Internet governance.[57] Moreover, Postel's sudden death in October 1998 "robbed the organization of its moral center, [and] a good part of its institutional memory . . . "[58] Postel's obituary, which begins, "A long time ago, in a network, far far away, a great adventure took place!," is published as RFC comment 2468.[59] Nevertheless, even with this troubled start, ICANN has persisted in performing several vital functions, including the allocation of IP address space and TLD DNSs along with IANA itself, if not always with solid footing.[60]

THE FORK: WHAT IF THE U.S. GOVERNMENT HAD NOT HELPED TO CREATE ICANN IN 1998 BUT INSTEAD HANDED OVER IANA FUNCTIONS TO AN INTERGOVERNMENTAL ORGANIZATION LIKE THE ITU?

ICANN operated under a joint program with the U.S. Department of Commerce until 2016, when the agreement was finally allowed to lapse, thus finally fulfilling Postel's original vision for an independent organization managing TLD DNSs (though still a nonprofit corporation subject to the laws of California).[61] But what if the U.S. government had followed the suggestions from the committee's original report nearly 20 years earlier? By removing the U.S. government's power to sign off on any changes to the root zone file such as new TLDs, it's possible that some tension might have been removed during the rapid scaling of what became the global Internet. But if the U.S. government had signed over the IANA functions—to an intergovernmental organization like the ITU—the Internet could have lost a great deal of its dynamism, leading to stepped-up cyber sovereignty. Although such a system could enhance accountability, it would have major—and potentially dire—implications for human rights and global integration.

Yet such a counterfactual is not without its potential problems. As seen since 2016, for example, the very fact that ICANN continues as a nonprofit registered in California means that the California Attorney General has remained under pressure to occasionally intervene in its decision-making, for example, in pressuring ICANN when the Internet Society tried to sell dot-org. Similar pressures could have played out in the intervening decades if ICANN had become independent earlier. Moreover, it's possible that calls for ICANN's functions to be subsumed under an intergovernmental organization might have taken longer to gather steam, but once they did the U.S. government may not have been able to resist such entreaties.

WIDER IMPLICATIONS

The decision to create ICANN and place it under the authority of the U.S. Department of Commerce has had long-standing and widespread implications not only for Internet governance but also geopolitics.

THE DIGITAL SILK ROAD TO CYBER SOVEREIGNTY

It is no secret that China's ambitious Belt and Road Initiative, which was launched in 2013 and now includes more than 100 nations with investments over $575 billion,[62] also has a less well-known Digital Silk Road (DSR) component.[63] Although not a particularly top-down endeavor given the wide array of tech investments that have been made (or previously made and later reclassified) under the DSR umbrella, it was announced in 2020 that the DSR would be increasingly centralized and that it "not only [would include] . . . the development of the digital service sector, such as . . . smart cities, telemedicine, and internet finance, but also accelerates technological progress including computing, big data, Internet of Things, artificial intelligence, blockchain, and quantum computing."[64] Although concerns about the DSR becoming a manifestation of China's plans for "techno-authoritarianism" may be overblown, it does seek to deepen its role in standard setting and Internet governance more broadly in a way that could "materially alter the course of global [cyber] norms away in ways the US and other democracies would not support."[65]

DIGITAL ISOLATION AND THE WAR IN UKRAINE

Europe maintains an interesting position in this regard, seeking to find a third way out of either, as described in 2018 by French President Emmanuel Macron, "on the one hand, of complete self-management, without governance, and that of a compartmented Internet, entirely monitored by strong and authoritarian states."[66] Instead, Europe has sought to apply its own values such as respect for human rights, including privacy onto the Internet, reshaping cyberspace "within its own political, social and cultural confines."[67]

In contrast, the United States has a stated policy of promoting a single global networked commons where freedom of speech is supposedly sacrosanct, as was discussed in Chapter 5. China, on the other hand, along with many other nations, is viewed as building digital barriers in the name of cyber sovereignty.[68] Or consider Russia, which has been preparing for years under its Sovereign Internet Law for the day that it might choose (or be forced) to decouple from the global DNS, and the Internet as a whole. It has conducted tests to this effect, claiming that it has the capability to still operate in a domestic intranet separate from ICANN. With the benefit of hindsight given the impacts of the war in Ukraine, these preparations seem integral to the Kremlin's plans to harden the Russian digital economy from the worst effects of a digital blockade. Indeed, pressure has been mounting on ICANN to suspend the dot-ru top-level country domain, while the EU is "seeking to all but wipe certain Russian outlets from the internet," including Russia Today (RT) and Sputnik.[69] Although such actions may not lead to a true "splinternet" scenario, it could represent a step away from the global networked commons envisioned by Tim-Berners Lee and so many others and toward a system of rival networks and governance bodies in which services are not just blocked but are indeed unavailable from country to country.[70] ICANN, after all, has no power to mandate that nations follow its decisions—actions are based on consensus, which is ponderous but has also kept a single, global domain name system humming for a generation.

INTERPLANETARY PROTOCOL

Concerns over a "splinternet" scenario playing out on earth may also have some resonance with the cosmos. Space is increasingly central to Internet access, so much so that Cerf has even worked to develop—in partnership with the Jet Propulsion Laboratory—an interplanetary protocol, which is an "interplanetary extension of the Internet to support manned and robotic exploration of the Solar System."[71] Over time, the interplanetary file system, an homage to J. C. R. Licklider's ideas for an "intergalactic computer network" from the 1960s, represents a step beyond TCP/IP given its lack of functionality in space since "the speed of light was too slow" given the distances involved, according to Vint Cerf[72]; the new system could, in fact, be a promising Web 3.0 candidate that could take the web and ICANN along with it into the next generation.[73]

WRAP UP

It's important to remember that the Internet has remarkably few true needs, such as recording protocol parameters, allocating blocks of IP addresses, recording domain names, and configuring the DNS root. Everything else is gravy, but this raises the stakes considerably for governance over these core functions such as removing a TLD or changing who manages it. ICANN has managed the DNS root for decades and has evolved considerably over that time, becoming after 2016 an institution close to Postel's 1990s-era vision. However, geopolitical pressures coming from the DSR and the war in Ukraine threaten to undermine the global domain name system and even have new Web 3.0 technologies provide new opportunities for decentralization. In other words, the next chapter of Internet governance may be the most interesting yet.

PART III

Curtains

8

Taking Stock

The Internet We Deserve

This concluding chapter summarizes the key decision points from Parts I and II. We map then these topics and trends to contemporary debates about how to better manage cybersecurity, privacy, disinformation, and critical infrastructure. From there, we look at the road ahead. There is certainly cause for hope for cyber peace in our time, but the decisions discussed in this book—along with so many others—have shaped cyber-space and with it, for better or worse, the daily lives of billions of people. Reflecting on those past choices can help inform upcoming decisions—such as how we can build a global culture of cybersecurity, or whether and how to regulate artificial intelligence or the metaverse. We thus start charting a path toward a more sustainable, secure, and equitable Internet for the 21st century by applying lessons learned—both successes and failures—from the 20th.

LESSONS LEARNED

Parts I and II of this book reviewed a series of technical and policy choices central to the development of the Internet. This section groups them into a series of lessons, which are unpacked in turn.

Forks in the Digital Road. Scott J. Shackelford and Scott O. Bradner, Oxford University Press. © Oxford University Press 2024.
DOI: 10.1093/oso/9780197617762.003.0008

The Path Not Taken Was Usually Not Taken for a Good Reason

The road not taken tends to focus our attention; it is all too easy to dwell on the "what ifs?" Robert Frost tells us that taking the unexpected route makes all the difference. As with hiking in the woods, so too in cyberspace? As has been shown, not necessarily. There were good reasons, for example, why IP was not encrypted as was discussed in Chapter 3, opening the door to a range of security vulnerabilities. As we discussed, even if Rivest-Shamir-Adleman (RSA)—or some version of it—had been available and built into TCP/IP, the drawbacks may well have outweighed the security benefits. For example, how might the loss of anonymity have impacted the rapid scaling of the global Internet, including the dot-com boom of the late '90s?

Similarly, as was discussed in Chapter 5, "Section 230 is responsible for the open Internet that Americans know today, as platforms are free to allow—or moderate—user content without fearing company-ending litigation."[1] If it had never existed, or had been interpreted differently by the courts, firms would likely have taken down content more readily, lest it be deemed objectionable to one group or another. There is also a case to be made that it would have been harder, if not impossible, for the next generation of social media firms such as Facebook to take root without the certainty that the broad reading of Section 230 afforded. The difficulties in reaching a consensus on how best to reform Section 230 in the United States showcases the challenging trade-offs and the good reasons why it has persisted for more than 20 years.

This is not to say that there is neither some wisdom of the crowds animating these choices nor a historical, "great persons" of Internet governance theory of the case to be made. Real life is not so clear-cut, and doubtless, there are myriad confounding forces and variables influencing each of these choices. But, as we've seen, they nevertheless had significant consequences, from fueling phishing to disinformation, even as they also helped create a global knowledge commons and social media networks.

Vision, Ethics (and Open Source) Matters

Tim Berners-Lee's Unitarian faith informed his choice to keep the World Wide Web patent-free, and open. As was discussed in Chapter 4, we are all still dealing with the torrent of innovation that Tim helped to unleash; if anything, he was more successful in promoting his vision than he ever could have imagined, saying at one point, "I had no idea that people would put literally everything on it [the web]."[2] Religion—and ethical considerations more generally—seem to be an underappreciated component of why some of these key digital forks were taken.

The concept of openness, particularly open source in this context, has been a driving force across many of these key chapters. Jon Postel, for example, seemed particularly keen on keeping "Internet standards and protocols consistent, open, and free."[3] Such openness is fundamental to effective research design,[4] but it is also an ethical principle in its own right, a belief in the value of communities to effectively govern—and police—themselves. Such open-source methodologies have their advantages, but do require firms to be proactive by implementing available patches, among other things; Equifax failed to do so in its Apache systems, for example, which led to one of the worst data breaches in history, compromising the credit reports of 143 million adult Americans.[5]

Communities Can (Sometimes) Govern Themselves

A key concern across many of the digital forks surveyed in this book has been the question of who should get to make the decisions about key aspects of cybersecurity and Internet governance, which, as was discussed in Chapter 7, includes the development of norms for Internet operators and increasingly content providers, along with technical standards underpinning internetworked systems. Some players approached this topic with either implicit or explicit bias, favoring one group or another. For example, as Senator Ron Wyden has said in reference to the Section 230 debate analyzed in Chapter 5, "Clearly, to guard the portals of cyberspace, the private sector is in a far better position than the federal government."[6] Yet, as we have seen, the scrappy tech startups of the late '90s and '00s evolve into the trillion-dollar behemoths of the 2020s, and questions have arisen about whether these companies are indeed the trusted gatekeepers keeping the best interests of users at the forefront of their decision-making. Facebook, for example, has been hit with several multibillion-dollar fines by the FTC for its shoddy privacy and security practices and is being investigated by countries around the world for its anticompetitive practices, including by the European Commission.

Yet even as calls have risen to rein in the worst abuses of tech companies—including from the likes of Elon Musk to permit uninhibited free speech on Twitter that would risk turning it into a cesspool, or for Google and YouTube to do more to pop algorithmic bubbles—we have also seen communities govern themselves rather well throughout the history of the Internet. Consider the Internet Engineering Task Force (IETF). This volunteer-driven group has been engineering new and updating old protocols since 1986 by developing, maintaining, and publishing Internet technical standards. So, what differentiates this organization from the likes of Facebook, and under what circumstances can communities govern themselves?

If Boeing is allowed to certify that a crash-prone aircraft is safe,[7] and Facebook can violate users' privacy expectations,[8] should companies and industries ever be allowed to police themselves?[9] The debate is heating up, particularly in the U.S. tech sector, with growing calls to regulate—or even break up—the likes of Google, Apple, and Amazon.[10]

It turns out to be possible, at least sometimes, for companies and industries to govern themselves, while still protecting the public interest. Groundbreaking work done by Nobel Prize–winning political economist Elinor Ostrom and her husband Vincent found a solution to a classic economic quandary, in which people—and businesses—self-interestedly enrich themselves as quickly as possible with certain resources, including personal data, thinking little about the secondary costs they might be inflicting on others.[11]

There are ways companies can become leaders by experimenting with business opportunities and collaborating with peers, while still working with regulators to protect the public, including both in the air and cyberspace.[12] Consider the classic economic problem commonly known as "the tragedy of the commons," in which a parcel of grassland is made available for a community to graze its livestock. Everyone tries to get the most benefit from it, and as a result, the land is overgrazed. What started as a resource for everyone becomes of little use to anyone. For many years, economists thought there were only two possible solutions. One was for the government to step in and limit how many people could graze their animals. The other was to split the land up among private owners who had exclusive use of it and could sustainably manage it for their benefit.

The Ostroms, however, found a third way. In some cases, they revealed, self-organization can work well, especially when the various people and groups involved can communicate effectively. They developed design principles to help understand the dynamics involved, along with furthering the concept of "polycentric governance." For those new to the topic, the field of polycentric (multicentered) governance is a multilevel, multipurpose, multifunctional, and multisectoral model,[13] which has been championed by scholars including Nobel laureate Professor Elinor Ostrom and Professor Vincent Ostrom. According to Professor Michael McGinnis, "[t]he basic idea [of polycentric governance] is that any group . . . facing some collective problem should be able to address that problem in whatever way they best see fit," which could include using existing governance structures or crafting new systems.[14] This robust model challenges orthodoxy by demonstrating both the benefits of self-organization, understood here as networking regulations "at multiple levels," and the extent to which national and private control can coexist with communal management.[15] It also posits that, due to the existence of free riders in a multipolar world, "a single governmental unit" is often incapable of managing global collective action problems.

Instead, a polycentric approach recognizes that diverse organizations working at multiple levels can create different types of policies that can increase levels of cooperation and compliance, enhancing "flexibility across issues and adaptability over time."[16] As Professor Fikret Berkes has stated, "Polycentric and multilayered institutions improve the fit between knowledge and action in a social-ecological system in ways that allow societies to respond adaptively to change."[17] Yet such networks can also be "inefficient"[18] and are susceptible to institutional fragmentation and gridlock caused by an overlapping authority that must still "meet standards of coherence, effectiveness, [and] . . . sustainability."[19]

The concept can seem complicated, but in practice it is increasingly popular in federal programs and even as a goal for governing the Internet.[20] Scholars such as Elinor Ostrom produced a broad swath of research over the decades, looking at public schools and police department performance in Midwestern U.S. cities, coastal overfishing, forest management in nations like Nepal, and even traffic jams in New York City. They identified commonalities among all these studies, including whether the group's members can help set the rules by which their shared resources are governed, how much control they have over who gets to share it, how disputes are resolved, and how everyone's use is monitored. All of these factors can help predict whether individuals or groups will successfully self-regulate, whether the challenge they're facing is climate change, cybersecurity, or data privacy. Trust is key, as Lin Ostrom said, and an excellent way to build trust is to let smaller groups make their own decisions as was discussed in Chapter 7.[21]

Polycentric governance's embrace of self-regulation involves relying on human ingenuity and collaboration skills to solve difficult problems—while focusing on practical measures to address specific challenges. Self-regulation does have its limits, though—as discussed throughout this book, and more recently in how the Federal Aviation Administration allowed Boeing to certify the safety.[22] Facebook has also been heavily criticized for failing to block an anonymous horde of users across the globe from manipulating people's political views.[23]

Polycentric regulation is a departure from the idea of "keep it simple, stupid"—rather, it is a call for engagement by numerous groups to grapple with the complexities of the real world, both online and offline. Ostrom's ideas suggest they could begin to do this by engaging with peers and industry groups to set rules and ensure they are enforced. Consider the smart-device business, with tens of billions of connected devices around the world, and little to no concern for user security or privacy as was discussed in Chapters 4 and 5. Customers often buy the cheapest smart home camera or digital sensor, without looking at competitors' security and privacy protections. The results are predictable—hackers have hijacked thousands of Internet-connected devices and used them to attack the physical network of the Internet, take control of industrial equipment, and spy on private citizens through their smartphones and baby monitors. Some governments are starting to get involved. The state of California and the European Union are exploring laws that promote "reasonable" security requirements, at least as a baseline. The EU is encouraging companies to band together to establish industry-wide codes of conduct through General Data Protection Regulation (GDPR).

Effective self-governance may seem impossible in our hyperconnected present because of the scale and variety of groups and industries involved, but polycentric governance does provide a useful lens through which to view these problems. Ostrom has asserted that this approach may be the most flexible and adaptable way to manage rapidly changing industries. It may also help avoid conflicting government regulations that risk stifling innovation in the name of protecting consumers without helping either cause.

But success is not certain. It requires active engagement by all parties, who must share a sense of responsibility with the customers and mutual trust in one another. That's not easy to build in any community, let alone the dynamic tech industry. Government involvement can help build bridges and solidify trust across the private sector, as happened with cybersecurity efforts from the National Institute for Standards and Technology. Some states, like Ohio, are even rewarding firms for using appropriate self-regulation in their cybersecurity decision-making.[24] Polycentric governance can be flexible, adapting to new technologies more appropriately—and often more quickly—than pure governmental regulation. It also can be more efficient and cost-effective, though it's not a cure for all regulatory ills. And it's important to note that regulation can spur innovation as well as protect consumers, especially when the rules are simple and outcome focused.

Consider the North American Electric Reliability Council (NERC). That organization was originally created as a group of companies that came together voluntarily to protect against blackouts and more cynically get ahead of government regulation. NERC standards, however, were eventually made legally enforceable in the aftermath of the Northeast blackout of 2003. They are an example of an organic code of conduct that was voluntarily adopted and subsequently reinforced by the government, consistent with professor Ostrom's ideas. Ideally, it should not require such a crisis to spur this process forward.

Ultimately, what's needed—and what professor Ostrom and her colleagues and successors have called for—is more experimentation and less theorizing. We can do more to put her insights to work, offering industries the opportunity to self-regulate where appropriate while leaving the door open for the possibility of government action, including antitrust enforcement, to protect the public and promote cyber peace.

THE INTERNET WE DESERVE

This section pivots from lessons learned to focus on the digital road ahead, including with regard to cyber peace, misinformation, AI, the metaverse, and opportunities for reforming global Internet governance.

Cyber Peace

As this book has demonstrated, the Internet has developed organically through a series of pivotal forks in the digital road. These choices have collectively led to a vision of cyberspace that some of the key decision makers featured in Parts I and II applaud, while others are raising alarms. For example, Vint Cerf has argued that "the Internet is for everyone,—but it won't be if Governments restrict access to it, so we must dedicate ourselves to keeping the network unrestricted, unfettered and unregulated. We must have the freedom to speak and the freedom to hear."[25] Such remarks bring in many of the key threads of cybersecurity and Internet governance discussed throughout this book, including the role of the public and private sectors in managing cyberspace in such hot topics as content moderation and cyberattacks. As we turn from diagnosing some of the key reasons for why the Internet we have toward conceptualizing the Internet we deserve, one core concept that can help lead the way is cyber peace.

In a world beset by pervasive cyber insecurity,[26] it may seem odd to discuss the prospects for cyber peace. From ransomware impacting communities around the world,[27] to state-sponsored attacks on electrical infrastructure,[28] to disinformation campaigns spreading virally on social media, we seem to have relatively little bandwidth left over for asking the big questions: what is the best we can hope for in terms of "peace" on the Internet, and how might we get there? Yet the stakes couldn't be higher. McKinsey, for example, has argued that "$9 trillion to $21 trillion of economic-value creation, worldwide, [will] depend on the robustness of the cybersecurity environment."[29] But the news is not all bleak, as has been seen, with the Internet user experience being secured through now near-ubiquitous encryption and biometric technologies enabling a step toward the long-fabled death of the password.[30]

Is the peaceful use of cyberspace possible, and what might it mean? "Cyber peace" is difficult to define, as difficult, if not more so than its offline comparator. The term "cyber peace" seems to have originated during a program "at the Vatican's Pontifical Academy of Sciences in December 2008."[31] However, it was being used before that date, indeed as early as 2005 as Professor Renée Marlin-Bennett has explored.[32] This conference, however, helped to crystallize the concept by releasing the "Erice Declaration on Principles for Cyber Stability and Cyber Peace" (Erice Declaration).[33] The declaration called for enhanced cooperation and stability in cyberspace by promoting six principles ranging from guaranteeing the "free flow of information" to forbidding exploitation and avoiding cyber conflict,[34] several of which mirror more recent efforts such as the 2018 Paris Call.

One throughline from 2012 to the present, though, is the focus on protecting critical infrastructure as a key element of cyber peace.[35] Still, a core facet of the understanding throughout this period was a negative cyber peace, for example, managing the damage caused by cyberattacks rather than conceptualizing and planning for a more sustainable and equitable status quo. The conceptual framework of polycentric governance introduced earlier was deployed to better contextualize the range of actors, architectures, and governance scales in play.[36] It argued

[C]yberpeace not as the absence of conflict, but as the creation of a network of multilevel regimes working together to promote global cybersecurity by clarifying norms for companies and countries alike to reduce the risk of conflict, crime, and espionage in cyberspace to levels comparable to other business and national security risks. Working together through polycentric partnerships, and with the leadership of engaged individuals and institutions, we can stop cyber war before it starts by laying the groundwork for a positive cyber peace that respects human rights, spreads Internet access, and strengthens governance mechanisms by fostering multi-stakeholder collaboration.[37]

Despite growing recognition of the positive role played by polycentric governance in attaining cyber peace,[38] there remain nearly as many different conceptions of "cyber peace" as there are other related and equally amorphous terms, such as "sustainable development,"[39] or even "cyberspace" itself.[40] Thus, while "cyber peace," sometimes also called "digital peace,"[41] is a term that is increasingly used, it remains little understood. It is clearly more than the "absence of violence" online, which was the starting point for how Professor Johan Galtung described the new field of peace studies he helped to found in 1969.[42] Similarly, Galtung argued that agreeing on universal definitions for "peace" or "violence" was unrealistic; instead, the goal should be landing on a "subjectivistic" definition agreed to by the majority.[43] Doing so, he recognized that as society and technology change, so too should our conceptions of peace and violence (an observation that's arguably equally applicable both online and offline). That is why he defined violence as "the cause of the difference between the potential and the actual, between what could have been and what is."[44]

Extrapolating from this logic, as technology advances, be it biometrics or blockchain, the opportunity cost of not acting to ameliorate suffering grows, as do the capabilities of attackers to cause harm. This highlights the fact that cyber peace is not a finish line but an ongoing process of due diligence and risk management, echoing Wegener's sentiments. In this way, a sense of positive cyber peace is defined here as a polycentric system that: (1) respects human rights and freedoms,[45] (2) spreads Internet access along with cybersecurity best practices,[46] (3) strengthens governance mechanisms by fostering multistakeholder collaboration,[47] and (4) promotes stability and relatedly sustainable development.[48]

These four pillars of cyber peace may be constructed by clarifying the rules of the road for companies and countries alike to help reduce the threats of cyber war, terrorism, crime, and espionage to levels comparable to other business and national security risks. This could encourage the movement along a cyber peace spectrum toward a more resilient, stable, and sustainable Internet ecosystem with systems in place to "deter hostile or malicious activity"[49] and in so doing promote both human and national security online and offline.[50] To achieve this goal, a new approach to cybersecurity is needed that seeks out best practices from the public and private sectors. This approach builds from the work of other scholars who have similarly criticized a fixation on Westphalian, national-security-centric models of enhancing cybersecurity, and it instead focuses on minimizing "structural forms of violence" across various governance scales and sectors.[51] Such an approach may be viewed as in keeping with the prevailing multistakeholder approach to Internet governance,[52] which is in contrast to the rise of so-called cyber sovereignty.[53]

A growing community of scholars, practitioners, and policymakers are looking beyond this baseline definition and are aiming at operationalizing a *positive* cyber peace as is explored throughout this edited volume. This new drive is being supported by a growing coalition, including the governments of France and New Zealand along with firms like Microsoft and NGOs such as the Cyberpeace Institute, which is coming together to promote stability, such as by leveraging codes of conduct and emerging international standards aimed at reducing cyber insecurity and promoting cybersecurity due diligence. These stakeholders, and others, are helping to create and promote myriad related efforts such as the Online Trust Alliance, ICT4Peace, and the Cyber Peace Alliance, which are backed by major funders such as the Hewlett Foundation and the Carnegie Endowment for International Peace. The Paris Call itself is a broad statement of principles that focus on improving "cyber hygiene," along with "the security of digital products and services" and the "integrity of the internet," among other topics.[54] Similarly, in the aftermath of the 2019 mass shooting at two mosques in Christchurch, New Zealand, the governments of 18 nations—along with more than a dozen well-known technology firms like Google and Facebook—adopted the Christchurch Call to Eliminate Terrorist and Violent Extremist Content Online. Yet neither of these calls, or other related efforts, binds the participants, though they do help find common ground that could, in time, be codified into laws or other enforceable standards, nor builds consensus about cyber peace including the vital task of fostering equitable Internet governance.

Equitable Internet Governance

There are a variety of approaches that have been suggested over the years to make Internet governance more representative, and equitable, along with even more barriers that have sprung up blocking their realization. For example, Malta has long argued that the global commons—including the Internet—should be treated as part of the common heritage of mankind (CHM).[55] Neither scholars nor policymakers have agreed on a common understanding of the CHM, but still, the term is used widely. In 2017, Pope Francis called the oceans "the common heritage of the human family."[56] Nevertheless, most conceptions of the CHM share five primary elements. First, there can be no private or public appropriation; no one legally owns common heritage spaces. Second, "representatives from all nations" must work together to manage global common pool resources.[57] Third, all nations must "actively share" in the "benefits acquired from [the] exploitation of the resources from the common heritage region."[58] Fourth, there can be no weaponry or military installations established in common heritage areas, as they should be used for "peaceful purposes."[59] Fifth, the commons "must be preserved for the benefit of future generations[.]"[60]

Yet applying CHM concepts outside of the oceans, or space, to cyberspace is problematic. For example, concerning representative governance, the closest analogue to an international regime in the cyber context would be the Internet Corporation for Assigned Names and Numbers (ICANN), the Internet Governance Forum (IGF), or possibly an intergovernmental organization from the International Telecommunication Union (ITU). However, expanding the mandate of these organizations or creating a new body is politically divisive. The extent to which sustainable development is replacing or giving new life to the CHM concept is an area of active debate, which is part of larger conversations about the role of the green movement in improving and informing Internet governance.

Aside from an unlikely Treaty for Cyberspace in the vein of the Outer Space Treaty or the Antarctic Treaty, a far more likely scenario is leveraging polycentric networks to push back against creeping Internet sovereignty and help keep cyberspace global. Yet, as a 2022 Council on Foreign Relations report concludes, "[t]he utopian vision of an open, reliable, and secure global network has not been achieved and is unlikely ever to be realized. Today, the Internet is less free, more fragmented, and less secure."[61] In essence, not only has the U.S. strategy to promote a global, open, and secure Internet been—at best—a limited success, but with it, the vision of many of the leading thinkers such as Tim Berners-Lee and Vint Cerf vision as was discussed in Parts I and II.

Are we doomed, then, to a vision of the 21st-century Internet that is more closed, less innovative, and free? Not necessarily. As Adam Segal and Jami Miscik have argued, some steps could be taken in the United States and across Western nations to consolidate support for a robust Internet freedom agenda. These steps could include a new round of "digital trade agreements among trusted partners," the U.S. government pursuing a version of GDPR to help close transatlantic divides on data governance and present a united front challenging Chinese and Russian models of state-centric Internet governance, and provide more aid and infrastructure development to developing nations in need of support.[62] Added to this list could be efforts to further globalize ICANN's governance bodies and potentially even create an international cybercrime center with some authority to address common concerns such as ransomware attacks on civilian critical infrastructure.[63] A key aspect to multistakeholder Internet governance going forward will be to ensure a diverse array of voices from around the world, especially from underrepresented groups and women, given how central diversity is to not only cybersecurity but more broadly to economic development.[64] As former U.S. President Barack Obama said, "The Internet is not a luxury, it is a necessity"[65] and, thus, even a human right to include privacy and cybersecurity.[66] Recognizing and enforcing such human rights, though, are two separate issues.[67] Some have pinned their hopes for the latter on Web 3.0 technologies including blockchain that cut out the middleman and promise self-enforcing capabilities. We feel, though, that the Internet of Things potentially has even more transformative power, which we turn to next.

Internet of Things

As was discussed in Chapter 3, there is a great deal of buzz surrounding the Internet of Things (IoT), which is the notion, simply put, that nearly everything not currently connected to the Internet from gym shorts to streetlights soon will be.[68] The rise of "smart products" such as Internet-enabled refrigerators and self-driving cars holds the promise to revolutionize business and society.[69] Applications are seemingly endless, as are the corresponding vulnerabilities. As the Council on Foreign Relations has argued, "As the Internet of Things (IoT) expands in coming years, the next iteration of the network will connect tens of billions of devices, digitally binding every aspect of day-to-day life, from heart monitors and refrigerators to traffic lights and agricultural methane emissions."[70] The resulting global technological ecosystem has many opportunities to open new business and industries even as it risks further blurring the line between the "real world" and cyberspace, as seen in the increasing number of cyberattacks that have had physical impacts as seen in the Russian cyberattacks on Ukrainian critical infrastructure, including its power grid, or ransomware attacks on hospitals during the Covid-19 pandemic, resulting in patient deaths.

A variety of approaches are being tried to enhance security and improve governance on the IoT. These include stepped-up efforts from the FTC to investigate firms with lax cybersecurity, the National Institute for Standards and Technology (NIST) developing IoT-specific frameworks to guide industry on governance best practices, and the state of California requiring "reasonable" cybersecurity for all Internet-connected devices. As the IoT matures, disparate smart residential and commercial networks will be able to communicate with one another, creating smart (and potentially more resilient) things, cities, and societies. Such an ultimate, macro-level outcome resembles the early days of networking when Cisco used multiprotocol routing to join dissimilar networks that eventually led to the widespread adoption of a common networking standard called the Internet Protocol, as was discussed in Part I, which we all rely on today every time we sign in online. The IoT looks set to follow a similar route, albeit on a larger scale, spanning myriad sectors and industries. In response, polycentric IoT cybersecurity regulations should be adapted and improved to better keep pace with these changes,[71] particularly with regard to data regulations monitoring private firms and companies that transfer Personally identifiable information (PII).[72] This includes standards—including a NIST IoT-specific effort—along with the Consumer Reports Digital Standard, and the use of corporate governance structures, such as sustainability, and international norms, including due diligence. Such an all-of-the-above, polycentric approach is essential to addressing governance gaps on the Internet of Things. As Professor Elinor Ostrom said, this is not a "keep it simple, stupid" response,[73] but a multifaceted one in keeping with the complexity of the crises in Internet governance.

Conclusion—Our Meta Future?

The metaverse. Depending on your perspective, it's either the future of the Internet, the next generation of video games, or even "a deeply uncomfortable, worse version of Zoom."[1] In many ways, the confusion, overpromising, and hype are reminiscent of how the Internet itself was envisioned in earlier epochs. After all, William Gibson, who coined the term "cyberspace" in his sci-fi novel *Neuromancer*, famously described it in part as "a consensual hallucination experienced daily by billions of legitimate operators in every nation."[2] From this vantage point, the metaverse is the ultimate realization of Gibson's original idea of cyberspace itself.

As *Wired* has argued, in most instances you can use "metaverse" and "cyberspace" interchangeably—it's not necessarily about a new fundamental technology but, rather, new ways of interacting with existing tech through virtual and augmented reality. But these technologies can also allow for new markets, and even economies, to flourish through the creation, purchase, and sale of digital assets, including so-called non-fungible tokens (NFTs). In its ultimate form, users would be able to take these assets across platforms, exploring infinite worlds with a constant avatar. Although many opportunities already exist for users to, for example, buy virtual goods and play games like those on *Fortnite*, that's only one application of the underlying tech. In short, "[s]aying that Fortnite is 'the metaverse' would be a bit like saying Google is 'the internet.'"[3]

A diverse range of firms are investing in metaverse tech, causing a digital gold rush since there is such a substantial first-mover advantage to

Forks in the Digital Road. Scott J. Shackelford and Scott O. Bradner, Oxford University Press. © Oxford University Press 2024.
DOI: 10.1093/oso/9780197617762.003.0009

CONCLUSION

be won, which *Forbes* has estimated to be north of a $1 trillion revenue opportunity.[4] These include not only Meta (formerly Facebook), but also Nvidia, Unity, Roblox, and even Snap, to name a few. Companies like Nike are already developing ways to equip avatars with digital, personalized sneakers. Prices for virtual parcels of land doubled to more than $12,000 in late 2021.[5] There's even now a "United Metaverse Nation," which professes its identity: "The United Metaverse Nation is the first decentralized autonomous organization DAO that acts as a virtual country."[6] In other words, the stakes are high, and confusion abounds.

How do we begin to govern the metaverse, especially if it's captured at an early stage by firms like Meta? This brings to the fore debates about the appropriate role of the private sector as gatekeeper, as was discussed in Chapter 5 in the context of Section 230. In other words, the same core questions and dynamics that have bedeviled the myriad forks in the history of the Internet continue to influence the key questions that will likely arise in the 21st century. Who should govern the metaverse? What is "reasonable" cybersecurity on the Internet of Things, and how do we protect privacy in such a hyperconnected future? How will blockchain applications and Web 3.0 more broadly reshape the trajectory of Internet governance? Addressing these questions, though, and so many more digital forks to come will have to be the subject of another book.

NOTES

PREFACE

1. See Lana Jelic, *This Is the First Ever Internet Message Sent*, TweakTown (Oct. 29, 2016), https://www.tweaktown.com/news/54662/first-internet-message-sent/index.html.
2. See, e.g., Internet Live Stats, https://www.internetlivestats.com/ (last visited Aug. 11, 2022); Jessica Gall Myrick, *Study: People Who Watch Cat Videos Are Shyer, Spend More Time Online*, SLATE (June 18, 2015), https://slate.com/technology/2015/06/study-people-who-watch-cat-videos-are-shyer-spend-more-time-online.html.
3. JEFF KOSSEFF, THE TWENTY-SIX WORDS THAT CREATED THE INTERNET (2019).
4. *The American Presidency Project*, UCSB, https://www.presidency.ucsb.edu/documents/message-for-american-education-week (last visited Aug. 11, 2022).

CHAPTER 1

1. JACQUES BERLEUR, MARKKU I. NURMINEN, & JOHN IMPAGLIAZZO, SOCIAL INFORMATICS: AN INFORMATION SOCIETY FOR ALL? 436 (2006).
2. *Chronological History of IBM*, IBM, https://www.ibm.com/ibm/history/history/decade_1950.html.
3. *SAGE: The First National Air Defense Network*, IBM, https://www.ibm.com/ibm/history/ibm100/us/en/icons/sage/.
4. Vannevar Bush, *As We May Think*, ATLANTIC, July 1945, https://www.theatlantic.com/magazine/archive/1945/07/as-we-may-think/303881/.
5. J.C.R. Licklider, *Man-Computer Symbiosis*, HFE-1 IRE TRANSACTIONS ON HUM. FACTORS IN ELECS. 4 (1960), https://groups.csail.mit.edu/medg/people/psz/Licklider.html.
6. JAMES GILLIS ET AL., HOW THE WEB WAS BORN: THE STORY OF THE WORLD WIDE WEB 46 (2000).
7. Paul Baran, *On Distributed Communications Networks*, RAND (1962), https://www.rand.org/pubs/papers/P2626.html.
8. If the origin and destination telephones were connected to the same telephone switch, then the connections could be internal to that switch.
9. Circuit Switching, https://erg.abdn.ac.uk/users/gorry/course/intro-pages/cs.html (last visited Dec. 7, 2022).

10. Vinton Cerf, *Cerf's Up: Back to the Future, Part II*, 62(7) COMM. OF THE ACM 6 (2019), https://cacm.acm.org/magazines/2019/7/237700-back-to-the-future-part-ii/fulltext.

11. *See, e.g.*, Thomas McMullan, *The World's First Hack: The Telegraph and the Invention of Privacy*, GUARDIAN (July 15, 2015), https://www.theguardian.com/technology/2015/jul/15/first-hack-telegraph-invention-privacy-gchq-nsa.

12. *See Paul Baran*, ENCYCLOPEDIA BRITTANICA, https://www.britannica.com/biography/Paul-Baran (last visited Dec. 8, 2022).

13. ILKKA TUOMI, THE MAKING OF THE INTERNET, IN NETWORKS OF INNOVATION 54 (2006).

14. *Id.*

15. *Id.*

16. *Paul Baran RAND (1960s)*, CYBERTELECOM FED. INTERNET L. & POL'Y: AN EDUC. PROJECT, https://www.cybertelecom.org/notes/baran.htm (last updated Oct. 7, 2019).

17. Virginia Campbell, *How RAND Invented the Postwar World*, RAND 58 (2004), https://www.rand.org/content/dam/rand/pubs/reprints/2009/RAND_RP1396.pdf.

18. *Donald Davies*, INTERNET HALL OF FAME, https://www.internethalloffame.org/inductees/donald-davies (last visited Dec. 8, 2022).

19. Larry Roberts, *The ARPANET & Computer Networks*, PROC. ACM CONF. 51, 53 (1986), https://dl.acm.org/doi/10.1145/12178.12182; *Oral History Interview with Paul Baran*, CHARLES BABBAGE INST. 19–21 (1990), https://conservancy.umn.edu/handle/11299/107101; Campbell, *supra* note 17, at 53.

20. Peter Grier, *In the Beginning, There Was the ARPANET*, AIR FORCE MAG. (1997), https://www.airforcemag.com/PDF/MagazineArchive/Documents/1997/January%201997/0197arpanet.pdf; Campbell, *supra* note 17, at 58.

21. James L. Pelkey, *The History of Computer Communications, in* NPL NETWORK AND DONALD DAVIES 1966–1971, https://historyofcomputercommunications.info/section/6.11/NPL-Network-and-Donald-Davies-1966-1971/.

22. *DARPA: Bridging the Gap—Powered by Ideas* http://www.dtic.mil/cgi-bin/GetTRDoc?Location=U2&doc=GetTRDoc.pdf&AD=ADA433949.

23. DoD Directive 5105.1, https://web.archive.org/web/20160613125249/http://semanticvoid.com/docs/darpa_directive.pdf.

24. Jeff Tollefson, *The Rise of "ARPA-Everything" and What It Means for Science*, NATURE (July 8, 2021), https://www.nature.com/articles/d41586-021-01878-z.

25. Arthur L. Norberg, *Larry Roberts Oral History Interview* (Apr. 4, 1989), at 18, https://conservancy.umn.edu/handle/11299/107608.

26. *Larry Roberts—Complete Biography, History and Inventions*, COMP. HISTORY (Jan. 4, 2021), https://history-computer.com/larry-roberts-complete-biography/.

27. James Pelkey, *Interviews of Lawrence G. "Larry" Roberts*, 1, 12, (1988) http://archive.computerhistory.org/resources/access/text/2013/04/102746626-05-01-acc.pdf.

28. Larry Roberts, *Multiple Computer Networks and Intercomputer Communications* (1967), https://www.researchgate.net/publication/234826251_Multiple_Computer_Networks_and_Intercomputer_Communications/link/546d0f2a0cf26e95bc3cac53/download.

NOTES

29. Larry Davies et al., *A Digital Communication Network for Computers Giving Rapid Response at Remote Terminals*, PROC. OF THE FIRST ACM SYMPOSIUM ON OPERATING SYSTEM PRINCIPLES, ed. J. Gosden, B. Randell, Association for Computing Machinery, New York, NY, United States (1967); *Larry Roberts Oral History Interview* conducted by Arthur L. Norberg, 1, 16–17 (Apr. 4, 1989), https://conservancy.umn.edu/handle/11299/107608; *On Packet Switching, Net History*, https://www.nethistory.info/Archives/packets.html.

30. Interview with Larry Roberts (on file with authors), 2023.

31. Sean Gallagher, *50 Years Ago Today, the Internet Was Born. Sort of*, ARS TECHNICA (Oct. 29, 2019), https://arstechnica.com/information-technology/2019/10/50-years-ago-today-the-internet-was-born-sort-of/.

32. WALTER ISAACSON, THE INNOVATORS: HOW A GROUP OF HACKERS, GENIUSES, AND GEEKS CREATED THE DIGITAL REVOLUTION 249 (2014).

33. Mark Crispin, *Universal Host Table*, RFC 752, https://rfc-editor.org/rfc/rfc752.txt.

34. Pelkey, *supra* note 32, at 14.

35. *Number of Connected Devices Reached 22 Billion, Where Is the Revenue?*, STRATEGY ANALYTICS (2019), https://www.helpnetsecurity.com/2019/05/23/connected-devices-growth/.

36. Bradley Mitchell, *What Internet and Network Backbones Do*, LIFEWIRE (2020), https://www.lifewire.com/definition-of-backbone-817777.

37. James L. Pelkey, *Interview with Robert William "Bob" Taylor*, 1, 2 (2017), https://archive.computerhistory.org/resources/access/text/2017/12/102738691-05-01-acc.pdf.

38. Thomas Marill & Lawrence G. Roberts, *Towards a Cooperative Network of Time-Shared Computers*, at 430 (1966), https://dl.acm.org/doi/pdf/10.1145/1464291.1464336; James L. Pelkey, *Interviews with Lawrence G. "Larry" Roberts*, 1, 4, https://archive.computerhistory.org/resources/access/text/2013/04/102746626-05-01-acc.pdf.

39. Pelkey, *supra* note 44, at 8.

40. *The History of Computer Communications*, NETWORKING: VISION AND PACKET SWITCHING 1959–1968, https://historyofcomputercommunications.info/section/4.6/Packet-Switching//.

41. Pelkey, *supra* note 44, at 6.

42. Judy O'Neil, *An Interview with Wesley Clark*, 1, 27 (1990), https://lib-umedia-qat-01.oit.umn.edu/item/p16022coll92:70.

43. John Markoff, *Wesley A. Clark, Who Designed First Personal Computer, Dies at 88*, N.Y. TIMES (Feb. 27, 2016), https://www.nytimes.com/2016/02/28/business/wesley-a-clark-made-computing-personal-dies-at-88.html.

44. Paul Baran, *On Distributed Communications Networks*, RAND, 1, 28 (1962), https://www.rand.org/content/dam/rand/pubs/papers/2005/P2626.pdf (last visited Jan. 14, 2024).

45. *Birth of the ARPAnet: 1969*, CYBER TELECOM, https://www.cybertelecom.org/notes/internet_history69.htm.

46. *Id.*

47. Jon Postel, *Internet Protocol*, RFC 791, § 2.4 (September 1981), https://www.rfc-editor.org/rfc/rfc791.txt.

48. *Id.* at §1.4.

49. Chantal Lebrument & Fabian Soyez, The Inventions of Louis Pouzzin, v, xv (2020), https://link.springer.com/content/pdf/bfm%3A978-3-030-34836-6%2F1.pdf.

50. Peter Grief, *In the Beginning, There Was ARPANET*, Air & Space Forces Mag. (1997), https://www.airforcemag.com/article/0197arpanet/; Judy O'Neil, *An Interview with Robert E. Kahn*, 1, 25, 26 (1990), https://conservancy.umn.edu/bitstream/handle/11299/107387/oh192rek.pdf?sequence=1&isAllowed=y; Judy O'Neil, *An Interview with Vinton Cerf*, 1, 23, 24 (Apr. 24, 1990), https://conservancy.umn.edu/handle/11299/107214.

51. Judy O'Neil, *An Interview with Bob Kahn*, 1, 24–27 (Apr. 24, 1990), http://conservancy.umn.edu/handle/11299/107387.

52. *See* Robert E. Kahn, Nat'l Inventors Hall of Fame, https://www.invent.org/inductees/robert-e-kahn (last visited Jan. 10, 2022).

53. Robert Kahn, Internet Hall of Fame, https://www.internethalloffame.org/inductees/robert-kahn (last visited Jan. 10, 2022).

54. *A Technical History of the ARPANET—A Technical Tour: IMP-to-IMP Error Detection*, THINK Protocols Team (2003), https://web.archive.org/web/20120907210508/http://www.cs.utexas.edu/users/chris/think/ARPANET/Technical_Tour/ii_errdet.shtml.

55. *X.25 Protocol*, Network Encyclopedia, https://networkencyclopedia.com/x-25/ (last visited Jan. 14, 2024).

56. A. McKenzie, *A Host/Host Protocol for an ARPANET-Type Network*, RFC 714, 1, 2–3 (Apr. 1976), https://www.ietf.org/rfc/rfc714.txt.

57. *See* The Intelligent Network: A Joint Study by Bell Atlantic, IBM and Siemens (W.D. Ambrosch & Maher B. Sasscer eds.,1989).

58. *Louis Pouzin*, Comp. History Museum, https://computerhistory.org/profile/louis-pouzin/ (last visited Dec. 10, 2022).

59. *Id.*

60. James L. Pelkey, *Interview of Louis Pouzin*, 1, 6 (Nov. 28, 1988), https://archive.computerhistory.org/resources/access/text/2017/12/102740273-05-01-acc.pdf.

61. J.H. Saltzer et al., *End-to-End Arguments in System Design*, MIT (1984), https://web.mit.edu/Saltzer/www/publications/endtoend/endtoend.pdf.

62. Pelkey, *supra* note 66, at 11.

63. David Isenberg, *The Rise of the Stupid Network*, ACM Networker 2.0 (1997), http://www.rageboy.com/stupidnet.html.

64. Steve G. Steinberg, *Netheads vs Bellheads,* Wired (Oct. 1, 1996), https://www.wired.com/1996/10/atm-3/.

65. Adam Thierer, Permissionless Innovation and Public Policy 3 (2016), https://papers.ssrn.com/sol3/papers.cfm?abstract_id=2761139.

66. Bradley Mitchell, *Beginner's Guide to Asynchronous Transfer Mode (ATM)*, Lifewire (June 23, 2021), https://www.lifewire.com/asynchronous-transfer-mode-817942.

67. *ITU-T's Definition of NGN*, ITU-T, https://www.itu.int/en/ITU-T/gsi/ngn/Pages/definition.aspx (last visited Dec. 10, 2022).

68. *Everything You Need to Know About 5G*, Qualcomm, https://www.qualcomm.com/5g/what-is-5g (last visited Dec. 10, 2022).

NOTES

69. *A Brief Prehistory of VoIP*, A31 (2010), https://www.youtube.com/watch?v=av4K Flj-wp4.

70. A.C. Norwine & J. Murphy, *Characteristic Time Intervals in Telephonic Conversation*, 17 Bell System Tech. J. 281, 282 (1938), https://archive.org/details/bstj17-2-281.

71. *Id.*

72. *See, e.g., Tenth Broadband Progress of Inquiry*, FCC, 15 (2014), https://docs.fcc.gov/public/attachments/FCC-14-113A1.docx.

73. *Transmission Control Protocol*, IBM, https://www.ibm.com/docs/en/aix/7.2?topic=protocols-transmission-control-protocol (last visited Dec. 10, 2022).

74. Marc Weber, *Oral History of Danny Cohen*, at 21, (Nov. 18, 2011), https://archive.computerhistory.org/resources/access/text/2019/08/102746173-05-01-acc.pdf.

75. *A Brief Prehistory of VoIP, supra* note 75, at A12–18.

76. *Danny Cohen*, Internet Hall of Fame, https://www.internethalloffame.org/inductees/danny-cohen (last visited Dec. 10, 2022).

77. Weber, *supra* note 80, at 38–39.

78. *Id.* at 22.

79. Del Zoppo, *Packet-Voice-Conference* (1978), https://www.youtube.com/watch?v=MGat1jRQ_SM.

80. Vint Cerf et al., *Specification of Internet Transmission Control Program*, RFC 675 (Dec. 1974), https://www.rfc-editor.org/rfc/rfc675.txt.

81. *See Bob Kahn, the Bread Truck, and the Internet's First Communion*, Internet Hall of Fame (Aug. 13, 2012), https://www.internethalloffame.org//blog/2012/08/13/bob-kahn-bread-truck-and-internet%e2%80%99s-first-communion.

82. *Id.*

83. *Id.*

84. *Id.*

85. *Id.*

86. *A Brief Prehistory of VoIP, supra* note 75, at A28–34.

87. Weber, *supra* note 80, at 40.

88. David P. Reed, *The Law of the Pack*, Harv. Bus. Rev. (Feb. 2001), https://hbr.org/2001/02/the-law-of-the-pack.

89. *Jon Postel—Complete Biography, History, and Inventions*, HC (Jan. 16, 2022), https://history-computer.com/jon-postel-complete-biography/.

90. David Reed, *UDP & Me*, https://www.deepplum.com/blog-dpr/?page_id=6 (last visited Dec. 10, 2022).

91. *User Datagram Protocol*, RFC 768 (1980), https://www.rfc-editor.org/rfc/rfc768.txt; *Internet Protocol*, RFC 791 (1981), https://www.rfc-editor.org/rfc/rfc791.txt; *Internet Control Message Protocol*, RFC 792 (1981), https://www.rfc-editor.org/rfc/rfc792.txt; *Transmission Control Protocol*, RFC793 (1981), https://www.rfc-editor.org/rfc/rfc793.txt.

92. Gavin Clarke, *30 Years Ago, at Flip of a Switch, the Internet as We Know It WAS BORN* (Jan. 3, 2013), https://www.theregister.com/2013/01/03/operational_internet_anniversary/.

93. *Id.*

94. *Zoom Connection Process*, Zoom (2020), https://zoom.us/docs/doc/Zoom%20Connection%20Process%20Whitepaper.pdf.

95. Iyengar et al., *QUIC: A UDP-Based Multiplexed and Secure Transport*, RFC 9000 (May 2021), https://www.rfc-editor.org/rfc/rfc9000.txt.
96. J. Iyengar & M. Thomson, *QUIC: A UDP-Based Multiplexed and Secure Transport*, IETF RFC 9000 (May 2021), https://www.ietf.org/rfc/rfc9000.txt.

CHAPTER 2

1. GERALD SUSSMAN, COMMUNICATION, TECHNOLOGY, AND POLITICS IN THE INFORMATION AGE, ix (1977), ISBN 0-8039-5139-6.
2. John Day, *The Clamor Outside as INWG Debated: Economic War Comes to Networking*, IEEE ANNALS OF THE HISTORY OF COMPUTING 58, 61 (2016), https://arussell.org/INWG-Day.pdf.
3. *Statistics of Communications Common Carriers*, FCC, 1979, 1, 17 (1982), https://www.fcc.gov/file/11646/download.
4. *Id.* at 18.
5. *History of Computer Communications*, § 2.11 Computer Inquiry I and the Carterfone (1965–1973), https://historyofcomputercommunications.info/section/2.11/Computer-Inquiry-I-and-the-Carterfone-1965-1973/.
6. *Id.* at § 2.12 (*The FCC, Jurisdictional Disputes and Direct Connection of CPE* [1973–1978]).
7. Day, *supra* note 2, at 64.
8. DOROTHY M. CERNI, THE CCITT: ORGANIZATION, U.S. PARTICIPATION, AND STUDIES TOWARD THE ISDN 7–9 (1982).
9. *Id.* at 9.
10. Philipp Genschel and Raymund Werle, *From National Hierarchies to International Standardization*, 13(3) JOURNAL OF PUBLIC POLICY, 211 (1993), https://citeseerx.ist.psu.edu/viewdoc/download?doi=10.1.1.197.6950&rep=rep1&type=pdf.
11. ANDREW RUSSELL, OPEN STANDARDS AND THE DIGITAL AGE 171 (2014).
12. *About US*, ISO, https://www.iso.org/about-us.html (last visited Dec. 10, 2022).
13. Will Kenton, *International Organization for Standardization (ISO)*, Investopedia (2022), https://www.investopedia.com/terms/i/international-organization-for-standardization-iso.asp.
14. James Pelkey, *Interview of Hubert Zimmerman* 4 (1988), https://www.computerhistory.org/collections/catalog/102738698.
15. *Official Biography: Steve Crocker*, INTERNET HALL OF FAME, https://www.internethalloffame.org/official-biography-steve-crocker (last visited Dec. 10, 2022).
16. IETF, https://www.ietf.org (last visited Dec. 10, 2022).
17. RFC, IETF, https://www.ietf.org/rfc/rfc-index.txt (last visited Dec. 10, 2022).
18. Alex McKenzie, *INWG and the Conception of the Internet: An Eyewitness Account*, IEEE 66 (2011), https://ieeexplore.ieee.org/document/5723076.
19. *Id.* at 67.
20. *Id.* at 67–68. Cerf and Kahn later published an updated version of INWG 39 in the May 1974 edition of the *IEEE Transactions on Communications*.
21. McKenzie, *supra* note 18, at 69.

NOTES

22. *Id.* at 70.
23. RUSSELL, *supra* note 11, at 174.
24. *Id.* at 176.
25. *Id.* at 177.
26. Day, *supra* note 2, at 65.
27. MATTHIAS BARWOLF, END-TO-END ARGUMENTS IN THE INTERNET: PRINCIPLES, PRACTICES, AND THEORY 338–41 (2010).
28. Interview (on file with authors), Jan. 24, 2023.
29. Day, *supra* note 2, at 70.
30. Pelkey, *supra* note 14, at 3.
31. *BSD Unix: Power to the People, from the Code*, Andrew Leonard (2000), https://landley.net/history/mirror/books/andrewlenard/part4.html.
32. Vint Cerf, *DoD Protocol Standardization*, IEN 152, at 3, https://www.rfc-editor.org/ien/ien152.txt (July 1, 1980).
33. Warren Toomey, *The Strange Birth and Long Life of Unix*, IEEE SPECTRUM 36–37 (Nov. 28, 2011).
34. *Id.* at 52–53.
35. David Fiedler, *The Unix Tutorial: Part 3: Unix in the Marketplace*, BYTE (Oct. 1983), https://archive.org/stream/byte-magazine-1983-10/1983_10_BYTE_08-10_UNIX#page/n133/mode/2up.
36. *Berkeley Software Distribution*, Open Source Fandom, https://opensource.fandom.com/wiki/Berkeley_Software_Distribution (last visited Jan. 22, 2024).
37. *ARPA Becomes DARPA*, DARPA, https://www.darpa.mil/about-us/timeline/arpa-name-change (last visited Jan. 22, 2024).
38. MARSHALL MCKUSICK, OPEN SOURCES: VOICES FROM THE OPEN SOURCE REVOLUTION 35 (1999).
39. *Id.*
40. Nils Gjerull, *The HISP Case in Ethiopia*, *in* OPEN SOURCE SOFTWARE DEVELOPMENT IN DEVELOPING COUNTRIES: THE HISP CASE IN ETHIOPIA (2006), http://www.gjerull.net/site_media/static/html/masterthesis/.
41. IES NEWS (first issue), at 4 (Autumn 1985), http://aei.pitt.edu/82640/1/1985.1.pdf.
42. Interview (on file with authors).
43. *Id.*
44. *An Interview with Peter Denning: Building a Culture of Innovation*, UBIQUITY (April 2004), https://ubiquity.acm.org/article.cfm?id=991107 (the "dead cows" reference refers to Denning's story in the interview of Louis Pasteur developing an anthrax vaccine in response to French farmer's complaints of dead cows—"*When you are looking for opportunities, look for the dead cows*").
45. ARPANET, https://military-history.fandom.com/wiki/ARPANET (last visited Dec. 12, 2022).
46. E. Feinler & J. Postel, *ARPANET Resource Handbook*, NAT'L TECH. REP. LIBRARY 16 (1978).
47. Peter J. Denning et al., *History and Overview of CSNET*, PURDUE UNIV. COMP. SCI. 20 (1981), https://docs.lib.purdue.edu/cgi/viewcontent.cgi?article=1347&context=cstech.

48. J.A. PAYNE, ARPANET HOST TO HOST ACCESS AND DISENGAGEMENT MEASUREMENTS 5 (1978), https://www.its.bldrdoc.gov/publications/download/78-3.pdf.
49. Denning et al., *supra* note 47, at 2.
50. Lawrence Landweber's Internet Hall of Fame 2012 Profile, http://opentranscripts.org/transcript/lawrence-landweber-internet-hall-fame-2012-profile/ (last visited Dec. 12, 2022).
51. *Id.*
52. Denning et al., *supra* note 47, at 5, 6; Lawrence Landweber's Internet Hall of Fame 2012 Profile, *supra* note 50.
53. Lawrence Landweber's Internet Hall of Fame 2012 Profile, *supra* note 50.
54. Denning et al., *supra* note 47, at 5.
55. Peter J. Denning & Douglas E. Comer, *The CSNET User Environment*, PURDUE UNIV. COMP. SCI. (1981), https://docs.lib.purdue.edu/cgi/viewcontent.cgi?article=1374&context=cstech.
56. Interview with Larry Landweber (on file with authors).
57. *An Interview with Peter Denning Conducted by Jeffrey R. Yost*, 61 (Apr. 10, 2013), https://conservancy.umn.edu/handle/11299/156515.
58. *CSNET—Computer Science Network*, LIVINGINTERNET, https://www.livinginternet.com/i/ii_csnet.htm (last visited Dec. 12, 2022).
59. Jay P. Kesan & Rajiv C. Shah, *Fool Us Once Shame on You—Fool Us Twice Shame on Us: What We Can Learn from the Privatizations of the Internet Backbone Network and the Domain Name System*, 79 WASH. UNIV. L. REV. 89, 103 (2001).
60. Interview with Brian Carpenter (on file with authors).
61. *The Birth of the Web*, CERN, https://home.cern/science/computing/birth-web (last visited Dec. 12, 2022).
62. Conversation in Steve Wolf's office, likely in early 1989 (on file with authors).
63. *A Brief History of NSF and the Internet*, NSF (Aug. 13, 2003), https://www.nsf.gov/news/news_summ.jsp?cntn_id=103050.
64. *From Supercomputing to the TeraGrid*, NSF (Apr. 19, 2006), https://www.nsf.gov/news/news_summ.jsp?cntn_id=106875.
65. Al Brenner, *The John von Neumann Computer Center: An Analysis, in* FRONTIERS OF SUPERCOMPUTING 472 (1983), https://publishing.cdlib.org/ucpressebooks/view?docId=ft0f59n73z&chunk.id=d0e15283.
66. *Harvard to Receive Supercomputer Access*, HARVARD CRIMSON (Feb. 27, 1985), https://www.thecrimson.com/article/1985/2/27/harvard-to-receive-supercomputer-access-pthe/.
67. Doug Gale, *The NSFNET and the Evolution of a National Research and Education Network*, SIGUCCS NEWSLETTER 8 (1991), https://dl.acm.org/doi/pdf/10.1145/122230.122231.
68. *The Internet: Changing the Way We Communicate*, NSF, 11 (2001), https://www.nsf.gov/about/history/nsf0050/pdf/internet.pdf.
69. Kevin Werbach, *Digital Tornado: The Internet and Telecommunications Policy*, FCC, at 13 (1997), https://www.fcc.gov/reports-research/working-papers/digital-tornado-internet-and-telecommunications-policy.

NOTES

70. *The Internet, supra* note 68, at 11.
71. *Id.*
72. *Dennis Jennings Testimonial,* TECH ARCHIVES (1987), https://techarchives.irish/how-the-internet-came-to-ireland-1987-97/dennis-jennings/.
73. *The Internet, supra* note 68, at 13.
74. *NSFNET Backbone Acceptable Use Policy,* http://www2.nmcc.edu/pages/information-technology/policies/nsfnet-aup.php (last visited Dec. 12, 2022).
75. *Id.*
76. *Id.*
77. *Id.*
78. DAVID MOWERY, IS THE INTERNET A US INVENTION?—AN ECONOMIC AND TECHNOLOGICAL HISTORY OF COMPUTER NETWORKING 1376, n.11 (2002), https://citeseerx.ist.psu.edu/viewdoc/download?doi=10.1.1.121.478&rep=rep1&type=pdf.
79. Public Law 102-476 (Oct. 23, 1992), https://www.govinfo.gov/link/statute/106/2300.
80. *Id.* at §4.
81. *How the US NSFNET Regional Academic Networks Evolved to Become the Global Internet (1985–1995),* INTERNET ARCHIVE, at 28, https://archive.org/stream/12streams-6/i2internethistory_TRANSCRIPT_djvu.txt.
82. *A Brief History of NSF and the Internet, supra* note 63.
83. Robert Zakon, *Hobbes' Internet Timeline,* RFC 2235 17 (November 1997), https://www.ietf.org/rfc/rfc2235.txt.
84. IBM network engineer at a SHARE meeting in about 1992. SHARE is an enterprise information technology user group that generally focuses on IBM technology and users.
85. Scott Bradner, *Application of Bridges and Routers: Network Design & Product Survey,* PROC. TWENTY-FIRST INTERNET ENGINEERING TASK FORCE (1991).
86. *Internetworking Technology Overview,* CISCO SYS. (1994), http://ciscoarchive.lunaimaging.com/MediaManager/srvr?mediafile=/MISC/CHMC~5~5/106/78-1249-01.pdf.
87. *Id.*
88. Stephen Davis, *Focus on NSF Supercomputing, in* COMPUTERS IN PHYSICS 22 (1987), https://aip.scitation.org/doi/pdf/10.1063/1.4903429.
89. Paul Ginsparg, *It Was Twenty Years Ago Today...*, https://ar5iv.labs.arxiv.org/html/1108.2700 (last visited Dec. 12, 2022).
90. Jennings, *supra* note 72.
91. ANDREW TANENBAUM, COMPUTER NETWORKS 46 (4th ed., 1996).
92. *See* ANDREW RUSSELL, OPEN STANDARDS AND THE DIGITAL AGE: HISTORY, IDEOLOGY, AND NETWORKS, chapter 7 (2014).
93. Proc. of the IEEE (Dec. 1983), https://ieeexplore.ieee.org/xpl/tocresult.jsp?isnumber=31332.
94. *Id.* (Richard desJardins, *Afterword: Evolving Towards OSI*).
95. *Id.* (Harold Folts, *Scanning the Issue*).
96. Vint Cerf & Kevin Mills, *Explaining the Role of GOSIP,* RFC 1169, at § 5 (Aug. 1990), https://www.ietf.org/rfc/rfc1169.txt.
97. *Id.*

98. FIPS Publication 146-1, *GOSIP*, §11, https://nvlpubs.nist.gov/nistpubs/Legacy/FIPS/fipspub146-1.pdf.

99. OSI Ref. Model, https://www.studocu.com/in/document/mahatma-gandhi-university/bachelor-of-computer-applications/osi-reference-model-computer-networks/37283283.

100. Proc. of the IEEE, *supra* note 93, at 4, 6, 7, 38, 101.

101. *See, e.g.*, Phill Gross's presentation on ISO Transition Planning during the 3rd IETF meeting, July 23–24, 1986, https://www.ietf.org/proceedings/03.pdf, pages at 149–162.

102. *See, e.g.*, the agenda for the 8th IETF meeting in November 2–4, 1987, at 5, https://www.ietf.org/proceedings/08.pdf.

103. Dennis Livingston, *Software Links Multivendor Networks*, MINI-MICRO SYSTEMS, at 49 (Mar. 1988), http://bitsavers.informatik.uni-stuttgart.de/magazines/Mini-Micro_Systems/198803.pdf.

104. *Id.* at 50.

105. *Id.* at 54.

106. TANENBAUM, *supra* note 91, at 48.

107. *Internet History of the 1990s*, Computer History Museum, https://www.computerhistory.org/internethistory/1990s/ (last visited Jan. 14, 2024).

108. *Id.*

109. *The Singularity Is Near*, http://www.singularity.com/charts/page79.html (last visited Dec. 12, 2022).

110. Quoted by Guy Alms, who was at the meeting where Medin made the statement, in a private communication.

111. IESG Past Members, https://www.ietf.org/about/groups/iesg/past-members/ (last visited Dec. 12, 2022).

112. Nat'l Info. Infrastructure Progress Rep. (Sept. 1993–1994), at 11, https://ntrl.ntis.gov/NTRL/dashboard/searchResults/titleDetail/PB94209988.xhtml#.

113. 59 Fed. Reg. 177 (Sept. 14, 1994), https://www.govinfo.gov/content/pkg/FR-1994-09-14/html/94-22685.htm.

114. 60 Fed. Reg. 93 (May 15, 1995), https://www.govinfo.gov/content/pkg/FR-1995-05-15/html/95-11917.htm.

115. *Id.*

116. TANENBAUM, *supra* note 91, at 43–44.

117. Edwin Mier, *Current OSI Products Need Time to Mature*, 7(36) NETWORK WORLD 1, 1 (1990).

118. I. Maathuis & W.A. Smit, *The Battle Between Standards: TCP/IP vs OSI Victory Through Path Dependency of by Quality?*, IEEE EXPLORE, at 168 (2003).

119. *Id.* at 169–72.

CHAPTER 3

1. Craig Timberg, *A Flaw in the Design*, WASH. POST (May 30, 2015), https://www.washingtonpost.com/sf/business/2015/05/30/net-of-insecurity-part-1/ ("David D. Clark, an MIT scientist whose air of genial wisdom earned him the nickname

NOTES 171

'Albus Dumbledore,' can remember exactly when he grasped the Internet's dark side. He was presiding over a meeting of network engineers when news broke that a dangerous computer worm—the first to spread widely—was slithering across the wires.").

2. *See A History of Internet Security*, https://www.washingtonpost.com/graphics/national/security-of-the-internet/history/ (last visited Dec. 13, 2021). For further discussion on BBN, see Chapter 1.

3. For an expanded treatment of this topic, see Scott J. Shackelford, *5 Milestones That Created the Internet, 50 Years After the First Network Message,* CONVERSATION (Oct. 25, 2019), https://theconversation.com/5-milestones-that-created-the-internet-50-years-after-the-first-network-message-123114.

4. *See* Vinton G. Cerf & Edward Cain, *The DoD Internet Architecture Model,* 7 COMPUTER NETWORKS 307, 307 (1983).

5. ANDREW W. MURRAY, THE REGULATION OF CYBERSPACE: CONTROL IN THE ONLINE ENVIRONMENT 44 (2006).

6. *Viruses/Contaminant/Destructive Transmission Statutes,* NAT'L CONF. ST. LEGISLATURES, http://www.ncsl.org/IssuesResearch/TelecommunicationsInformationTechnology/StateVirusandComputerContaminantLaws/tabid/13487/Default.aspx (last updated Feb. 14, 2012). For a deeper dive on this topic, see chap. 3 of SCOTT J. SHACKELFORD, MANAGING CYBER ATTACKS IN INTERNATIONAL LAW, BUSINESS AND RELATIONS: IN SEARCH OF CYBER PEACE (2014).

7. Timberg, *supra* note 1.

8. *Id.*

9. For an expanded treatment of this topic, see Scott J. Shackelford, *30 Years Ago, the World's First Cyberattack Set the Stage for Modern Cybersecurity Challenges,* CONVERSATION (Nov. 1, 2018), https://theconversation.com/30-years-ago-the-worlds-first-cyberattack-set-the-stage-for-modern-cybersecurity-challenges-105449.

10. *See Five Interesting Facts About the Morris Worm (for Its 25th Anniversary),* WELIVESECURITY (Nov. 6, 2013), https://www.welivesecurity.com/2013/11/06/five-interesting-facts-about-the-morris-worm-for-its-25th-anniversary/.

11. Index of /Docs-Free/Morris-Worm, http://www.foo.be/docs-free/morris-worm/ (last visited Dec. 14, 2021).

12. *See* Scott Bradner, *Worms, Viruses, etc.: Things That Go Bump on the Net,* https://www.sobco.com/presentations/1989-08-06-worms-viruses.pdf.

13. Timothy B. Lee, *How a Grad Student Trying to Build the First Botnet Brought the Internet to Its Knees,* WASH. POST (Nov. 1, 2013), https://www.washingtonpost.com/news/the-switch/wp/2013/11/01/how-a-grad-student-trying-to-build-the-first-botnet-brought-the-internet-to-its-knees/.

14. *See* BRENDAN P. KEHOE, ZEN AND THE ART OF THE INTERNET (1992), https://legacy.cs.indiana.edu/docproject/zen/zen-1.0_toc.html.

15. *See* Lee, *supra* note 13.

16. *See Five Interesting Facts About the Morris Worm, supra* note 10.

17. *The Morris Worm: The First Significant Cyber Attack,* https://www.thinkreliability.com/InstructorBlogs/blog-MorrisWorm.pdf (last visited Dec. 14, 2021).

18. *See* Lee, *supra* note 13.

19. *See* Nicole Perlroth, This Is How They Tell Me the World Ends: The Cyberweapons Arms Race (2021); Andy Greenberg, Sandworm: A New Era of Cyberwar and the Hunt for the Kremlin's Most Dangerous Hackers (2019); Kim Zetter, Countdown to Zero Day: Stuxnet and the Launch of the World's First Digital Weapon (2015).

20. *See* Tony Long, *July 26, 1989: First Indictment Under Computer Fraud Act*, Wired (July 26, 2011), https://www.wired.com/2011/07/0726first-computer-fraud-ind ictment/.

21. *See, e.g.*, Fred Kaplan, The secret History of Cyber War (2017); Stephen Levy, Hackers: Heroes of the Computer Revolution (2010).

22. *See, e.g.*, Bruce Middleton, A History of Cyber Security Attacks: 1980 to Present (2017).

23. *See* Paul Marks, *Dot-Dash-Diss: The Gentleman Hacker's 1903 Lulz*, New Scientist (Dec. 20, 2011), https://institutions.newscientist.com/article/mg21228440-700-dot-dash-diss-the-gentleman-hackers-1903-lulz/ (noting that Maskelyne "would use Morse code in 'mind-reading' magic tricks to secretly communicate with a stooge. He worked out how to use a spark-gap transmitter to remotely ignite gunpowder. And in 1900, Maskelyne sent wireless messages between a ground station and a balloon 10 miles away. But, as author Sungook Hong relates in the book Wireless, his ambitions were frustrated by Marconi's broad patents, leaving him embittered towards the Italian. Maskelyne would soon find a way to vent his spleen.").

24. *Id.*

25. *Id.*

26. *Id.*

27. *See, e.g.*, Karen Epper Hoffman, *Hacking for the Public Good*, GCN (Oct. 7, 2019), https://cyware.com/news/hacking-for-the-public-good-9961c316.

28. *Hacking the Holocaust*, Ava Ex Machina (Sept. 22, 2017), https://medium.com/@ silicondomme/hacking-the-holocaust-abcd332947ae.

29. *Id.*

30. John von Neumann, *theory of self-reproducing automata* (Arthur W. Burks ed., 1966), https://cba.mit.edu/events/03.11.ASE/docs/VonNeumann.pdf.

31. *See* Elizabeth McCracken, *Dial-Tone Phreak*, N.Y. Times (Dec. 30, 2007), https:// www.nytimes.com/2007/12/30/magazine/30joybubbles-t.html.

32. *Id.*

33. *See, e.g.*, Walter Isaacson, The Innovators: How a Group of Hackers, Geniuses, and Geeks Created the Digital Revolution 202–4 (2015).

34. *Id.* at 202.

35. *See* Katie Chadd, *The History of Cybersecurity*, Avast (Nov. 24, 2020), https://blog. avast.com/history-of-cybersecurity-avast.

36. The engineer Paul Baran from the RAND Corporation, who founded packet switching, among other things, made the case for an internetworked, decentralized communication system that could survive a nuclear attack. *Id.* at 238; Mark Humphrys, *History of the Internet*, https://computing.dcu.ie/~humphrys/Notes/Internet/history.html (last visited Dec. 14, 2021). As computers were reduced in size and made more accessible,

NOTES   173

storing data under lock and key became harder to justify economically as more and more people needed to access them, giving rise to passwords. Baran argued that direct, secure communication pathways could be set up to allow for multiple users to access the same data from different points along a packet-switched line, permitting more efficient use of scarce computing resources. *Id.*

37. *See* Cade Metz, *Why Do We Call Them Internet Packets? His Name Was Donald Davies*, WIRED (Sept. 10, 2012), https://www.wired.com/2012/09/donald-davies/.

38. Timberg, *supra* note 1.

39. *Id.*

40. *See* Lana Jelic, *This Is the First Ever Internet Message Sent*, TWEAKTOWN (Oct. 29, 2016), https://www.tweaktown.com/news/54662/first-internet-message-sent/index.html.

41. Timberg, *supra* note 1.

42. *See Tech Trivia*, GCN, https://gcn.com/blogs/tech-trivia/2011/08/first-computer-virus.aspx (last visited Dec. 14, 2021).

43. *See* Dakota Murphey, *A History of Information Security*, IFSEC GLOBAL (June 27, 2019), https://www.ifsecglobal.com/cyber-security/a-history-of-information-security/.

44. Timberg, *supra* note 1 ("Metcalfe posted a formal message to the ARPANET Working Group in December 1973 warning that it was too easy for outsiders to log on to the network. 'All of this would be quite humorous and cause for raucous eye winking and elbow nudging, if it weren't for the fact that in recent weeks at least two major serving hosts were crashed under suspicious circumstances by people who knew what they were risking; on yet a third system, the system wheel password was compromised—by two high school students in Los Angeles no less. . . . We suspect that the number of dangerous security violations is larger than any of us know [and] is growing.' ").

45. *Id.*

46. *See* SECURE COMPUTER SYSTEM: UNIFIED EXPOSITION AND MULTICS INTERPRETATION, U.S. AIR FORCE (Mar. 1976), https://csrc.nist.gov/csrc/media/publications/conference-paper/1998/10/08/proceedings-of-the-21st-nissc-1998/documents/early-cs-papers/bell76.pdf.

47. Theodore A. Linden, *Operating System Structures to Support Security and Reliable Software*, 8 ACM COMPUTING SURVEYS 409, 410 (1976).

48. *See, e.g.*, Tomas C. Greene, *Chapter One: Kevin's Story*, REGISTER (Jan. 13, 2003), https://www.theregister.com/2003/01/13/chapter_one_kevin_mitnicks_story/.

49. Timberg, *supra* note 1.

50. *Id.*

51. *Id.* (citing JANE ABBATE, INVENTING THE INTERNET [2000]).

52. *Id.*

53. *Id.*

54. *Id.*

55. *See A History of Internet Security*, *supra* note 2.

56. *See* Markus Pössel, *The Creation of the Internet, Privacy, and a Geek Joke: Interview with Vint Cerf*, SCI. AM. BLOG (Sept. 27, 2013), https://blogs.scientificamerican.

com/guest-blog/the-creation-of-the-internet-privacy-and-a-geek-joke-interv
iew-with-vint-cerf/ (noting that the British intelligence agency Government
Communications Headquarters [GCHQ] had in fact developed the same algo-
rithm some years earlier but kept it classified).

57. *Hangout with Vint Cerf,* https://www.youtube.com/watch?v=17GtmwyvmWE&t=
1381s (Apr. 2, 2014).

58. Troy Wolverton, *The Internet's "Father" Says It Was Born with Two Big Flaws,* Bus.
Insider (Jan. 20, 2019), https://www.businessinsider.com/google-vint-cerf-expla
ins-why-early-internet-lacked-security-and-room-2019-1.

59. However, national security clearly played a role, as illuminated by Steve Crocker,
a lifelong friend of Cerf who also worked on early networking technology for
DARPA, who has said, "Back in those days, the NSA still had the ability to visit a
professor and say, 'Do not publish that paper on cryptography.'" Ryan Singel, *Vint
Cerf: We Knew What We Were Unleashing on the World,* Wired (Apr. 23, 2012),
https://www.wired.com/2012/04/epicenter-isoc-famers-qa-cerf/.

60. Wolverton, *supra* note 58 (according to Cerf: "We might not have been able to
get much traction to adopt and use the network, because it would have been too
difficult.").

61. *Bob Kahn, the Bread Truck, and the Internet's First Communion, supra* note 87.

62. Cerf & Cain, *supra* note 4.

63. Singel, *supra* note 59.

64. Wolverton, *supra* note 58.

65. Dawn Parzych, *The Fallacy of Move Fast and Break Things,* DevOps (Feb. 11, 2020),
https://devops.com/the-fallacy-of-move-fast-and-break-things/.

66. Vint Cerf, *"Father of the Internet" Vint Cerf Says We Need to Be Less Naive If We're
Going to Fix It,* Quartz (Sept. 6, 2019), https://qz.com/1703322/internet-pioneer-
vint-cerf-on-what-we-need-to-do-to-fix-the-web/.

67. *See* Nicole Wetsman, *Hospitals Say Cyberattacks Increase Death Rates and Delay
Patient Care,* Verge (Sept. 27, 2021), https://www.theverge.com/2021/9/27/22696
097/hospital-ransomware-cyberattack-death-rates-patients.

68. *See Ukraine Cyber-Attack: Russia to Blame for Hack, Says Kyiv,* BBC (Jan. 14, 2022),
https://www.bbc.com/news/world-europe-59992531.

69. *See, e.g.,* Adam Segal, *Cyber Conflict After Stuxnet,* Council on Foreign Rel.
(June 27, 2016), https://www.cfr.org/blog/cyber-conflict-after-stuxnet.

70. *See, e.g.,* Alex Scroxton, *A Trillion Dollars Lost to Cyber Crime Every Year,* Comp.
Wkl'y (Dec. 7, 2020), https://www.computerweekly.com/news/252493157/A-trill
ion-dollars-lost-to-cyber-crime-every-year; *North Korea Hackers Stole $400m of
Cryptocurrency in 2021, Report Says,* BBC (Jan. 13, 2022), https://www.bbc.com/
news/business-59990477.

71. Timberg, *supra* note 1.

72. *Id.*

73. *Id.*

74. Fran Korten, *No Panaceas! Elinor Ostrom Talks with Fran Korten,* Shareable
(Mar. 18, 2010), https://www.shareable.net/no-panaceas-elinor-ostrom-talks-with-
fran-korten/.

NOTES 175

75. *See, e.g.*, Jacob Hoffman-Andrews, *Why Public Wi-Fi Is a Lot Safer than You Think*, EFF (Jan. 29, 2020), https://www.eff.org/deeplinks/2020/01/why-public-wi-fi-lot-safer-you-think.

76. *See* Scott J. Shackelford, *We Urgently Need a NTSB for Cybersecurity*, WALL ST. J. (Mar. 2, 2021), https://www.wsj.com/articles/we-urgently-need-a-ntsb-for-cybersecurity-11614726398.

77. *See, e.g.*, Scott J. Shackelford, *"NotPetya" Ransomware Attack Shows Corporate Social Responsibility Should Include Cybersecurity*, CONVERSATION (June 27, 2017), https://theconversation.com/notpetya-ransomware-attack-shows-corporate-social-responsibility-should-include-cybersecurity-79810.

78. SCOTT J. SHACKELFORD, THE INTERNET OF THINGS: WHAT EVERYONE NEEDS TO KNOW xvii (2020).

79. *Id.* (citing Neena Kapur, *The Rise of IoT Botnets*, AM. SEC. PROJECT [Jan. 13, 2017], https://www.americansecurityproject.org/the-rise-of-iot-botnets/ ("A bot is defined as a computer or internet-connected device that is infected with malware and controlled by a central command-and-control (C2) server. A botnet is the term used for all devices controlled by the C2 server, and they can be used to carry out large scale distributed denial of service (DDoS) attacks against websites, resulting in an overload of traffic on the website that renders it unusable."); Garrett M. Graff, *How a Dorm Room Minecraft Scam Brought Down the Internet*, WIRED (Dec. 13, 2017), https://www.wired.com/story/mirai-botnet-minecraft-scam-brought-down-the-internet/).

80. *The Internet's "Father" Says It Was Born with Two Big Flaws*, KNOWBE4 (Jan. 2020), https://blog.knowbe4.com/the-internets-father-says-it-was-born-with-two-big-flaws.

81. Created in 1981, IPv4 allowed the creation of more than four billion IP addresses, which early Internet architects thought would be sufficient for expansion. They were wrong. Europe started rationing IPv4 addresses in September 2012. *See, e.g.*, Robert McMillan, *Coming This Summer: U.S. Will Run Out of Internet Addresses*, WALL ST. J. (May 13, 2015), http://www.wsj.com/articles/coming-this-summer-u-s-will-run-out-of-internet-addresses-1431479401; John Brzozowski, *IPv4 Depletion Not the Beginning of the End, It's Just the End of the Beginning*, COMCAST (Sept. 24, 2015), http://corporate.comcast.com/comcast-voices/ipv4-depletion-not-the-beginning-of-the-end-its-just-the-end-of-the-beginning. Since 1992, engineers have been designing and attempting to implement a new system called IPv6, which features a larger address space—on the order of billions of IP addresses for each person alive in 2022. Architects again imagine this scale to be inexhaustible. Time will tell whether this view is accurate.

82. Encryption Backdoors, https://cs.stanford.edu/people/eroberts/cs181/projects/ethics-of-surveillance/tech_encryptionbackdoors.html (last visited Jan. 14, 2022).

83. *See* Parker Higgins, *On the Clipper Chip's Birthday, Looking Back on Decades of Key Escrow Failures*, EFF (Apr. 16, 2015), https://www.eff.org/deeplinks/2015/04/clipper-chips-birthday-looking-back-22-years-key-escrow-failures.

84. *Id.*

85. *See* Mitchell Clark, *Here's How the FBI Managed to Get into the San Bernardino Shooter's iPhone*, VERGE (Apr. 14, 2021), https://www.theverge.com/2021/4/14/22383957/fbi-san-bernadino-iphone-hack-shooting-investigation.

86. Grant Gross, *Cerf Calls Encryption Back Doors "Super Risky,"* COMPUTER WORLD (May 4, 2015), https://www.computerworld.com/article/2918394/cerf-calls-encryption-back-doors-super-risky.html.
87. Hay Newman, *Australia's Encryption-Busting Law Could Impact Global Privacy*, WIRED (Dec. 7, 2018), https://www.wired.com/story/australia-encryption-law-global-impact/.
88. *See* Andi Wilson Thompson, *The "Five Eyes" Still Can't See Straight on Encryption*, NEW AMERICA FOUND. (Oct. 15, 2020), https://www.newamerica.org/oti/blog/the-five-eyes-still-cant-see-straight-on-encryption/.
89. Robert E. Kahn, *The Role of Architecture in Internet Defense, in* AMERICA'S CYBER FUTURE: SECURITY AND PROSPERITY IN THE INFORMATION AGE 205, 208 (Kristin Lord & Travis Sharp eds., 2011).
90. *See* Jennifer L. Schenker, *Re-Engineering the Internet*, INNOVATOR (June 21, 2018), https://innovator.news/re-engineering-the-internet-2e0e0d331007.
91. VINT CERF & JOSEPH MENN, FATAL SYSTEM ERROR: THE HUNT FOR THE NEW CRIME LORDS WHO ARE BRINGING DOWN THE INTERNET 245 (2010).
92. Patricia Lyons & Robert Kahn, *Blocks as Digital Entities: A Standards Perspective*, 38 INFO. SERV. & USE 173 (2018), https://content.iospress.com/articles/information-services-and-use/isu180021.
93. *See* Adam Mann, *Google's Chief Internet Evangelist on Creating the Interplanetary Internet*, WIRED (May 6, 2013), https://www.wired.com/2013/05/vint-cerf-interplanetary-internet/.

CHAPTER 4

1. TIM BERNERS-LEE & MARK FISCHETTI, WEAVING THE WEB: THE ORIGINAL DESIGN AND ULTIMATE DESTINY OF THE WORLD WIDE WEB BY ITS INVENTOR (1999) (cover blurb by *TIME* magazine).
2. Nikhilesh Dholakia et al., *Internet Diffusion*, INTERNET ENCYCLOPEDIA (Feb. 2003), https://www.researchgate.net/publication/236784798_Internet_diffusion.
3. *See World Wide Web Timeline*, PEW RESEARCH CTR. (Mar. 11, 2014), https://www.pewresearch.org/internet/2014/03/11/world-wide-web-timeline/.
4. *See Ted Nelson Coins the Terms Hypertext, Hypermedia, and Hyperlink*, History of Information, https://www.historyofinformation.com/detail.php?id=830 (last visited Jan. 8, 2024).
5. BERNERS-LEE & FISCHETTI, *supra* note 1.
6. Sir Timothy Berners-Lee, *Longer Biography*, W3C https://www.w3.org/People/Berners-Lee/Longer.html (last visited Sept. 15, 2021).
7. *See The Birth of the Web*, CERN, https://home.cern/science/computing/birth-web (last visited Sept. 17, 2021).
8. *A Little History of the World Wide Web*, https://www.w3.org/People/Berners-Lee/History.html (last visited Sept. 17, 2021).
9. *Id.*
10. *Id.*

NOTES

11. Tim Berners-Lee, *Long Live the Web: A Call for Continued Open Standards and Neutrality*, Sci. Am. (Dec. 1, 2010), https://www.scientificamerican.com/article/long-live-the-web/.

12. Berners-Lee & Fischetti, *supra* note 5, at 61–62.

13. *Id.*

14. *See* Isaac Asimov, Foundation 7 (1966).

15. Berners-Lee & Fischetti, *supra* note 5, at 61–62 (emphasis added).

16. It became clear in the web's development that strings of digits were needed to be distinguished between addresses, and other resources and identifiers. What emerged was a system by which a URI identifies specific resources such as a page number in a book, while a URL "tells you how to access it" such as through HTTPS.
    See, e.g., Daniel Miessler, *What's the Difference Between a URI and a URL?*, https://danielmiessler.com/study/difference-between-uri-url/ (last visited Oct. 15, 2021) ("All URLs are URIs, but not all URIs are URLs.").

17. Berners-Lee, *Long Live the Web, supra* note 11.

18. Walter Isaacson, The Innovators: How a Group of Hackers, Geniuses, and Geeks Created the Digital Revolution 412 (2014).

19. *Id.*

20. *Id.*

21. *Id.*

22. *Id.*; Jack Goldsmith & Tim Wu, Who Controls the Internet? Illusions of a Borderless World 52 (2006).

23. Isaacson, *supra* note 19, at 413.

24. *Id.*

25. *Id.*

26. *Id.* at 414.

27. *Id.*

28. Berners-Lee, *Long Live the Web, supra* note 11.

29. *Id.*

30. Isaacson, *supra* note 18, at 413.

31. *Id.*

32. *Id.*

33. *See* CERN Convention (1953), https://home.cern/about/who-we-are/our-history (last visited Jan. 14, 2024).

34. *Id.*

35. *Id.*

36. *Id.*

37. *See, e.g.*, Pieter Verdegem, *Tim Berners-Lee's Plan to Save the Internet: Give Us Back Control of Our Data*, Conversation (Feb. 5, 2021), https://theconversation.com/tim-berners-lees-plan-to-save-the-internet-give-us-back-control-of-our-data-154 130; Scott J. Shackelford, Governing New Frontiers in the Information Age: Toward Cyber Peace (2020).

38. *See* Tim Gihring, *The Rise and Fall of the Gopher Protocol*, MinnPost, (Aug. 11, 2016), https://www.minnpost.com/business/2016/08/rise-and-fall-gopher-proto

col/?utm_source=thenewstack&utm_medium=website&utm_campaign=platf orm ("With minimal computer knowledge, you could download an interface—the Gopher—and begin searching the internet, retrieving information linked to it from anywhere in the world. It was like the Web but more straightforward, and it was already working.").

39. ISAACSON, *supra* note 18, at 413.

40. *Id.*

41. *See Software Release of WWW into Public Domain*, CERN DOCUMENT SERV. (Apr. 30, 1993), https://cds.cern.ch/record/1164399.

42. BERNERS-LEE & FISCHETTI, *supra* note 5, at 62.

43. *See* Marina Giampietro, *Twenty Years of a Free, Open Web*, CERN (Apr. 30, 2013), https://home.cern/news/news/computing/twenty-years-free-open-web.

44. *See, e.g., Mosaic Browser—History of the NCSA Mosaic Internet Web Browser*, HISTORY OF COMPUTING, https://history-computer.com/software/mosaic-brow ser-history-of-the-ncsa-mosaic-internet-web-browser/ (last updated July 15, 2021).

45. Global Digital Population as of January 2021, https://www.statista.com/statistics/ 617136/digital-population-worldwide/ (last visited Jan. 14, 2024).

46. *See, e.g.,* Sarah Phillips, *A Brief History of Facebook*, GUARDIAN (July 25, 2007), https://www.theguardian.com/technology/2007/jul/25/media.newmedia.

47. For an introduction to cyber sovereignty, see Adam Segal, *China's Vision for Cyber Sovereignty and the Global Governance of Cyberspace, in* AN EMERGING CHINA-CENTRIC ORDER: CHINA'S VISION FOR A NEW WORLD ORDER IN PRACTICE NBR SPECIAL REP. ed. Nadège Rolland #87 at 85, 86 (2020). *See also* Scott J. Shackelford & Frank W. Alexander, *China's Cyber Sovereignty: Paper Tiger or Rising Dragon?*, POL'Y F. (Jan. 12, 2018), https://www.policyforum.net/chinas-cyber-sovereignty/; Scott J. Shackelford et al., *Back to the Future of Internet Governance?*, 16 Geo. J. Int'l Aff. 83 (2015).

48. *See Visitor Fees in the National Park System: A Legislative and Administrative History*, NAT'L PARK SYS. https://www.nps.gov/parkhistory/online_books/mack intosh3/fees2.htm (last visited Oct. 19, 2021).

49. *See Highway History*, U.S. DEP'T TRANSPORTATION, https://www.fhwa.dot.gov/inf rastructure/tollroad.cfm (last visited Oct. 19, 2021).

50. *See* Adam Smeltz, *50 Years Ago, Touch-Tone Phones Began a Communication Revolution*, TRIBLIVE (Nov. 17, 2013), https://archive.triblive.com/news/50-years-ago-touch-tone-phones-began-a-communication-revolution/.

51. British Telecommunications v. Prodigy Communs., 217 F. Supp. 2d 399 (S.D.N.Y. 2002).

52. *"Tim Berners-Lee Explains What It Will Take to Make the Internet More Accessible*, ECONOMIST, https://www.dailymotion.com/video/x6fbn4k (last visited Sept. 14, 2021).

53. *See Internet Access Is a "Human Right,"* BBC (Mar. 8, 2010), http://news.bbc.co.uk/ 2/hi/technology/8548190.stm.

54. Vinton G. Cerf, *Internet Access Is Not a Human Right*, N.Y. TIMES (Jan. 4, 2012), http://www.nytimes.com/2012/01/05/opinion/internet-access-is-not-a-human-right.html.

NOTES

55. *See* David Rothkopf, *Is Unrestricted Internet Access a Modern Human Right?*, Foreign Pol'y (Feb. 2, 2015, 11:26 AM), http://foreignpolicy.com/2015/02/02/unrestricted-internet-access-human-rights-technology-constitution/.

56. *Id.*

57. Berners-Lee, *Long Live the Web, supra* note 11.

58. *See Internet Access Is a "Human Right," supra* note 54.

59. *See id.*

60. *See* Jack J. Barry, *COVID-19 Exposes Why Access to the Internet Is a Human Right*, OpenGlobalRights (May 26, 2020), https://www.openglobalrights.org/covid-19-exposes-why-access-to-internet-is-human-right/.

61. Berners-Lee, *supra* note 6.

62. *Id.*

63. 2018 Paris Call for Trust and Security in Cyberspace, https://pariscall.internatio nal/en/ (last visited Jan. 22, 2024).

64. Tim Berners-Lee, *Long Live the Web, supra* note 11 ("By 'open standards' I mean standards that can have any committed expert involved in the design, that have been widely reviewed as acceptable, that are available for free on the Web, and that are royalty-free (no need to pay) for developers and users.").

65. *Id.*

66. Giampietro, *supra* note 43.

67. Berners-Lee, *Long Live the Web, supra* note 11.

68. *See The WIRED Guide to Net Neutrality*, Wired (May 5, 2020), https://www.wired.com/story/guide-net-neutrality/.

69. *Id.*

70. Berners-Lee, *Long Live the Web, supra* note 11 ("Net neutrality maintains that if I have paid for an Internet connection at a certain quality, say, 300 Mbps, and you have paid for that quality, then our communications should take place at that quality. Protecting this concept would prevent a big ISP from sending you video from a media company it may own at 300 Mbps but sending video from a competing media company at a slower rate.").

71. *See* Michael Koziol, *Countries Around the World Tackled Net Neutrality in Different Ways*, IEEE Spectrum (Dec. 7, 2017), https://spectrum.ieee.org/countries-around-the-world-tackled-net-neutrality-in-different-ways; Sascha Meinrath & Nathalia Foditsch, *How Other Countries Deal With Net Neutrality*, Smithsonian Mag. (Dec. 15, 2017), https://www.smithsonianmag.com/innovation/how-other-countr ies-deal-net-neutrality-180967558/.

72. *See The WIRED Guide to Net Neutrality, supra* note 68.

73. *See, e.g.*, Charlie Terenzio, *How Walled Gardens Like Facebook Are Cannibalizing Media Publishers*, Forbes (June 6, 2018), https://www.forbes.com/sites/forbesco mmunicationscouncil/2018/06/06/how-walled-gardens-like-facebook-are-cannib alizing-media-publishers/?sh=5074a5615101.

74. *Id.*

75. *Id.*

76. Berners-Lee, *Long Live the Web, supra* note 11.

77. *Cf.* Chris Anderson & Michael Wolff, *The Web Is Dead. Long Live the Internet*, Wired (Aug. 17, 2010), https://www.wired.com/2010/08/ff-webrip/.
78. *See* John Divine, *The 10 Biggest Tech Companies in the World*, U.S. News & World Rep. (Sept. 20, 2021), https://money.usnews.com/investing/stock-market-news/sli deshows/most-valuable-tech-companies-in-the-world?slide=12.
79. *See* Caleb Silver, *The Top 25 Economies in the World*, Investopedia, (Dec. 24, 2020), https://www.investopedia.com/insights/worlds-top-economies/.
80. *See* Maya Villasenor, *Is Global Antitrust Up to the Challenge of Big Tech?*, Council on Foreign Rel. (Dec. 7, 2020), https://www.cfr.org/blog/global-antitrust-challe nge-big-tech.
81. *Id.*
82. Berners-Lee, *Long Live the Web*, *supra* note 11.
83. Chris Bing, *Trump Administration Wants Larger Role in Shaping International Data Laws*, Cyber Scoop (Jan. 29, 2018), https://www.cyberscoop.com/trump-intern ational-data-laws-rob-joyce/.
84. *See Russia: Growing Internet Isolation, Control, Censorship*, Human Rights Watch (June 18, 2020), https://www.hrw.org/news/2020/06/18/russia-growing-internet-isolation-control-censorship.
85. *See* Segal, *supra* note 48, at 86.
86. Andrea Little Limbago, *China's Global Charm Offensive*, War on the Rocks (Aug. 28, 2017), https://warontherocks.com/2017/08/chinas-global-charm-offensive/.
87. Segal, *supra* note 47.
88. Berners-Lee, *Long Live the Web*, *supra* note 11.
89. *Id.*
90. Berners-Lee, *supra* note 6.
91. *See Inventor of World Wide Web Receives ACM A.M. Turing Award*, Assoc. Computing Machinery (Apr. 4, 2017), https://awards.acm.org/about/2016-turing.
92. *Inrupt, Tim Berners-Lee's Solid, and Me*, Schneier on Sec. (Feb. 21, 2020), https://www.schneier.com/blog/archives/2020/02/inrupt_tim_bern.html.

Chapter 5

1. *Franklin and the Free Press*, Heritage Found. (Apr. 4, 2017), https://www.heritage.org/american-founders/commentary/franklin-and-the-free-press.
2. *Free Speech Quotes*, Pew Research Ctr. (Oct. 19, 2017), https://www.pewresearch.org/internet/2017/10/19/shareable-quotes-from-experts-on-the-future-of-truth-and-misinformation-online/.
3. *Online Use*, Pew Research Ctr. (Dec. 16, 1996), https://www.pewresearch.org/politics/1996/12/16/online-use/.
4. *Section 230*, EFF, https://www.eff.org/issues/cda230#:~:text=47%20U.S.C.,of%20the%20Communication%20Decency%20Act&text=Section%20230%20says%20t hat%20%22No,%C2%A7%20230).
5. Jeff Kosseff, The Twenty-Six Words That Created the Internet (2019).
6. Jeff Kosseff, *A User's Guide to Section 230, and a Legislator's Guide to Amending It (or Not)*, Berkeley J. L. & Tech. 1, 3 (2022).

NOTES

7. Kosseff, *supra* note 43, at 5; 361 U.S. 147, 148 (1959) (the ordinance stated that: "any person to have in his possession any obscene or indecent writing, [or] book . . . [i]n any place of business where . . . books . . . are sold or kept for sale.").

8. *Smith*, 361 U.S. at 151 (noting that to rule otherwise "may tend to work a substantial restriction on the freedom of speech and of the press.").

9. Kosseff, *supra* note 43, at 5.

10. *Id.* at 6 (citing Ginsberg v. New York, 390 U.S. 629, 646 [1968]).

11. 418 U.S. 87, 119 (1974).

12. Restatement (Second) of Torts, § 581. A comment elaborates that: a distributor "is not liable, if there are no facts or circumstances known to him which would suggest to him, as a reasonable man, that a particular book contains matter which upon inspection, he would recognize as defamatory." *Id.* at (e); Kosseff, *supra* note 43, at 7.

13. Kosseff, *supra* note 6, at 8.

14. *Id.*; Cubby v. CompuServe, 776 F. Supp. 135 (S.D.N.Y. 1991).

15. Kosseff, *supra* note 6, at 8.

16. Allen S. Hammond, *Private Networks, Public Speech: Constitutional Speech Dimensions of Access to Private Networks*, 55 U. PITT. L. R. 1085, 1117–18 (1994).

17. Kosseff, *supra* note 43, at 9.

18. *Id.*; Stratton Oakmont v. Prodigy Servs Co., Trial IAS Part 34, 1995 WL 323710, at 1 (May 24, 1995).

19. *See* Kosseff, *supra* note 43, at 10.

20. Brief of Chris Cox, Former Member of Congress and Co-Author of CDA Section 230, and NetChoice as Amici Curiae in Support of Defendants and Affirmance, at 2–3 (Sept. 27, 2018), https://netchoice.org/wp-content/uploads/2020/04/La-Park-Amicus-Brief-FILED.pdf.

21. Kosseff, *supra* note 6, at 11.

22. *Id.*

23. *Id.*

24. 104 Cong. (1995-96), 141 DAILY EDITION (Feb. 1, 1995), https://www.congress.gov/congressional-record/1995/02/01/senate-section/article/S1944-1 ("Once passed, our children and families will be better protected from those who would electronically cruise the digital world to engage children in inappropriate communications and introductions.").

25. *See* Tim Murphy, *How Newt Gingrich Saved Porn*, MOTHER JONES (Dec. 2, 2011), https://www.motherjones.com/politics/2011/12/how-newt-gingrich-saved-porn/.

26. Kosseff, *supra* note 6, at 11.

27. *See* Cox, Charles Christopher (1952-), U.S. House of Representatives, https://history.house.gov/People/Listing/C/COX,-Charles-Christopher-(C000830)/.

28. Ron Wyden, U.S. Senator, https://www.wyden.senate.gov/meet-ron (last visited Feb. 10, 2022).

29. KOSSEFF, *supra* note 5, at 69.

30. H.R. 1978 (104th Congress, 1995).

31. 47 U.S.C. § 230(c)(1); KOSSEFF, *supra* note 5.

32. Kosseff, *supra* note 6, at 12.

33. 47 U.S.C. § 230(e)(4).

34. 47 U.S.C. § 230(a)(4).
35. Kosseff, *supra* note 6, at 13 (citing INTERACTIVE WORKING GROUP REPORT, PARENTAL EMPOWERMENT, CHILD PROTECTION, AND FREE SPEECH IN INTERACTIVE MEDIA [1995]).
36. Kosseff, *supra* note 6, at 14.
37. Among other things, the bill did include several last-minute revisions, including the Hyde Amendment, which "extended the federal obscenity laws to cover interactive computer services" and was criticized, including by the Department of Justice. Robert Cannon, *The Legislative History of Senator Exon's Communications Decency Act: Regulating Barbarians on the Information Superhighway*, 49 FED. COMM. L.J. 51 (1996), https://www.cybertelecom.org/cda/cannon2.htm. Cox was likewise an early and public detractor of the CDA, saying that it was "doomed to fail because their idea of a Federal Internet Police will make the Keystone Cops look like crack crime fighters." *News Oct 95*, GOVTECH (Aug. 12, 2010), https://www.govtech.com/magazines/gt/news-oct-95.html.
38. *See* Christopher Cox, *The Origins and Original Intent of Section 230 of the Communications Decency Act*, UNIV. RICH. J. L. & TECH. (Aug. 27, 2020), https://jolt.richmond.edu/2020/08/27/the-origins-and-original-intent-of-section-230-of-the-communications-decency-act/.
39. Reno v. American Civil Liberties Union, 521 U.S. 844, 875 (1997).
40. *Id.* at 885. The public also almost immediately soured on the CDA, with hackers defacing the U.S. Department of Justice site in protest. *See Hackers Deface Web Site of U.S. Justice Department*, L.A. TIMES (Aug. 18, 1996), https://www.latimes.com/archives/la-xpm-1996-08-18-mn-35440-story.html ("The official World Wide Web site—https://www.usdoj.gov—was changed to read "United States Department of Injustice" next to a red, black, and white flag bearing a swastika. The text of the page was written over a background of gray swastikas, and at the top declared in red letters was "This page is in violation of the Communications Decency Act.").
41. Kosseff, *supra* note 6, at 4.
42. *Id.*; Danielle Keats Citron & Mary Anne Franks, *The Internet as a Speech Machine and Other Myths Confounding Section 230 Reform*, 2020 U. CHI. LEGAL F. 45, 46–47 (2020).
43. Kosseff, *supra* note 6, at 3.
44. *Id.* at 16.
45. *Id.* (citing Ian Ballon, *Zeran v. AOL: Why the Fourth Circuit Is Wrong*, J. INTERNET L. [1998]).
46. *Id.*
47. *Id.*
48. Zeran v. America Online, 129 F.3d 327, 329 (4th Cir. 1997).
49. Zeran v. America Online, 958 F. Supp. 1124, 1133 (E.D.Va. 1997).
50. Kosseff, *supra* note 6, at 17.
51. Eric Goldman, *The Ten Most Important Section 230 Rulings*, 20 TUL. J. TECH. & INTELL. PROP. 1, 3 (2017).

NOTES

52. Barnes v. Yahoo!, 570 F.3d 1096, 1105 (9th Cir. 2009) (holding that Section 230 "shields from liability all publication decisions, whether to edit, to remove, or to post, with respect to content generated entirely by third parties.").

53. Kosseff, *supra* note 6, at 21. Another example involves situations in which another claim is included in the dispute that does not require courts "to treat the interactive computer service providers as publishers," such as in a 2009 case involving a woman who had been promised by a Yahoo! executive that the firm would take down a post but then failed to do so. Barnes v. Yahoo!, 570 F.3d 1096, 1098 (9th Cir. 2009).

54. Kosseff, *supra* note 6, at 4.

55. Testimony of Jeff Kosseff, Assistant Professor, Cyber Science Department, U.S. Naval Academy before the Senate Commerce, Science, and Transportation Committee (July 28, 2020), https://www.commerce.senate.gov/services/files/444EFF87-84E3-46DB-B8DB-24DC9A424869.

56. *See* Kosseff, *supra* note 6, at 3 (citing Ali Sternburg, *Why Do So Many Section 230 Stories Contain Corrections*, Disruptive Comp. Project [Sept. 3, 2019]).

57. *Id.* (citing 1 Corrections, N.Y. Times [July 9, 2021]).

58. Order, Papataros v. Amazon.com, Civ. No. 17-9836 (D. N.J. Aug. 26, 2019).

59. *Id.* (citing Meghan Anand et al., *All the Ways Congress Wants to Change Section 230*, Slate [last updated June 2, 2021], https://slate.com/technology/2021/03/section-230-reform-legislative-tracker.html).

60. *Id.* at 30.

61. *Id.*

62. *See* United States v. Alvarez, 567 U.S. 709, 732 (2012) (plurality) ("The remedy for speech that is false is speech that is true. This is the ordinary course in a free society. The response to the unreasoned is the rational; to the uninformed, the enlightened; to the straight out lie, the simple truth.").

63. Ron Wyden, *I Wrote This Law to Protect Free Speech. Now Trump Wants to Revoke It*, CNN (June 9, 2020), https://www.cnn.com/2020/06/09/perspectives/ron-wyden-section-230/index.html?fbclid=IwAR1mOHxR8yebkuhMTiHv_qbM96ZboVarU146poPVrlPrZqkLVwRJeK519Fg.

64. Kosseff, *supra* note 6, at 31.

65. *Id.* at 34 (citing S. 299 [117th Congress]).

66. *Id.* at 35.

67. *Id.* at 37.

68. Malwarebytes v. Enigma Software Group, 141 S. Ct. 13 (2020) (statement of Thomas, J.).

69. *See, e.g.*, Tate Ryan-Mosley, *Four Ways the Supreme Court Could Reshape the Web*, MIT Tech. Rev. (Feb. 27, 2023), https://www.technologyreview.com/2023/02/27/1069146/four-ways-supreme-court-reshape-web-section-230-gonzalez-taamneh/.

70. Sanne Roeven, *Exploring the History of Section 230 of the Communications Decency Act of 1996*, Ballotpedia (June 8, 2021), https://news.ballotpedia.org/2021/06/08/exploring-the-history-of-section-230-of-the-communications-decency-act-of-1996/.

71. *Id.*

72. John Borland, *As Europe Went to the Polls, Cyber Election Efforts Paid Off*, SYMANTEC (June 5, 2019), https://www.symantec.com/blogs/election-security/europe-went-polls-cyber-election-efforts-paid (noting that Microsoft has also expressed its desire to join the Code).

73. Code of Practice on Disinformation, Eur. Comm'n, https://ec.europa.eu/digital-single-market/en/news/code-practice-disinformation (last visited Sept. 10, 2019).

74. *Id.*

75. *Id.*

76. Kevin Townsend, *Research Shows Twitter Manipulation in Weeks Before EU Elections*, SEC. WK. (May 28, 2019), https://www.securityweek.com/research-shows-twitter-manipulation-weeks-eu-elections.

77. Borland, *supra* note 72. This research was first published as Scott J. Shackelford et al., *Defending Democracy: Taking Stock of the Global Fight Against Digital Repression, Disinformation, and Election Insecurity*, 77 WASH. & LEE L. REV. 1747 (2021).

78. *See* Seth Copen Goldstein, *Solving the Political Ad Problem with Transparency*, CONVERSATION (Oct. 17, 2017), https://theconversation.com/solving-the-political-ad-problem-with-transparency-85366.

79. Australian Govt. Dep't of Foreign Aff. & Trade, Cyber Cooperation Program, Pacific Cyber Security Operational Network (PaCSON), https://dfat.gov.au/international-relations/themes/cyber-affairs/cyber-cooperation-program/Pages/pacific-cyber-security-operational-network-pacson.aspx.

80. Christchurch Call to Eliminate Terrorist and Violent Extremist Content Online (Christchurch Call) (2019), www.christchurchcall.com/ (last visited Apr. 8, 2020).

81. *About*, CHRISTCHURCH CALL, https://www.christchurchcall.com (last visited Jan. 8, 2024) ("Counter the drivers of terrorism through resilience, inclusiveness of societies, education and building media literacy. Ensure effective enforcement of applicable laws that prohibit terrorism in a manner consistent with the rule of law and international human rights law. Encourage media outlets to apply ethical standards when depicting terrorist content and support frameworks for reporting that do not amplify terrorist content. Consider appropriate and collaborative actions to prevent the use of online services to disseminate terrorist content." Commitments by online service providers: "Provide greater transparency in the setting of community standards. Enforce community standards in a manner consistent with human rights and fundamental freedoms. Implement effective measures to mitigate risks of terrorist content disseminated through live streaming. Implement regular and transparent public reporting."). For more on this topic, see Scott J. Shackelford, *Inside the Drive for Cyber Peace: Unpacking Implications for Practitioners and Policymakers*, 21 UNIV. OF CAL. DAVIS BUS. L.J. 285 (2021).

82. Daniel Funke & Daniela Flamini, *A Guide to Anti-Misinformation Actions Around the World*, Poynter, https://www.poynter.org/ifcn/anti-misinformation-actions/ (last visited Jan. 4, 2020).

83. *Id.*; *Tactics to Fight Disinformation in Thailand, Indonesia, Japan, the Philippines and India*, GLOBAL GROUND MEDIA (Apr. 23, 2019), https://www.globalgroundme

NOTES 185

dia.com/2019/04/23/tactics-to-fight-disinformation-in-thailand-indonesia-japan-the-philippines-and-india/.

84. Funke & Flamini, *supra* note 82.

85. *Id.*

86. *See* Samir Patil, *India Has a Public Health Crisis. It's Called Fake News.*, N.Y. TIMES (Apr. 29, 2019), https://www.nytimes.com/2019/04/29/opinion/india-elections-dis information.html.

87. *Microsoft Releases Digital Civility Index on Safer Internet Day*, MICROSOFT (Feb. 5, 2019), https://news.microsoft.com/en-in/microsoft-digital-civility-index-safer-internet-day-2019/.

88. *Child-Lifting Rumours Caused 69 Mob Attacks, 33 Deaths in Last 18 Months*, BUS. STANDARD (July 9, 2018), https://www.business-standard.com/article/current-affa irs/69-mob-attacks-on-child-lifting-rumours-since-jan-17-only-one-before-that-118070900081_1.html.

89. Funke & Flamini, *supra* note 82; Vindu Goel, *India Proposes Chinese-Style Internet Censorship*, N.Y. TIMES (Feb. 14, 2019), https://www.nytimes.com/2019/02/14/tec hnology/india-internet-censorship.html.

90. Reply Comments of Co-Authors of Section 230 of the Communications Act of 1934, FCC (Sept. 17. 2020), https://ecfsapi.fcc.gov/file/10917190303687/2020-09-17%20 Cox-Wyden%20FCC%20Reply%20Comments%20Final%20as%20Filed.pdf.

91. *See* Chris Cox, *Policing the Internet: A Bad Idea in 1996—and Today*, REALCLEARPOLITICS (June 25, 2020), https://www.realclearpolitics.com/articles/ 2020/06/25/policing_the_internet_a_bad_idea_in_1996_--_and_today.html.

92. Shane Tews, *The Past, Present, and Future of Section 230: Highlights from My Conversation with Former Rep. Chris Cox (R-CA)*, AM. ENT. INST. (Nov. 8, 2021), https://www.aei.org/technology-and-innovation/the-past-present-and-future-of-section-230-highlights-from-my-conversation-with-former-rep-chris-cox-r-ca/.

93. *See* Marc L. Caden & Stephanie E. Lucas, *Accidents on the Information Superhighway: On-Line Liability and Regulation*, 2 RICH. J.L. & TECH. 3 (1996), http://jolt.richmond.edu/jolt-archive/v2i1/caden_lucas.html#IIIC1.

94. Felix Gillette, *Section 230 Was Supposed to Make the Internet a Better Place. It Failed*, BLOOMBERG (Aug. 7, 2019), https://www.bloomberg.com/news/features/2019-08-07/section-230-was-supposed-to-make-the-internet-a-better-place-it-failed.

95. *See* Dylan Byers, *How Facebook and Twitter Decided to Take Down Trump's Accounts*, NBC NEWS (Jan. 14, 2021), https://www.nbcnews.com/tech/tech-news/ how-facebook-twitter-decided-take-down-trump-s-accounts-n1254317.

96. According to Notre Dame Professor Don Howard, different online communities "have a complicated topology and geography, with overlap, hierarchy, varying degrees of mutual isolation and mutual interaction. There are also communities of corporations or corporate persons, gangs of thieves, and . . . on scales small and large." Don Howard, *Civic Virtue and Cybersecurity* 15 (Working Paper, 2014). What is more, Professor Howard argues that these communities will each construct norms in their own ways, and at their own rates, but that this process has the potential to make positive progress toward addressing multifaceted issues such as enhancing cybersecurity. *Id.* at 22.

97. *See, e.g.*, Maya Villasenor, *Is Global Antitrust Up to the Challenge of Big Tech?*, CFR (Dec. 7, 2020), https://www.cfr.org/blog/global-antitrust-challenge-big-tech.

98. Hoaxy, https://hoaxy.osome.iu.edu/ (last visited Feb. 20, 2022).

99. Ben Popken, *Factory of Lies: Russia's Disinformation Playbook Exposed*, NBC News (Nov. 5, 2018), https://www.nbcnews.com/business/consumer/factory-lies-russia-s-disinformation-playbook-exposed-n910316.

100. *Id.*

101. *Id.*

CHAPTER 6

1. *FCC Announces Plan to Protect Access to an Open Internet*, GOOGLE PUBLIC POLICY BLOG (Sept. 21, 2009), https://publicpolicy.googleblog.com/2009/09/fcc-announces-plan-to-protect-access-to.html.

2. *See* Stephanie Mlot, *Comcast Is America's Most Hated Company*, PC MAG. (Jan. 12, 2017), https://www.pcmag.com/news/comcast-is-americas-most-hated-company.

3. *See* Arshad Mohammed, *SBC Head Ignites Access Debate*, WASH. POST, (Nov. 4, 2005), https://www.washingtonpost.com/archive/business/2005/11/04/sbc-head-ignites-access-debate/a21d3eaa-9579-4d8a-9473-cac0cbed540d/ ("Now what they would like to do is use my pipes free, but I ain't going to let them do that because we have spent this capital and we have to have a return on it. So there's going to have to be some mechanism for these people who use these pipes to pay for the portion they're using.").

4. *See, e.g.,* Thiago Garrett et al., *A Survey of Network Neutrality Regulations Worldwide*, 44 COMP. L. SEC. REV. (2022).

5. *See, e.g., 1990s Internet & World Wide Web*, https://nostalgiacafe.proboards.com/thread/133/1990s-internet-world-wide-web (last visited Mar. 4, 2022).

6. These included: ARPANET (ARPA), NSFNet (National Science Foundation), Esnet (Department of Energy), NASA Science Internet (NASA), etc.

7. MEERA GOYAL & NISHIT MATHUR, INFORMATION TECHNOLOGY & ITS IMPLICATIONS IN BUSINESS 269 (2021).

8. *See* Barry M. Leiner et al., *A Brief History of the Internet*, INTERNET SOC'Y (1997), https://drive.google.com/file/d/1_tQYRtg7wItHdukNAnxYEGemPJZ3By9Z/view.

9. *Id.*

10. *A Timeline of NSF History*, NSF, https://nsf.gov/about/history/timeline80s.jsp#1980s (last visited June 1, 2022).

11. *See Vint Cerf—Co-Creator of the Internet and Email*, ABILITY MAG., https://abilitymagazine.com/vint-cerf-co-creator-of-the-internet-and-email/.

12. *Id.*

13. *Id.*

14. Scott Bradner, *Forks: Decisions That Got Us the Internet We Have*, ISOC TECH SERIES (June 25, 2020).

15. Steve Case, Encyclopedia Britannica, https://www.britannica.com/biography/Steve-Case (last visited May 29, 2022).

NOTES

16. *A Brief Guide to the Tumultuous 30-Year History of AOL*, Time (May 22, 2015), https://time.com/3857628/aol-1985-history/.
17. *Id.*
18. *See* NSFNET Bringing the World of Ideas Together (1992) ("The National Science Foundation Network (NSFNET) provides the opportunity for students, scientists, business people—individuals from literally all walks of life—to access resources ranging from electronic community bulletin boards to supercomputers scattered across the continent and around the world. The NSFNET offers access to the nation's largest and fastest network for research, education, and technology transfer."); *see also* Leiner et al., *supra* note 8, at 11: ("NSF's privatization policy culminated in April, 1995, with the defunding of the NSFNET Backbone. The funds thereby recovered were (competitively) redistributed to regional networks to buy national-scale Internet.").
19. *See* Jason Kaiaran, *By the Numbers: AOL Then and Now*, Quartz (May 12, 2015), https://qz.com/403266/by-the-numbers-aol-then-and-now/; *AOL Still Has 1.5 Million Subscribers, Somehow*, Input Mag. (May 2021), https://www.inputmag.com/tech/aol-still-has-1-point-5-million-subscribers-somehow#:~:text=Still%20a%20moneymaker%20%E2%80%94%20Despite%20years,AOL%20Advantage%2C%20according%20to%20CNBC.
20. *See* Guise Bule, *A Short History of the Internet*, ItSec, https://itsec.group/blog-post-short-history-of-the-internet.html; *The Complete List of Internet Companies in the US*, BroadbandNow, https://broadbandnow.com/All-Providers (last visited June 3, 2022).
21. *See, e.g.,* Lawrence Lessig, *Voice-Over-IP's Unlikely Hero*, Wired (May 1, 2005), https://www.wired.com/2005/05/voice-over-ips-unlikely-hero/.
22. Leiner et al., *supra* note 8; B. Kahlin, *The Commercialization and Privatization of the Internet*, RFC 1192 (Nov. 1990), https://www.rfc-editor.org/rfc/rfc1192.
23. Tim Wu, *Network Neutrality FAQ*, http://www.timwu.org/network_neutrality.html (last visited June 1, 2022). For a deeper academic analysis, see Tim Wu, Network Neutrality, Broadband Discrimination, 2 J. Telecom. & High Tech. L. 141, 142 (2003).
24. Tyler Elliott Bettiylon, *Network Neutrality: A History of Common Carrier Laws 1884–2018*, Medium (Dec. 12, 2017), https://medium.com/@TebbaVonMathenstien/network-neutrality-a-history-of-common-carrier-laws-1884-2018-2b592f22ed2e.
25. *See* Garrett, *supra* note 4.
26. *Id.*
27. *Id.* (citing Federal Communications Commission [FCC], Appropriate Framework for Broadband Access to the Internet Over Wireline Facilities [2005], https://www.fcc.gov/document/appropriate-framework-broadband-access-internet-over-wireline-0).
28. *Id.*
29. Powell Urges Industry to Adopt "Net Freedom" Principles, FCC Press Release (Feb. 9, 2004), https://www.fcc.gov/document/powell-urges-industry-adopt-net-freedom-principles.

30. *Id.* (citing Federal Communications Commission [FCC], Preserving the Open Internet Final Rule (2010), https://www.fcc.gov/document/preserving-open-internet-final-rule).

31. *Id.* (citing Letter to FCC Chairman Tom Wheeler [2014], https://www.wyden.senate.gov/imo/media/doc/OpenInternetInvestorsLetter.pdf).

32. *Id.* (citing Federal Communications Commission [FCC], FCC Releases Open Internet Order [2015], https://www.fcc.gov/document/fcc-releases-open-internet-order).

33. *Id.* (noting that the revised net neutrality rules included: "(i) No blocking: consumers must have access to all legal content in the Internet. (ii) No throttling: ISPs cannot degrade traffic based on origin, destination, or content, and cannot prioritize their own services. (iii) No paid prioritization: ISPs cannot be paid (directly or indirectly) in order to prioritize certain types of traffic. (iv) Transparency: consumers must be fully informed about the services they are contracting.").

34. *Id.* (citing Federal Communications Commission [FCC], Statement of Chairman Pai on Revoking Midnight Regulations [2017], https://www.fcc.gov/document/statement-chairman-pai-revoking-midnight-regulations).

35. *See, e.g.,* T. J. York, *FCC's Simington Welcomes Congressional Action on Net Neutrality,* Broadband Breakfast (June 1, 2022), https://broadbandbreakfast.com/2022/06/fccs-simington-welcomes-congressional-action-on-net-neutrality/.

36. *See Net Neutrality 2021 Legislation,* Nat'l Conf. St. Legislatures, https://www.ncsl.org/research/telecommunications-and-information-technology/net-neutrality-2021-legislation.aspx (last visited June 2, 2022) ("Sixteen states have introduced net neutrality legislation in the 2021 legislative session.").

37. *See* Garrett, *supra* note 4.

38. Zero-rating refers to the practice of permitting free/unlimited use of specific services, which does not then count toward a subscriber's data limits. *See* Davide Banis, *How "Zero-Rating" Offers Threaten Net-Neutrality in the Developing World,* Forbes (Feb. 18, 2019), https://www.forbes.com/sites/davidebanis/2019/02/18/how-zero-rating-offers-threaten-net-neutrality-in-the-developing-world/?sh=2f338fd33b41.

39. *Id.*

40. *Id.*

41. *Id.* (noting that "[i]t is easy to use slicing to break NN principles, by downgrading/upgrading the QoS settings of each slice. It is thus important to monitor and detect whether slicing is promoting unfair traffic differentiation.").

42. *See* Sam Sabin, *About Half the Public Thinks Local Governments Should Be Able to Pursue Their Own Broadband Network Build-Outs,* Morning Consult (Apr. 26, 2021), https://morningconsult.com/2021/04/26/municipal-broadband-private-isps-poll/.

43. *Id.*

44. *See* Floyd Norris, *Goodbye to Reforms of 2002,* N.Y. Times (Nov. 5, 2009), https://www.nytimes.com/2009/11/06/business/06norris.html; Rachel A. Elkins, *From Independence to Regulation: A Look Into Major Accounting Scandals and the Changes Implemented by the Sarbanes-Oxley Act,* Univ. Tenn. Research &

NOTES

CREATIVE EXCHANGE (2014), https://trace.tennessee.edu/cgi/viewcontent.cgi?arti
cle=2767&context=utk_chanhonoproj.

45. *The WorldCom Scandal*, INT'L BANKER (Sept. 29, 2021), https://internationalban
ker.com/history-of-financial-crises/the-worldcom-scandal-2002/.

CHAPTER 7

1. Mitch Kapor: Politics is Architecture, and Architecture is Politics, https://worlda
rchitecture.org/architecture-news/pzpvn/mitch-kapor-politics-is-architecture-
and-architecture-is-politics.html. Selections of this chapter were first published in
chap. 1 of SCOTT J. SHACKELFORD, MANAGING CYBER ATTACKS IN INTERNATIONAL
LAW, BUSINESS AND RELATIONS: IN SEARCH OF CYBER PEACE (2014).

2. IP addresses are made up of 32-bit binary strings. "Bits" are the 1s and 0s (electronic
pulses and nonpulses) of computer-speak. An IPv4 address is the equivalent rep-
resentation of a 32-bit binary string, which is split into four 8-bit sequences known
as "bytes" that also correspond to one of the decimal strings. *Internet History*,
COMPUTER HIST. MUSEUM, http://www.computerhistory.org/internet_history/
#1964 (last visited Jan. 24, 2021); *Internet Protocol, DARPA Internet Program
Protocol Specification*, UNIV. SOUTHERN CAL. INFO. SCI. INST. (Sept. 1981), http://
tools.ietf.org/html/rfc791. IPv6 addresses are 128 bits represented as eight 4-digit
hex values (each of which represents 16 bits).

3. WILLIAM GIBSON, NEUROMANCER 52 (1984).

4. *See, e.g.*, John Perry Barlow, *Declaration of Cyberspace Independence* (Feb. 8, 1996),
https://projects.eff.org/~barlow/Declaration-Final.html. For a good overview, see
JACK GOLDSMITH & TIM WU, WHO CONTROLS THE INTERNET? ILLUSIONS OF A
BORDERLESS WORLD (2008).

5. Jonathan Masters, *What Is Internet Governance?*, CFR (Apr. 23, 2014), https://www.
cfr.org/backgrounder/what-internet-governance.

6. Larry Downes, *Requiem for Failed UN Telecom Treaty: No One Mourns the WCIT*,
FORBES (Dec. 17, 2012), http://www.forbes.com/sites/larrydownes/2012/12/17/no-
one-mourns-the-wcit/.

7. About, Web 3 Foundation, https://web3.foundation/about/ (last visited June
23, 2022).

8. *Lawrence Roberts*, INTERNET HALL OF FAME, https://www.internethalloffame.org/
inductees/lawrence-roberts (last visited June 23, 2022).

9. *See* Giovanni Navarria, *How the Internet Was Born: The Network Begins to Take
Shape*, CONVERSATION (Oct. 30, 2016), https://theconversation.com/how-the-inter
net-was-born-the-network-begins-to-take-shape-67904.

10. *Id.*

11. A variety of RFCs are relevant to understanding IANA functions: the first RFC,
issued on April 7, 1969, with Jon Postel as the series editor and relating to host software, through to RFC 717 from July 1976, which deals with assigned network numbers and is still being regularly updated. But there were other important items to
assign, including IP addresses and top-level domains, the former being defined by

RFC 791 in September 1981 involving a 32-bit IP address. Later RFCs accomplished other things, such as RFC 1591, which adopted the DNS structure itself.

12. Anyone who wants to can join the IETF at any time for free, and everyone who is a "member" is a volunteer who is welcome to join in the discussion and submit a proposal for a new standard or an alteration to an existing standard in the form of an RFC.

13. *Sci/Tech "God of the Internet" Is Dead*, BBC News, Oct. 19, 1998, http://news.bbc.co.uk/2/hi/science/nature/196487.stm.

14. *Heavenly Father of the NET*, Economist (Summer 1997).

15. *See* David G. Post, In Search of Jefferson's Moose: Notes on the State of Cyberspace 148 (2009).

16. Jon Postel, Internet Hall of Fame, https://internethalloffame.org/inductees/jon-postel (last visited June 25, 2022).

17. *Id.*

18. *Id.* at 100–101. Domain requirements were established by RFC 920, including for dot-gov, dot-edu, dot-com, and dot-mil.

19. *See* Post, *supra* note 15, at 144.

20. *First New Generic Top-Level Domains Delegated*, ICANN (Oct. 23, 2013), http://www.icann.org/en/news/press/releases/release-23oct13-en; *New Generic Top-Level Domains*, ICANN, http://newgtlds.icann.org/en/announcements-and-media/video/overview-en (last visited Jan. 24, 2014). There are more country codes than countries because country code TLDs are sometimes given to disputed territories. For a list of current TLDs, see *Root Zone Database*, IANA, http://www.iana.org/domains/root/db/ (last visited Sept. 23, 2012).

21. Charles M. Kozierok, The TCP/IP Guide: A Comprehensive, Illustrated Internet Protocols Reference 887 (2005).

22. *See* Post, *supra* note 15, at 148. How a DNS query is resolved is best illustrated through an example. Suppose a host computer's resolver queries www.indiana.edu, which is located at the address 12.34.56.78. The resolver will first query the authoritative root name servers for the IP address of the TLD DNS servers, and then it will query the TLD DNS server to get the IP address of the subdomain DNS servers, etc., until it identifies the target computer itself. These results can be "cached," or put into short-term memory, to help speed the process along. Id. at 152. For each level in the DNS name, there are "authoritative" servers, which have the most updated versions of address records for their indexes, and there are servers that periodically receive updated information from authoritative servers and cache answers that they can pass along in response to client queries.

23. The name servers that point to the TLD name servers (many thousands of them) are coordinated by ICANN. The name servers for each of the TLDs are run by separate organizations, and the name servers for the second-level domains are run by other organizations, such as Indiana University for www.iu.edu and Harvard University www.harvard.edu.

24. *See id.* at 148; J. Klensin, Role of the Domain Name System, IETF RFC 3467 (2003), http://tools.ietf.org/html/rfc3467#page-4.

NOTES

25. The root is a text file that lists all of the TLDs and the IP addresses of their authoritative name servers. When compressed, the file is a mere 20 kilobytes—about the size of a long email—but contains "the Internet's most strategic point of control." Craig Simon, *The Privatization of the Internet's Domain Name System and the Implications for Global Politics*, ROOTS OF POWER (2008), https://www.scribd.com/document/58805571/Launching-the-DNS-War-Dot-Com-Privatization-and-the-Rise-of-Global-Internet-Governance. TLDs exist only because the root says they do. *See DNS Root Name Servers FAQ*, INTERNET SOC'Y, http://www.isoc.org/briefings/020/ (last visited Nov. 1, 2012).

26. *See* POST, *supra* note 15, at 152.

27. ANDREW W. MURRAY, THE REGULATION OF CYBERSPACE: CONTROL IN THE ONLINE ENVIRONMENT 92, 234 (2006).

28. KATHY BOWREY, LAW AND INTERNET CULTURES 56 (2005).

29. *See* ANDREW W. MURRAY, THE REGULATION OF CYBERSPACE: CONTROL IN THE ONLINE ENVIRONMENT 91 (2006).

30. *See* MILTON L. MUELLER, RULING THE ROOT: INTERNET GOVERNANCE AND THE TAMING OF CYBERSPACE 90–92 (2002) (chronicling the growth of IETF meetings from 50 people in 1987 to more than 650 in 1992).

31. *See* MURRAY, *supra* note 27, at 91.

32. *See* Brian Carpenter, *The Internet Engineering Task Force: Overview, Activities, Priorities*, INTERNET SOC'Y (Feb. 10, 2006), http://www.isoc.org/isoc/general/trustees/docs/Feb2006/IETF-BoT-20060210.pdf; *Overview of the IETF*, INTERNET ENG'G TASK FORCE, http://www.ietf.org/old/2009/overview.html (last visited Mar. 28, 2013).

33. BOWREY, *supra* note 28, at 56.

34. *Id.*

35. IETF Meetings, https://www.ietf.org/how/meetings/past/ (last visited June 26, 2022).

36. *China Again Signals Desire to Shape IPv6 Standards*, REGISTER (Apr. 26, 2022), https://www.theregister.com/2022/04/26/china_ipv6_plan/.

37. *See* Hans Klein, *ICANN and Internet Governance: Leveraging Technical Coordination to Realize Global Public Policy*, INFO. SOC'Y 193, 198–99 (2002).

38. *See* POST, *supra* note 15, at 149.

39. *Id.* at 149–52.

40. JACK GOLDSMITH & TIM WU, WHO CONTROLS THE INTERNET?: ILLUSIONS OF A BORDERLESS WORLD 36, 58 (2006).

41. *See* JOYCE REYNOLDS & JON POSTEL, NETWORK WORKING GROUP, IETF RFC 1000 (1987), http://www.rfc-editor.org/rfc/rfc1000.txt.

42. MUELLER, *supra* note 30, at 89.

43. *Id.* at 90–97.

44. *Id.* at 93.

45. *Id.* at 95–96.

46. GOLDSMITH & WU, *supra* note 40, at 37.

47. *See* MURRAY, *supra* note 29, at 104–7.

48. *See* Sai Anand Balu, *Controller of Internet Names Is Sued*, NANDO (Feb. 28, 1997).

49. Scott O. Bradner, *Institutionalizing the IANA Functions to Deliver a Stable and Accessible Global Internet for Mission Critical Business Traffic and Transactions*, HARVARD UNIV., https://www.sobco.com/presentations/iana.01.pdf (last visited Jan. 14, 2024).

50. GOLDSMITH & WU, *supra* note 40, at 42–44.

51. *See, e.g.*, Ted Bridis, *Internet Reconfiguration Turns Out to Be Rogue*, DAILY NEWS (Feb. 5, 1998).

52. *Id.* at 147–50; MUELLER, *supra* note 30, at 151.

53. MUELLER, *supra* note 30, at 170–72.

54. *Id.* at 170–74.

55. *See* MURRAY, *supra* note 29, at 106; ICANN Bylaws, ICANN, http://www.icann.org/en/about/governance/bylaws (last visited Oct. 15, 2021).

56. *See* MUELLER, *supra* note 30, at 175, 183–84; *Management of Internet Names and Addresses*, U.S. DEP'T COM. (1998), https://www.federalregister.gov/documents/1998/06/10/98-15392/management-of-internet-names-and-addresses.

57. ROBERT K. KNAKE, COUNCIL ON FOREIGN RELATIONS, INTERNET GOVERNANCE IN AN AGE OF CYBER INSECURITY 5 (2010), http://i.cfr.org/content/publications/atta chments/Cybersecurity_CSR56.pdf.

58. *See* MUELLER, *supra* note 30, at 181.

59. Vint Cerf, I REMEMBER IANA, IETF RFC 2468 (Oct. 17, 1998), www.ietf.org/rfc/rfc2468.txt.

60. *See* Peter Loshin, *What Is ICANN?*, https://www.techtarget.com/whatis/definition/ICANN-Internet-Corporation-for-Assigned-Names-and-Numbers (last visited June 30, 2022).

61. *See, e.g.*, Jason Kelley & Mitch Stoltz, *After Nonprofits Protest at ICANN, California's Attorney General Steps into the .ORG Battle*, EFF (Jan. 31, 2020), https://www.eff.org/deeplinks/2020/01/after-nonprofits-protest-icann-californias-attorney-gene ral-steps-org-battle.

62. *Belt and Road Initiative*, WORLD BANK (Mar. 28, 2018), https://www.worldbank.org/en/topic/regional-integration/brief/belt-and-road-initiative.

63. *See* Robert Greene & Paul Triolo, *Will China Control the Global Internet Via its Digital Silk Road?*, CARNEGIE ENDOWMENT (May 8, 2020), https://carneg ieendowment.org/2020/05/08/will-china-control-global-internet-via-its-digi tal-silk-road-pub-81857.

64. *Id.*

65. *Id.*

66. Konstantinos Komaitis, *EU Internet Regulations Are Falling into the "China Trap,"* POLITICO (June 28, 2022), https://www.politico.eu/article/eu-internet-regulation-falling-into-china-trap/.

67. *Id.*

68. For more on this topic, see Scott J. Shackelford, *The Coming Age of Internet Sovereignty?*, *in* OPPOSING VIEWPOINTS: INTERNET CENSORSHIP (Lynn M. Zott ed., 2014).

NOTES

69. James Ball, *Russia Is Risking the Creation of a "Splinternet"—and It Could Be Irreversible*, MIT Tech. Rev. (Mar. 17, 2022), https://www.technologyreview.com/2022/03/17/1047352/russia-splinternet-risk/ (ICANN rejected the proposal, arguing that "[T]he internet is a decentralized system. No one actor has the ability to control it or shut it down.").

70. *Id.*

71. Vint Cerf, *Remembering Jon: Looking Beyond the Decade*, ICANN (Oct. 1, 2008), https://www.icann.org/en/blogs/details/remembering-jon-looking-beyond-the-decade-1-10-2008-en.

72. Susan D'Agostino, *To Boldly Go Where No Internet Protocol Has Gone Before*, Quant Mag. (Oct. 21, 2020), https://www.quantamagazine.org/vint-cerfs-plan-for-building-an-internet-in-space-20201021/.

73. *Id.*

Chapter 8

1. Jeff Kosseff, *A User's Guide to Section 230, and a Legislator's Guide to Amending It (Or Not)*, 37 Berkeley J. L. & Tech. 1, 3 (2022).

2. *Id.*

3. *Jonathan B. Postel: 1943–1998*, USC News (Feb. 1, 1999), https://news.usc.edu/9329/Jonathan-B-Postel-1943-1998/.

4. *See, e.g.*, Openness in Research, Stanford University, https://doresearch.stanford.edu/policies/research-policy-handbook/conduct-research/openness-research (last visited July 7, 2022).

5. *See, e.g.*, Kate Fazzini, *In a Decade of Cybersecurity Alarms, These Are the Breaches That Actually Mattered*, CNBC (Dec. 23, 2019), https://www.cnbc.com/2019/12/23/stuxnet-target-equifax-worst-breaches-of-2010s.html.

6. Felix Gillette, *Section 230 Was Supposed to Make the Internet a Better Place. It Failed*, Bloomberg (Aug. 7, 2019), https://www.bloomberg.com/news/features/2019-08-07/section-230-was-supposed-to-make-the-internet-a-better-place-it-failed.

7. *See* Aaron C. Davis & Marina Lopes, *How the FAA Allows Jetmakers to "Self Certify" That Planes Meet U.S. Safety Requirements*, Wash. Post (Mar. 15, 2019), https://www.washingtonpost.com/investigations/how-the-faa-allows-jetmakers-to-self-certify-that-planes-meet-us-safety-requirements/2019/03/15/96d24d4a-46e6-11e9-90f0-0ccfeec87a61_story.html.

8. *See* Zeynep Tufekci, *Zuckerberg's So-Called Shift Toward Privacy*, N.Y. Times (Mar. 7, 2019), https://www.nytimes.com/2019/03/07/opinion/zuckerberg-privacy-facebook.html.

9. *See, e.g.*, Amit Narang, *Corporate Self-Regulation Is Failing*, Hill (Mar. 28, 2019), https://thehill.com/blogs/congress-blog/the-administration/436328-corporate-self-regulation-is-failing/.

10. *See* Jan Wolfe, *Explainer: Should Big Tech Fear U.S. Antitrust Enforcers?*, Reuters (June 5, 2019), https://www.reuters.com/article/us-tech-antitrust-legal-explainer/explainer-should-big-tech-fear-u-s-antitrust-enforcers-idUSKCN1T62K3.

11. *See, e.g.*, Kenneth J. Arrow, Robert O. Keohane, & Simon A. Levin, *Elinor Ostrom: An Uncommon Woman for the Commons*, 109 PNAS 13135–36 (July 30, 2012), https://www.pnas.org/doi/10.1073/pnas.1210827109.

12. *See, e.g.*, Scott J. Shackelford, Amanda Craig, & Janine Hiller, *Proactive Cybersecurity: A Comparative Industry and Regulatory Analysis*, 18 Am. Bus. L.J. 721 (2015).

13. Michael D. McGinnis, *An Introduction to IAD and the Language of the Ostrom Workshop: A Simple Guide to a Complex Framework*, 39 Pol'y Stud. J. 163, 171–72 (2011), http://php.indiana.edu/~mcginnis/iad_guide.pdf.

14. Michael D. McGinnis, *Costs and Challenges of Polycentric Governance: An Equilibrium Concept and Examples from U.S. Health Care*, Workshop on Self-Governance, Polycentricity, and Development, at 1–2 (Conference on Self-Governance, Polycentricity, and Development, Renmin University, in Beijing, China, 2011), http://php.indiana.edu/~mcginnis/Beijing_core.pdf.

15. *See* Elinor Ostrom, *Polycentric Systems as One Approach for Solving Collective-Action Problems* 1–2 (Ind. Univ. Workshop in Pol. Theory and Pol'y Analysis, Working Paper Series No. 08–6, 2008), http://dlc.dlib.indiana.edu/dlc/bitstream/handle/10535/4417/W08-6_Ostrom_DLC.pdf.

16. Robert O. Keohane & David G. Victor, *The Regime Complex for Climate Change*, 9 Persp. on Pol. 7, 15 (2011).

17. Fikret Berkes, Coasts for People: Interdisciplinary Approaches to Coastal and Marine Resource Management 129 (2015).

18. *Id.*

19. Keohane & Victor, *supra* note 16, at 7 (arguing that "the structural and interest diversity inherent in contemporary world politics tends to generate the formation of a regime complex rather than a comprehensive, integrated regime.").

20. *See, e.g.*, Scott J. Shackelford & Scott O. Bradner, *Have You Updated Your Toaster? Transatlantic Approaches to Governing the Internet of Everything*, 72 Hastings L.J. 628 (2021); Scott J. Shackelford, *Governing the Internet of Everything*, 37 Cardozo Arts & Entertainment L.J. 701 (2019).

21. *See* Daniel H. Cole, *Advantages of a Polycentric Approach to Climate Change Policy*, 5 Nature Climate Change 114–118 (Jan. 28, 2015), https://www.nature.com/articles/nclimate2490.

22. *See* Sinéad Baker, *FAA Boss Says It Let Boeing Partly Self-Regulate the Software Thought to Be Behind Both Fatal 737 Max Crashes*, Bus. Insider (Mar. 28, 2019), https://www.businessinsider.com/faa-let-boeing-self-regulate-software-believed-737-max-crashes-2019-3.

23. *See, e.g.*, Scott J. Shackelford, *Facebook's Social Responsibility Should Include Privacy Protection*, Conversation (Apr. 12, 2018), https://theconversation.com/facebooks-social-responsibility-should-include-privacy-protection-94549.

24. *See* Hannah Oswald & Molly McGinnis Stine, *"Safe Harbor" Ports in a Cybersecurity Litigation Storm*, JD Supra (Oct. 11, 2021), https://www.jdsupra.com/legalnews/safe-harbor-ports-in-a-cybersecurity-7125929/.

25. *See* Vint Cerf, *The Internet Is for Everyone*, Internet Soc'y (Apr. 7, 1999), https://www.internetsociety.org/news/speeches/2011/the-internet-is-for-everyone/.

NOTES

26. This section is republished from Scott J. Shackelford, *Inside the Drive for Cyber Peace: Unpacking Implications for Practitioners and Policyma*kers, 21 UNIVERSITY OF CALIFORNIA DAVIS BUSINESS LAW JOURNAL 285 (2021).

    See, e.g., The Growing Threat of Cyberattacks, HERITAGE FOUND., https://www.heritage.org/cybersecurity/heritage-explains/the-growing-threat-cyberattacks (last visited Feb. 20, 2020).

27. *See* Luke Broadwater, *Baltimore Transfers $6 Million to Pay for Ransomware Attack; City Considers Insurance Against Hacks*, BALTIMORE SUN (Aug. 28, 2019), https://www.baltimoresun.com/politics/bs-md-ci-ransomware-expenses-20190828-njg znd7dsfaxbbaglnvnbkgjhe-story.html; Karen Husa, *Panama-Buena Vista Union School District Computers and Phones Attacked by Ransomware*, KGET (Jan. 17, 2020), https://www.kget.com/news/local-news/panama-buena-vista-union-sch ool-district-computers-and-phones-attacked-by-ransomware/.

28. *See, e.g.,* ANDY GREENBERG, SANDWORM: A NEW ERA OF CYBERWAR AND THE HUNT FOR THE KREMLIN'S MOST DANGEROUS HACKERS 2 (2020).

29. *See* Tucker Bailey et al., *The Rising Strategic Risks of Cyberattacks*, MCKINSEY Q. (2014), https://www.mckinsey.com/business-functions/mckinsey-digital/our-insig hts/the-rising-strategic-risks-of-cyberattacks.

30. *See, e.g.,* Melissa Angell, *Is Apple's Passkey the Death of the Password? Not Quite, but It Will Make Hackers Work Harder*, INC. MAG. (June 15, 2022), https://www.inc.com/melissa-angell/apple-passkey-password-cybersecurity.html.

31. Jody R. Westby, *Conclusion, in* THE QUEST FOR CYBER PEACE 112, 112 (Int'l Telecomm. Union & Permanent Monitoring Panel on Info. Sec. eds., 2011), http://www.itu.int/dms_pub/itu-s/opb/gen/S-GEN-WFS.01-1-2011-PDF-E.pdf.

32. Renee Marlin-Bennett, *Cyber Peace: Is That a Thing?, in* CYBER PEACE: CHARTING A PATH TOWARD A SUSTAINABLE, STABLE, AND SECURE CYBERSPACE (Scott Shackelford, Frederick Douzet, and Chris Ankersen eds., Cambridge University Press, 2022).

33. *Id.; see* WORLD FED'N OF SCI., ERICE DECLARATION ON PRINCIPLES FOR CYBER STABILITY AND CYBER PEACE (2009), www.ewi.info/system/files/Erice.pdf.

34. Henning Wegener, *A Concept of Cyber Peace, in* THE QUEST FOR CYBER PEACE, *supra* note 31, at 77, 79–80.

35. *See id.;* Scott J. Shackelford, *In Search of Cyber Peace: A Response to the Cybersecurity Act of 2012*, 64 STAN. L. REV. ONLINE 106 (Mar. 8, 2012), http://www.stanfordlawrev iew.org/online/cyber-peace.

36. Scott J. Shackelford, *The Meaning of Cyber Peace*, 2 NOTRE DAME INST. FOR ADV. STUDY Q. (Oct. 2013), https://ndias.nd.edu/news-publications/ndias-quarterly/the-meaning-of-cyber-peace/.

37. Scott J. Shackelford, *Toward Cyberpeace: Managing Cyber Attacks Through Polycentric Governance*, 62 AM. UNIV. L. REV. 1273, 1280 (2013) (cited by BRUCE SCHNEIER, CLICK HERE TO KILL EVERYBODY 213 [2018]).

38. *See, e.g.,* Julien Chaisse & Cristen Bauer, *Cybersecurity and the Protection of Digital Assets: Assessing the Role of International Investment Law and Arbitration*, 21 VAND. J. ENT. & TECH. L. 550, 551 (2019).

39. The World Commission on Environment and Development: Our Common Future 37 (1987). *See also* Gabcikovo-Nagymaros Project (Hung. v. Slovk.), 1997 I.C.J. 7, 78 (Sept. 25) (defining sustainable development as "[the] need to reconcile economic development with protection of the environment").

40. Damir Rajnovic, *Cyberspace—What Is It?* Cisco Blog (July 26, 2012), http://blogs.cisco.com/security/cyberspace-what-is-it.

41. Digital Peace, Microsoft, https://digitalpeace.microsoft.com/ (last visited Nov. 5, 2018).

42. Johan Galtung, *Violence, Peace, and Peace Research*, 6 J. Peace Res. 167, 168 (1969).

43. *Id.*

44. *Id.* ("[I]f a person died from tuberculosis in the eighteenth century it would be hard to conceive of this as violence since it might have been quite unavoidable, but if he dies from it today, despite all the medical resources in the world, then violence is present according to our definition.") This argument was first published, and is expanded upon, in Scott J. Shackelford, Governing New Frontiers in the Information Age: Toward Cyber Peace (2020). *See also* Scott J. Shackelford & Steve Myers, *Block-by-Block: Leveraging the Power of Blockchain Technology to Build Trust and Promote Cyber Peace*, 19 Yale Journal of Law and Technology 334 (2017).

45. *See* Shackelford, *supra* note 47.

46. Though, there is a case to be made that Internet access itself should be considered a human right. *See* Carl Bode, *The Case for Internet Access as a Human Right*, Vice (Nov. 13, 2019), https://www.vice.com/en_us/article/3kxmm5/the-case-for-internet-access-as-a-human-right.

47. *See* Shackelford, *supra* note 41.

48. Global Commission on the Stability of Cyberspace, Advancing Cyberstability, 13 (2019), https://www.eastwest.ngo/in-focus/global-commiss ion-stability-cyberspace#:~:text=The%20Global%20Commission%20on%20 the,non%2Dstate%20behavior%20in%20cyberspace. ("Stability of cyberspace means everyone can be reasonably confident in their ability to use cyberspace safely and securely, where the availability and integrity of services and information provided in and through cyberspace are generally assured, where change is managed in relative peace, and where tensions are resolved in a non-escalatory manner.").

49. Obama White House, *The Comprehensive National Cybersecurity Initiative*, https://obamawhitehouse.archives.gov/node/233086 (last visited Nov. 10, 2017).

50. Heather M. Roff, Cyber Peace: Cybersecurity Through the Lens of Positive Peace 3 (2016), https://static.newamerica.org/attachments/12554-cyber-peace/FOR%20PRINTING-Cyber_Peace_Roff.2fbbb0b16b69482e8b6312937607a d66.pdf (arguing for a human security approach to cyber peace). Yet the notion of including humans in conceptions of cyberspace and cybersecurity is nothing new. *See* James A. Winnfield, Jr., Christopher Kirchhoff, & David M. Upton, *Cybersecurity's Human Factor: Lessons from the Pentagon*, Harv. Bus. Rev. (Sept. 2015), https://hbr.org/2015/09/cybersecuritys-human-factor-lessons-from-the-pentagon, along with the work on human factors.

51. Roff, *supra* note 50, at 3, 5.

NOTES

52. *See, e.g., Is Multistakeholderism Advancing, Dying or Evolving?*, UNESCO (Jan. 6, 2018), https://en.unesco.org/news/multistakeholderism-advancing-dying-evolving; Stuart N. Brotman, *Multistakeholder Internet Governance: A Pathway Completed, the Road Ahead*, BROOKINGS INST. (2015), https://www.brookings.edu/wp-content/uploads/2016/06/multistakeholder-1.pdf.

53. *See, e.g.*, Justin Sherman, *How Much Cyber Sovereignty Is Too Much Cyber Sovereignty?*, CFR (Oct. 30, 2019), https://www.cfr.org/blog/how-much-cyber-sovereignty-too-much-cyber-sovereignty.

54. Paris Call for Trust and Security in Cyberspace, https://pariscall.international/en/.

55. *See Malta Urges the UN to Consider the Internet as Common Heritage of Mankind*, TIMES OF MALTA (Dec. 21, 2015), http://www.timesofmalta.com/articles/view/20151221/local/malta-urges-the-un-to-consider-the-internet-as-common-heritage-of.596497. However, there have been efforts to include CHM elements in a new multilateral treaty on biodiversity protection. *See* Elizabeth Nyman et al., *71 Countries Are Negotiating a New Biodiversity Treaty. Here's What You Need to Know.*, WASH. POST (Sept. 19, 2018), https://www.washingtonpost.com/news/monkey-cage/wp/2018/09/19/the-world-has-begun-negotiating-a-marine-biodiversity-treaty-heres-what-you-need-to-know/?utm_term=.0ecc780a1ad6.

56. Massimo Costa, *Pope Francis Emphasizes Need to Care for Oceans in Message to Our Oceans Conference*, MALTA TODAY (Oct. 6, 2017), http://fore.yale.edu/news/item/pope-francis-emphasises-need-to-care-for-oceans-in-message-to-our-oceans-co/.

57. Jennifer Frakes, *The Common Heritage of Mankind Principle and the Deep Seabed, Outer Space, and Antarctica: Will Developed and Developing Nations Reach a Compromise?*, 21 WIS. INT'L. L.J. 409, 412 (2003).

58. *Id.*

59. *Id.* at 413.

60. *Id.*

61. Adam Segal & Jami Miscik, *Confronting Reality in Cyberspace: Foreign Policy for a Fragmented Internet, Council on Foreign Rel.* (July 2022), https://www.cfr.org/report/confronting-reality-in-cyberspace.

62. *Id.*

63. *Id.*

64. *See, e.g.*, Lauren Zabierek & Algirde Pipikaite, *Why Cybersecurity Needs a More Diverse and Inclusive Workforce*, WORLD ECON. F. (Oct. 26, 2021), https://www.weforum.org/agenda/2021/10/why-cybersecurity-needs-a-more-diverse-and-inclusive-workforce/.

65. Drew Alanoff, *President Obama: "The Internet Is Not a Luxury, It's a Necessity,"* TECH CRUNCH (July 15, 2015), https://techcrunch.com/2015/07/15/internet-for-everyone/?guccounter=1.

66. *See, e.g.*, Scott J. Shackelford, *Should Cybersecurity Be a Human Right? Exploring the "Shared Responsibility" of Cyber Peace*, 55 STANFORD JOURNAL OF INTERNATIONAL LAW 155 (2019).

67. *See, e.g.*, Oona A. Hathaway, Do Human Rights Treaties Make a Difference?, 111 YALE L.J. 1935, 1936 (2002).

68. *See* Daniel Burrus, *The Internet of Things Is Far Bigger than Anyone Realizes*, Wired (Nov. 2014), http://www.wired.com/2014/11/the-internet-of-things-bigger/; Lawrence J. Trautman, *Cybersecurity: What About U.S. Policy?*, 2015 U. Ill. J.L. Tech. & Pol'y 341, 348 (2015).

69. *See* Chris Welch, *Tesla's Model S Will Add Self-Driving "Autopilot" Mode in Three Months*, Verge (Mar. 19, 2015), http://www.theverge.com/2015/3/19/8257933/tesla-model-s-autopilot-release-date.

70. Segal & Miscik, *supra* note 61.

71. *See* Adam Thierer, *Putting Privacy Concerns About the Internet of Things in Perspective*, Int'l Assoc. Privacy Prof. (Feb. 3, 2014), https://iapp.org/news/a/putting-privacy-concerns-about-the-internet-of-things-in-perspective.

72. *See* Paul M. Schwartz & Edward J. Janger, *Notification of Data Security Breaches*, 105 Mich. L. Rev. 913, 922 (2007).

73. Jeffrey Weiss, *Elinor Ostrom and the Triumph of the Commons*, Politics Daily (2009), http://www.politicsdaily.com/2009/10/14/elinor-ostrom-and-the-triumph-of-the-commons/.

Conclusion—Our Meta Future?

1. Eric Ravenscraft, *What Is the Metaverse, Exactly?*, Wired (Nov. 25, 2021), https://www.wired.com/story/what-is-the-metaverse/.

2. William Gibson, Neuromancer 6 (2000).

3. *Id.*

4. Frank Holmes, *The Metaverse Is a $1 Trillion Revenue Opportunity. Here's How to Invest . . .* , Forbes (Dec. 20, 2021), https://www.forbes.com/sites/greatspeculati ons/2021/12/20/the-metaverse-is-a-1-trillion-revenue-opportunity-heres-how-to-invest/?sh=3bdcf2124df9.

5. *Conventional Economists Sound Alarm Over Cryptocurrency's Volatility*, PBS (Apr. 8, 2022), https://www.pbs.org/newshour/show/conventional-economists-sound-alarm-over-cryptocurrencys-volatility.

6. *What Is Metaverse Nation?*, https://readyformetaverse.com/Unitedmetaversenat ion#:~:text=What%20is%20United%20Metaverse%20Nation,are%20transpar ent%20and%20fully%20public (last visited June 1, 2022).

INDEX

For the benefit of digital users, indexed terms that span two pages (e.g., 52–53) may, on occasion, appear on only one of those pages.

Figures are indicated by *f* following the page number

Abbate, Janet, 77–78
acceptable use policy (AUP)
  for ARPANET, 46
  for CSNET, 47–48
  for NSFNET, 50–52, 117, 121
ACM. *See* Association for Computing
    Machinery
Advanced Projects Research Agency
    (ARPA), 11–12, 13, 17, 20–21, 24
  AUP for, 46
  Network Working Group, 38–39, 129
  NSC program, 28, 30
  student use of, enabling, 45–49
Advanced Research Projects Agency
    Network (ARPANET), 4, 5, 11–12,
    13–14, 16, 18, 20–22, 29
  AT&T and, 78
  AUP for, 46
  BBN and, 67, 129
  CCITT and, 40
  competing with, 35
  CSNET and, 46–49, 117
  Geographic Map, 14*f*, 14, 15
  NSC program and, 28
  NSF supercomputer centers linked to, 50
  Pentagon and, 75

  Postel and, 129–30
  Roberts and, 12–13, 18
  TCP/IP and, 30–31, 40, 47, 58–59, 62,
    79–80, 130
  Unix and, 43
  Usenet servers and, 117
AIDS, 113
Amazon, 24, 96, 146
American National Standards Institute
    (ANSI), 57
ANSI. *See* American National Standards
    Institute
anticompetitive behavior, 96
AOL, 104–5, 118–20
Apple, 53, 74, 96, 146
ARPA. *See* Advanced Projects Research
    Agency
ARPANET. *See* Advanced Research
    Projects Agency Network
ARPANET Resource Handbook, 46
Asian democracies, Internet regulations
    in, 110–11
Asimov, Isaac, 88
Association for Computing Machinery
    (ACM), 98
Asynchronous Transfer Mode (ATM), 24–25

ATM. *See* Asynchronous Transfer Mode
AT&T, 15, 36, 42, 43, 74, 76, 78, 92, 115–16
AT&T Bell Labs, 26, 42
AUP. *See* acceptable use policy
Avaaz, 109

backdoors, 80, 83–84
Baran, Paul, 10–11, 11*f*, 15, 18, 75, 172–73n.36
BBN. *See* Bolt Beranek and Newman Inc.
Berkeley
    DARPA and, 43–45
    networking release, 43
    UNIX at, 43, 62
Berkeley Software Distribution (BSD), 43
Berkes, Fikret, 147–48
Berners-Lee, Tim, 49, 86–98, 114*f*, 138, 145, 179n.70
Biden, Joe, 108, 123
blockchain, 84–85, 137, 153, 155–56
Bolt Beranek and Newman Inc. (BBN), 18, 67, 129
Boucher Amendment, 51–52
Bradner, Scott, 49
"Bread Truck," the, 29, 29*f*
browsers, 87–88, 91–92, 98
BSD. *See* Berkeley Software Distribution

Cailliau, Robert, 88–89
Carmille, René, 72–74
carriers and users, in network of the future, 20–21
Carterfone decision, FCC, 36–37
Case, Steve, 118–19
CBS Evening News, 113
CCITT. *See* Consultative Committee for International Telephony and Telegraphy
CDA. *See* Communications Decency Act
CDNs. *See* content delivery networks
censorship, 84–85, 96–97, 108, 110–11
Center for Democracy and Technology, 103–4
Cerf, Vint, 5, 20–21, 31–32, 39, 40, 56, 77–78, 115
    on backdoors, 83–84

on FNC, MCI Mail and, 117–18, 119–21
on Internet access, 150–51
on interplanetary Internet protocol, 139
on IoT, 83
Kahn and, 18–19, 21, 22, 24–26, 28–31, 67, 78–79, 80, 81, 85, 133–34
TCP/IP and, 31–32
on technology and rights, 92–93
CERN. *See* European Organization for Nuclear Research
China
    cyber sovereignty and, 96–97, 137, 138
    IETF and, 131–32
    Internet censorship in, 110–11
CHM. *See* common heritage of mankind
Christchurch Call to Eliminate Terrorist and Violent Extremist Content Online, 109–10, 153–54, 184n.81
circuit switching, 5–8, 9, 14–17, 39–40
Cisco, 53, 157
Clark, David D., 67, 69, 77–78, 170–71n.1
Clark, Wesley, 16, 17–18, 19–21
Clipper Chip, 83–84
"Code of Practice on Disinformation," 109
Cohen, Danny, 25, 27–28, 30
Cold War, 13, 79–80, 113
commercial Internet, 49–52, 103–4, 119–21, 120*f*, 124
common heritage of mankind (CHM), 154–55
Communications Decency Act of 1996 (CDA), 99–100, 102–3, 104, 113–14, 182n.37, 182n.40
    Section 230, 99–100, 102–8, 111, 112, 144, 145–46, 159
CompuServe, 101–2, 116–17
Computer Science and Artificial Intelligence Laboratory (CSAIL), 98
Computer Science Network (CSNET), 46–49, 117
Consultative Committee for International Telephony and Telegraphy (CCITT), 35–41, 56, 62
Consumer Reports Digital Standard, 157
content delivery networks (CDNs), 123–24

INDEX

Council on Foreign Relations, 155, 156–57
Covid-19 pandemic, 80, 92–93, 112–13,
  115–16, 156–57
Cox, Chris, 102–3, 111, 113–14, 182n.37
Craigslist, 107
Creeper, 75–76, 76f
Crocker, Steve, 38, 129, 174n.59
cryptography, 83–85
CSAIL. *See* Computer Science and
  Artificial Intelligence Laboratory
CSNET. *See* Computer Science Network
Cubby v. CompuServe (1991), 101–2
cyber attacks, 72–77, 150–51
  bugs and, 69
  Creeper, 75–76, 76f
  IoT and, 156–57
  Morris worm, 70–71
cyber peace, 150–54
cybersecurity, 67–69, 157
  cyber conflict and, 80–82
  encryption, 72, 77–80, 81, 85
  literacy, 70–71
  TCP/IP and, 80
cyber sovereignty, 96–97, 113, 128–29, 136,
  137, 138, 153
cyberspace, 88, 138, 143–44
  Berners-Lee on threats of, 94
  CDA on, 99–100, 103–4, 106, 108–9
  CHM and, 155
  cyber peace and, 150–53
  Gibson on, 127–28, 158
  infrastructure, critical *versus*
    noncritical, 80–81
  IoT and, 156–57
  Paris Call on, 93–94, 151, 153–54
  treaty for, 155

DAO. *See* decentralized autonomous
  organization
DARPA. *See* Defense Advanced Research
  Projects Agency
datagrams, 5, 23, 24, 25, 37, 41
data networks and data networking, 4–5,
  18, 56, 62
  CCITT and, 38, 40, 56

CSNET and, 48–49
IBM and, 37
INWG and, 39, 40, 56
ISO and, 38
NSF and, 49–50
NSFNET and, 52
OSI and, 56
packet, 39, 48–49, 52
regulatory framework for, 118
Davies, Donald, 11, 12–13, 15, 39–40, 48–
  49, 75
Day, John, 35–36
DDoS. *See* Distributed Denial of Service
decentralized autonomous organization
  (DAO), 158–59
DECnet, 53–54, 55
DEC VAX supercomputers, 54
Defense Advanced Research Projects
  Agency (DARPA), 21, 41–45, 47, 67, 131
Denning, Pete, 45
Denning, Peter, 47
Department of Commerce, U.S., 127
Department of Defense (DoD), 12, 13, 42,
  45, 46
Diffie, Whitfield, 78–79
digital divide, 15, 128–29
Digital Equipment Corporation, 75–76, 77
digital isolation, 138
Digital Silk Road (DSR), 137, 139
disinformation, 97, 100, 105, 106–7, 108–11,
  112–13, 143, 151
Distributed Denial of Service (DDoS), 68–
  69, 82–83, 175n.79
distributed network concept, of Baran,
  10, 11f
DNS. *See* domain name system
DNS servers, 130–31, 190n.22
DNS Wars, 133–36
DoD. *See* Department of Defense
domain name system (DNS), 130, 136, 138,
  190n.22
DSR. *See* Digital Silk Road
Dyn, 82–83

e2e. *See* end-to-end model

Eisenhower, Dwight, 12
encryption, 69, 72, 77–80, 81, 85
end-to-end (e2e) model, 24
Engressia, Joe, 74
ENQUIRE, 86–87
Erice Declaration on Principles for Cyber
 Stability and Cyber Peace, 151–52
ESPRIT. *See* European Strategic
 Programme on Research in
 Information Technology
Estrin, Gerald, 21
Ethernet, 76
European Commission, 44–45, 109, 145–46
European Organization for Nuclear
 Research (CERN), 49, 86–87, 88–93,
 119
European Strategic Programme on
 Research in Information Technology
 (ESPRIT), 44–45
European Union, 109, 148–49
Executive Order 13925: Preventing Online
 Censorship, 108
Exon, James, 102

Facebook, 91–92, 105, 145–46, 148, 158–59
Farber, Dave, 47
FBI, 82–83
Federal Communications Commission
 (FCC), 36–37, 108, 122–23
Federal Information Processing Standard
 (FIPS), 57–58
Federal Internetworking Requirements
 Panel, 59
Federalnaya Sluzhba Bezopasnosti (FSB),
 113
Federal Networking Council (FNC), 117–
 18, 119–21
Federal Trade Commission (FTC), 95,
 145–46, 157
FIPS. *See* Federal Information Processing
 Standard
First Amendment, 100–1, 106–7
5G networks, 123–24
FNC. *See* Federal Networking Council
Fortnite, 158
Franklin, Benjamin, 99

free code, 35
FSB. *See* Federalnaya Sluzhba
 Bezopasnosti
FTC. *See* Federal Trade Commission

Galtung, Johan, 152–53
General Data Protection Regulation
 (GDPR), 148–49, 155–56
Gibson, William, 127–28, 158
Gingrich, Newt, 102
Ginsberg v. United States (1968), 101
Goltz, John R., 116–17
Google, 96, 115–16, 146
Government Open Systems
 Interconnection Profile (GOSIP), 35,
 56–63
government-sponsored networks, access
 to, 35, 42–45
Greenberg, Andy, 70–71
Grudin, Jonathan, 99

hacking and hackers, 72–75
Hamling v. United States (1975), 101
Hammond, Allen S., 101
Hellman, Marty, 78–79
Heuer, Rolf, 93–94
HTML. *See* hypertext markup language
HTTP. *See* hypertext transfer protocol
human conversation, 26
human rights, 79, 84–85, 92–93, 94, 107,
 109–10, 136, 138, 153, 155–56, 184n.81
Hyde Amendment, 182n.37
hyperlinks, 86
hypertext, 87, 88–89
hypertext markup language (HTML), 89
hypertext transfer protocol (HTTP), 89

IAB. *See* Internet Architecture Board
IANA. *See* Internet Assigned Numbers
 Authority
IBM, 4, 35–37, 53–54
IBM 704, 74–75
ICANN. *See* Internet Corporation for
 Assigned Names and Numbers
IEEE. *See* Institute of Electrical and
 Electronics Engineers

INDEX

IETF. *See* Internet Engineering Task Force

IGF. *See* Internet Governance Forum

IMPs. *See* Interface Message Processors

India, Internet disinformation in, 110–11

Information Sciences Institute (ISI), 28, 30

Inrupt, 98

Instagram, 95–96

Institute of Electrical and Electronics
    Engineers (IEEE), 56–57

Interface Message Processors (IMPs), 18–
    19, 20, 22, 30–31

International Organization for
    Standardization (ISO), 38, 40, 41,
    44–45
  OSI and, 58
  SC16, 56–57

International Packet Network Working
    Group (INWG), 39, 40–41, 56

international standardization, 35

International Telegraph Union (ITU), 37–
    38, 84–85, 131–32, 134, 135–37, 155

Internet address system, 126–27, 129–31

Internet Architecture Board (IAB), 133–34

Internet Assigned Numbers Authority
    (IANA), 130, 131–32, 133–34, 135–36

Internet Corporation for Assigned Names
    and Numbers (ICANN), 124–25,
    127, 128–29, 131, 133, 135–37, 138–39,
    155–56

Internet Engineering Task Force (IETF),
    90, 128–29
  Berners-Lee and, 88, 90–91
  Facebook *versus*, 146
  IANA and, 131–32
  ICANN and, 131
  IPs and, 68
  ISOC and, 133–34
  ITU and, 131–32
  OSI protocols and, 58, 59
  QUIC and, 32
  RFCs, 38–39, 129
  TCP/IP and, 58, 60

Internet governance, 127–32, 133–37, 144,
    145–50, 157
  equitable, 154–56
  polycentric, 148–50, 152–53

Internet Governance Forum (IGF), 155

Internet of Everything, 123–24

Internet of Things (IoT), 29–30, 80, 82–83

Internet Protocol (IP), 18–19, 24–26, 52–55,
    68, 90, 139, 157. *See also* Transmission
    Control Program/Internet Protocol;
    Voice over Internet Protocol
  encryption of, 69, 72, 77–80, 81, 84–85

Internet Protocol addresses (IP addresses),
    68, 83, 129–30, 131, 133–34, 135–36,
    139, 175n.81, 189n.2, 189–90n.11,
    190n.22

Internet Protocol version 4 (IPv4), 175n.81

Internet Protocol version 6 (IPv6), 83,
    84–85

Internet Research Task Force (IRTF),
    133–34

Internet service providers (ISPs), 19, 32–
    33, 51, 52, 115–16
  AOL, 119
  CDNs and, 123–24
  net neutrality and, 121–23
  regulation of, 123–24

Internet standards development, 38–39

Internetwork Packet Exchange (IPX), 55

INWG. *See* International Packet Network
    Working Group

IoT. *See* Internet of Things

IP addresses. *See* Internet Protocol
    addresses

IPv4. *See* Internet Protocol version 4

IPv6. *See* Internet Protocol version 6

IPX. *See* Internetwork Packet Exchange

IRTF. *See* Internet Research Task Force

Isaacson, Walter, 74–75, 88–89, 90

Isenberg, David, 24

ISI. *See* Information Sciences Institute

ISO. *See* International Organization for
    Standardization

ISOC, 133–34

ISPs. *See* Internet service providers

ISP Wars, 116, 119, 121, 124–25

ITU. *See* International Telegraph Union

January 6 insurrection on the U.S. Capitol,
    112

Jennings, Dennis, 44–45, 50, 54–55
Jet Propulsion Laboratory, 139
Jobs, Steve, 74
John von Neuman Center (JvNC), 54
Joyce, Rob, 96–97
JvNC. *See* John von Neuman Center

Kahn, Robert, 20–21, 39, 48, 84
  on blockchain, 84–85
  Cerf and, 18–19, 21, 22, 24–26, 28–31, 67, 78–79, 80, 81, 85, 133–34
Kapor, Mitchell, 126
Kennedy, Ted, 18
KGB, 113
Kleinrock, Leonard, 21, 75
Kline, Charley, 75
Kosseff, Jeff, 104, 106–7

Landweber, Larry, 46–47
Leonard, Andrew, 41–42
Licklider, J. C. R., 3, 4, 139

Macron, Emmanuel, 138
Magaziner, Ira, 134
malware, 75–76, 175n.79
Marconi, Guglielmo, 72
Marlin-Bennett, Renée, 151
Maskelyne, Nevil, 72, 73f, 172n.23
McGinnis, Michael, 147
MCI Mail, 21, 117–18, 119–21
McKinsey, 151
Medin, Milo, 59
message switching, 8–9, 12–13, 14–17
Meta, 158–59
metaverse, 158–59
Metcalfe, Robert, 76, 173n.44
Microsoft, 55, 79–80, 96, 110–11, 146, 153–54
Mine of Information (MOI), 88–89
Mirai botnet, 82–83
Miscik, Jami, 155–56
misinformation, 105, 110, 111, 112–13
MIT, 4, 12, 69
Mitnick, Kevin, 77
MOI. *See* Mine of Information

Morris, Robert Tappan, 70, 71f, 81
Morris worm, 67–68, 70–71, 81–82
Morse code, 72
Musk, Elon, 146
Muslim Cyber Army, 110

NASA, 59
National Center for Supercomputing Applications (NCSA), 91
National Institute of Standards and Technology (NIST), 57–58, 59, 60, 61–62, 149–50, 157
National Science Foundation (NSF), 46–47, 49–50, 117, 133
National Science Foundation Network (NSFNET), 35, 49–52, 119, 187n.18
  AUP for, 50–52, 117, 121
  commercial Internet and, 49–52
  common vendor network protocols and, 53–55
  IPs permitted on, 52–55
  supercomputer centers, 54
  TCP/IP and, 50, 54–55, 62
National Security Agency (NSA), 67–68, 78–79, 174n.59
National Telecommunications and Information Administration (NTIA), 108, 135
NATO, 79–80
NCSA. *See* National Center for Supercomputing Applications
Nelson, Ted, 86
NERC. *See* North American Electric Reliability Council
net neutrality, 95, 116, 121, 122–24, 179n.70
network of networks, 18–19, 20, 24, 28
Network Secure Communication (NSC) program, of ARPA, 28, 30
Network Solutions, Inc. (NSI), 133
network topology, 16, 17–18
Neumann, Jon von, 74
Neuromancer (Gibson), 127–28, 158
New Zealand, Internet regulations in, 109–10
NFTs. *See* non-fungible tokens

INDEX

NGN, 24–25
NIST. *See* National Institute of Standards and Technology
non-fungible tokens (NFTs), 158
North American Electric Reliability Council (NERC), 150
NSA. *See* National Security Agency
NSC. *See* Network Secure Communication program, of ARPA
NSF. *See* National Science Foundation
NSFNET. *See* National Science Foundation Network
NSI. *See* Network Solutions, Inc.
NTIA. *See* National Telecommunications and Information Administration

Obama, Barack, 155–56
Observatory on Social Media, at Indiana University, 112–13
O'Dell, Mike, 20, 24
open source, 145
Open System Interconnection (OSI) protocol suite, 40, 44–45, 56
  GOSIP and, 57–61
  government mandate for, 56–63
  standards, 56–57
  TCP/IP and, 56, 58–61
OSI. *See* Open System Interconnection
Ostrom, Elinor, 81, 90, 146, 147, 148–49, 150, 157
Ostrom, Vincent, 146, 147
Oxford, 86–87, 98

Pacific Cyber Security Operational Network (PaCSON), 109–10
packet data networking, 39, 48–49, 52
packet radio network, 20–21
packets, 4, 11, 13–14, 19, 20, 22
  datagrams and, 23
  lost, 27, 31
packet switching, 5–6, 10–12, 13–14, 16, 38, 40
packet voice technology, 28
PaCSON. *See* Pacific Cyber Security Operational Network

Pai, Ajit, 123
Paris Call for Trust and Security in Cyberspace, 93–94, 151, 153–54
Pentagon, 13, 75
Performance Systems International (PSINET), 51
Perlroth, Nicole, 70–71
personally identifiable information (PII), 157
Phase 3, 128–29
phishing, 69, 78, 144
PII. *See* personally identifiable information
polycentric governance, 147–50, 152–53
postal, telegraph, and telephone services (PTTs), 35–36, 37–38, 40–41
Postel, Jon, 21, 30–31, 127, 129–35, 132*f*, 139, 145
Pouzin, Louis, 23, 24, 37, 39
Powell, Michael, 122
private sector, as Internet gatekeeper, 112
Prodigy, 101–3, 106, 118
PSINET. *See* Performance Systems International
PTTs. *See* postal, telegraph, and telephone services

QoS. *See* Quality of Service
Quality of Service (QoS), 123–24
Quantum Computer Services, 118–19
Quick User Datagram Protocol Internet Connections (QUIC) protocol, 32

RAND, 10
ransomware, 67–68, 80, 151, 155–57
RARE. *See* Réseaux Associés pour la Recherche Européenne
Rather, Dan, 113
Reaper, 75–76
Reed, David, 30–31
re-engineering the Internet, 80, 84–85
reliability, protocol and, 25–26
reliable information transfer, 27, 28, 31
Request for Comments (RFCs), 38–39, 129, 135–36, 189–90n.11
request for quotation (RFQ), 18

Research Open System for Europe (ROSE), 44–45
Réseaux Associés pour la Recherche Européenne (RARE), 117
RFCs. *See* Request for Comments
RFQ. *See* request for quotation
Richie, Dennis, 42
Rivest-Shamir-Adleman (RSA), 78–79, 144
Roberts, Larry, 12–13, 14–17, 18, 20, 39, 129
ROSE. *See* Research Open System for Europe
routers, 5, 18–19
RSA. *See* Rivest-Shamir-Adleman
RT. *See* Russia Today
Russia
  cyber sovereignty and, 96–97, 113, 138
  disinformation of, 113
Russia Today (RT), 138

SAGE. *See* Semi-Automatic Ground Environment
Saltzer, J.H., 24
Sarbanes-Oxley Act of 2002, 124–25
SC6. *See* subcommittee 6
SC16. *See* subcommittee 16
Scantlebury, Roger, 12–13
Schneier, Bruce, 98
Section 230, of CDA, 99–100, 102–8, 111, 112, 144, 145–46, 159
Secure Sockets Layer (SSL), 83–84
Segal, Adam, 97, 155–56
Semi-Automatic Ground Environment (SAGE), 4
Shoch, John, 30
Simington, Nathan, 123
smart network, 21, 22, 23, 24
smartphones, 19, 32–33, 67–68, 69, 127–28, 148–49
Smith v. California (1959), 100–1
SNA. *See* System Network Architecture
Snowden, Edward, 67–68
social networks and social media platforms, 95–96, 104–5, 144
special-purpose computers, 17–18
speech regulation, 100–11

splinternet, 138–39
split TCP, 5
SSL. *See* Secure Sockets Layer
Stanford University, 21, 29–30, 75, 78–79, 102–3
star topology, 17
Stratton Oakmont v. Prodigy (1995), 101–3, 106–7, 113–14
Stuxnet, 67–68, 80–81
subcommittee 6 (SC6), 38, 41
subcommittee 16 (SC16), 56–57
supercomputers, 50, 53, 54
Supreme Court, U.S., 99–101, 104, 106–7, 108, 122
Sussman, Gerald, 34
System Network Architecture (SNA), 22, 53–54

Tanenbaum, Andrew, 56, 58, 60–61
TCP. *See* Transmission Control Program
TCP/IP. *See* Transmission Control Program/Internet Protocol
Tech Model Railroad Club, 74–75
telegraph transmission, 8–9
telephone standards development, 37–38
The Information Mine (TIM), 88–89
Thomas, Bob, 75–76
Thomas, Clarence, 108
Thompson, Ken, 42
3Com, 76
TIM. *See* The Information Mine
TLDs. *See* top-level domains
Tomilson, Ray, 75–76
top-level domains (TLDs), 130–31, 132*f*, 134, 135–36, 139, 190n.22
Transmission Control Program (TCP), 25–26, 28–32
Transmission Control Program/Internet Protocol (TCP/IP), 21, 24, 52, 53, 116, 118, 126–27, 133
  ARPANET and, 30–31, 40, 47, 58–59, 62, 79–80, 130
  CCITT and, 35–41, 62
  Cerf and, 31–32
  cybersecurity and, 80

DARPA, UNIX and, 41–45
diagram of working process, 31*f*
encryption and, 72, 77, 79–80, 81, 85
IBM, 53–54
IETF and, 58, 60
JvNC and, 54
NSFNET and, 50, 54–55, 62
OSI and, 56, 58–62
RSA and, 78–79, 144
telephone world and, 36–41
UDP and, 30–31, 32
updates, 84
Trojan horses, 68–69
Trump, Donald, 95, 108, 112
Twitter, 112–13, 146
TX-2 computer, 16

UCLA, 21, 30, 38, 129–30
UDI. *See* universal document identifier
UDP. *See* User Datagram Protocol
uniform resource identifier (URI), 88,
177n.16
universal document identifier (UDI), 88
universal resource locator (URL), 88, 92,
177n.16
UNIX, 41–45, 61, 62–63
Unix to Unix NETwork (UUNET), 51
URI. *See* uniform resource identifier
URL. *See* universal resource locator
Usenet servers, 117, 118
User Datagram Protocol (UDP), 30–32
UUNET. *See* Unix to Unix NETwork

VAX supercomputers, 53, 54
VINES. *See* Virtual Integrated NEtwork
Service
virtual circuits, 22, 39–40
Virtual Integrated NEtwork Service
(VINES), 53
virtual private networks (VPNs), 119–20
viruses, 68–69, 70, 75–76
Vocoders, 27

Voice over Internet Protocol (VoIP), 25–
26, 119–20
VPNs. *See* virtual private networks

W3C. *See* World Wide Web Consortium
Walton, Bill, 82–83
War in Ukraine, 138, 139, 156–57
Web 2.0, 128–29
Web 3.0, 128–29, 139, 155–56, 159
web browsers, 87–88, 91–92, 98
WeIABb, 89
WhatsApp, 110–11
Wheeler, Tom, 122–23
Whitacre, Edward, Jr., 115–16
Widodo, Joko, 110
Wilkins, Jeffrey, 116–17
Wolf, Steve, 49, 51–52
WorldCom, 124–25
World Summit on the Information Society,
127–28
World War II, 4, 72–74
World Wide Web (WWW), 49, 86–89, 87*f*,
96–97, 98, 101
patenting, 89–92, 145
World Wide Web Consortium (W3C), 68,
98, 133–34
worms, 68–69, 70
Morris worm, 67–68, 70–71, 81–82
Wozniak, Steve, 74
Wu, Tim, 95
WWW. *See* World Wide Web
Wyden, Ron, 102–3, 111, 112, 113–14, 145–46

X.25, 22, 24–26, 39–41, 56
Xerox Network Systems (XNS), 39–40, 53

YouTube, 146
You've Got Mail, 118

Zeran v. America Online, Inc. (1997), 104–
5, 106, 108
Zuckerberg, Mark, 91–92

The manufacturer's authorised representative in the EU for product safety is Oxford
University Press España S.A. of El Parque Empresarial San Fernando de Henares,
Avenida de Castilla, 2 – 28830 Madrid (www.oup.es/en or product.safety@oup.com).
OUP España S.A. also acts as importer into Spain of products made by the manufacturer.

Printed in the USA/Agawam, MA
May 16, 2025

887590.007